Violence in Early Modern Europe

This latest addition to the successful textbook series *New Approaches to European History* offers students a broad-ranging survey of violence in western Europe from the Reformation to the French Revolution. Julius Ruff summarizes a huge body of research and provides readers with a clear, accessible, and engaging introduction to the topic of violence in early modern Europe. His book, enriched with fascinating illustrations, underlines the fact that modern preoccupations with the problem of violence are not unique, and that late medieval and early modern European societies produced levels of violence that may have exceeded those in the most violent modern inner-city neighborhoods. Julius Ruff examines the role of the emerging state in controlling violence; the roots and forms of the period's widespread interpersonal violence; violence and its impact on women; and rioting. His book will be of great value to students of European history, criminal justice sciences, and anthropology.

JULIUS R. RUFF is Associate Professor of History at Marquette University, Wisconsin. He is the author of *Crime, Justice and Public Order in Old Regime France* (1984) and co-author of *Discovering the Western Past: A Look at the Evidence* (fourth edition, 2000).

ʃʋ

NEW APPROACHES TO EUROPEAN HISTORY

Series editors
WILLIAM BEIK *Emory University*
T. C. W. BLANNING *Sidney Sussex College, Cambridge*

New Approaches to European History is an important new textbook series, which provides concise but authoritative surveys of major themes and problems in European history since the Renaissance. Written at a level and length accessible to advanced school students and undergraduates, each book in the series addresses topics or themes that students of European history encounter daily: the series embraces both some of the more "traditional" subjects of study, and those cultural and social issues to which increasing numbers of school and college courses are devoted. A particular effort will be made to consider the wider international implications of the subject under scrutiny.

To aid the student reader scholarly apparatus and annotation is light, but each work has full supplementary bibliographies and notes for further reading: where appropriate, chronologies, maps, diagrams and other illustrative material are also provided.

For a list of titles published in the series, please see end of book.

Violence in
Early Modern Europe

Julius R. Ruff

Marquette University, Milwaukee, Wisconsin

CAMBRIDGE
UNIVERSITY PRESS

2008/37

PUBLISHED BY THE PRESS SYNDICATE OF THE UNIVERSITY OF CAMBRIDGE
The Pitt Building, Trumpington Street, Cambridge, United Kingdom

CAMBRIDGE UNIVERSITY PRESS
The Edinburgh Building, Cambridge CB2 2RU, UK
40 West 20th Street, New York, NY 10011-4211, USA
10 Stamford Road, Oakleigh, VIC 3166, Australia
Ruiz de Alarcón 13, 28014 Madrid, Spain
Dock House, The Waterfront, Cape Town 8001, South Africa

http://www.cambridge.org

First published 2001

Printed in the United Kingdom at the University Press, Cambridge

Typeface Plantin 10/12 pt   *System* QuarkXPress™   [SE]

A catalogue record for this book is available from the British Library

Library of Congress Cataloguing in Publication data
Ruff, Julius R. (Julius Ralph)
Violence in early modern Europe, 1500–1800 / Julius R. Ruff.
    p.   cm. – (New approaches to European history)
Includes bibliographical references and index.
ISBN 0 521 59119 8 – ISBN 0 521 59894 X (pbk.)
1. Violence – Europe – History.   2. Violent crimes – Europe – History.
3. Political violence – Europe – History.   4. Europe – History.   I. Title.
II. Series.

HN380.Z9 V537 2001
303.6′094–dc21   00-067489

ISBN 0 521 59119 8 hardback
ISBN 0 521 59894 X paperback

Dedicated to
Laura Blair Ruff, *in thanks*
Julius Lincoln Ruff and Ruth B. Ruff, *in memory*
Julia Blair Ruff and Charles Williams Ruff, *in hope*
Chester and Ora Lee Williams Blair, *in tribute*

Contents

Illustrations

Acknowledgements

This is an unusually broad work, a study of violence in western Europe over a period of three centuries, and its completion would not have been possible without the aid of a number of institutions and persons. It is a pleasure to acknowledge that assistance here.

Marquette University provided considerable support in the writing of this book. Most especially, Academic Vice-President David R. Buckholdt and Dean of the College of Arts and Sciences Thomas E. Hachey made possible the sabbatical leave during which I began research; and my chairman, the Reverend Dr. Steven Avella, facilitated my writing by his arrangement of my instructional duties when I returned to the classroom. The university also provided financial support to the project, and I thank the Reverend Dr. Thaddeus J. Burch, S. J., Dean of the Graduate School, and the university's Committee on Research for a summer grant in 1997, as well as the university's Bradley Institute for Democracy and Public Values for research support in 1997–98. Various departments of the university and members of its community also aided my work: the Interlibrary Loan Department of Memorial Library tracked down numerous obscure works in an array of languages for my use; Dr. Curtis L. Carter, Director, and Mr. James R. Kieselburg, Registrar, kindly opened the collection of the Patrick and Beatrice Haggerty Museum of Art for the preparation of this work; and Mr. Dan Johnson of Photographic Services in the Instructional Media Center aided in the preparation of illustrations.

A large part of the information and insights on France contained in this volume is the result of my research on several projects over the years in the libraries and archives of that nation. I must therefore acknowledge support for these past endeavors from the American Philosophical Society, the Institut francophone de Paris, and the National Endowment for the Humanities.

My debts to individual scholars are numerous, too. William Beik suggested that I write this book, and his editorial skills and kind assistance were key in its preparation. I also must acknowledge the assistance of a number of historians, some of them intellectual companions of long standing, who generously aided in this project as in earlier ones. Albert Hamscher, Jeffrey Merrick, and Steven G. Reinhardt read the complete manuscript and provided considerable advice for its improvement from their respective perspectives on the early modern period. In addition, Jeffrey Merrick very kindly shared with me his work in progress on domestic conflict and political culture. Cynthia A. Bouton, Martha Carlin, the Reverend Dr. John Patrick Donnelly, S. J., J. Michael Phayer, and Merry Wiesner-Hanks also greatly aided the development of the book. My colleagues German Carillo and Lance Grahn gave me essential assistance with Spanish literary sources, and a former student, Dr. Monique I. Septon of Brussels, aided me in obtaining vital Belgian materials. My editor at Cambridge, Mrs. Elizabeth Howard, also provided great assistance during a writing process that took longer than expected. Finally, my students in History/Philosophy/Criminology and Legal Studies 151 ("Crime and Punishment") over the past fifteen years unwittingly furnished me with a critical forum for testing a number of ideas explored in this book.

Ultimately, however, any book is a very personal work. Despite all of this assistance, the responsibility for the final execution of the work is mine, and my greatest obligation is a personal one because of the stresses and strains that a writing project imposes on an author's family. Thus I owe my greatest thanks to my wife, Laura Blair Ruff, and to the rest of my family, immediate and extended; the dedication is an expression of gratitude for their love and support over many years.

Introduction: The problem of violence in early modern Europe

Most modern western Europeans and North Americans are acutely aware of violence in their midst, and public opinion polls consistently show that fear of violence is one of their primary concerns. The preoccupation of modern print and electronic media with the many forms of violence in society only heightens public concern about personal safety. Domestic violence, assaults and robberies, rape, the violence of organized crime, assassinations, riots, and acts of political terrorism all seize headlines and provide "lead-ins" for television and radio news, serving to convince many in their audiences that they live in the most violent of times.

Indeed, media focus on such news seems to have contributed to the belief among much of the public that not only are these the most violent of times, but they are also inexorably growing worse. A Gallup poll taken in the United States in 1996 is indicative of contemporary public perceptions of crime. Despite generally declining crime rates, 71 percent of those polled believed crime had increased in the United States in the past year, and 8 percent opined that crime rates were at least the same as those of the previous year. Nonetheless, 96 percent of respondents professed to have been unaffected by physical or sexual violence and such serious property crimes as housebreaking and car theft in the year ending in July 1996.[1]

Modern social theorists have reinforced this impression. From Ferdinand Tönnies and Emile Durkheim to late twentieth-century scholars, they have emphasized the criminogenic nature of many aspects of modern society, most especially industrialization, urbanization, and the attendant decay of the stabilizing institutions of family and community. And, certainly, the criminal justice statistics annually issued by all modern western governments have sustained the perception of a steadily worsening state of public safety. These data have shown dramatic increases since about 1960 in all forms of reported offenses, constituting

---

[1] George Gallup, Jr. (ed.), *The Gallup Poll: Public Opinion 1996* (Wilmington, DE: Scholarly Resources, 1997), pp. 195–96.

1

a post-World War II crime wave extending into the early 1990s in many western countries. These statistics also suggest that violent human conflict has become not only more frequent in the second half of the twentieth century but more lethal as well, the result of the firepower of a modern weaponry more and more available to the public, particularly in the United States.

But the focus of the journalist and sociologist, who after all seek to explain modern crime problems, must necessarily be on the present, and they are unprepared to undertake long-term studies of human behavior that might allow them to interpret today's crime wave in a broader chronological context. Beginning in the late 1950s, historians have now provided the foundation for just such an analysis in their research on the behavior of medieval and early modern Europeans. That research reveals that Europeans half a millennium ago constituted a society far more violent than that of their modern descendants. Violence, as we will see, was part of the discourse of early modern interpersonal relations. Thus overall rates of violent offenses, inflated by a plethora of often minor altercations, were higher than those of twentieth-century Europe. And Europeans of all social strata were prone to violent behavior, a situation quite different from that obtaining in our own time, when a large portion of reported violence is the work of those economically, ethnically, or politically marginalized in modern society.[2] These findings must ultimately impel a reconsideration of modern social theory because they also reveal the general decrease of violence in western Europe over the two or three centuries preceding the precipitate rise in the rates of all reported crime beginning about 1960. In this broader perspective, our current crime wave, with its increase in violence, must for now appear as an interruption in a long-term diminution of violence. Ours are not, at least yet, the most violent of times according to historians.

Our goal in the present volume is to assess the nature and extent of violence in early modern times, to examine its causes, and to weigh the reasons for its generally decreasing incidence until the twentieth-century crime wave. But certain aspects of our undertaking need definition, and first we must note the geographic scope of the present volume. The state

---

[2] For historians' findings on the criminogenic character of such marginalization, see, for example, on the Netherlands Pieter Spierenburg, "Long-Term Trends in Homicide: Theoretical Reflections and Dutch Evidence, Fifteenth to Twentieth Centuries" in Eric A. Johnson and Eric H. Monkkonen (eds.), *The Civilization of Crime: Violence in Town and Country since the Middle Ages* (Urbana: University of Illinois Press, 1996), p. 95; on Imperial Germany Eric A. Johnson, *Urbanization and Crime: Germany 1871–1914* (Cambridge University Press, 1995), pp. 178–79; and on the United States Roger Lane, *Violent Death in the City: Suicide, Accident, and Murder in Nineteenth-Century Philadelphia* (Cambridge, MA: Harvard University Press, 1979), especially pp. 104–14.

of historical research at the end of the twentieth century essentially defines the geographic limits of this study. Very little research has been done yet on crime and justice in eastern Europe, and as a consequence this volume must draw on the results of such studies in western Europe: that is, in England, France, Germany, Italy, the Low Countries, Scandinavia, and Spain.

The chronological scope of this volume is intentionally broad, and it encompasses the entire early modern period, from 1500 to 1800. We have chosen such a long period for two reasons. First, it will allow us to examine human behavior over the long term, permitting us to identify slow, but real, evolution in the violence of Europeans, individually and collectively, over three centuries. More importantly, however, our period encompasses an era of extraordinary changes in western Europe. Social and economic historians have now come to understand that many of these changes had profound impacts on violent behavior and state responses to it, which we will gauge in this book.

Politically, the western European state was perfecting and strengthening its institutions in this period, a process particularly marked in the assertion of its judicial power. This was an age in which many states codified their criminal laws (Germany's *Constitutio Criminalis Carolina* of 1532, France's Criminal Ordinance of Villers-Cotterêts of 1539 and that of 1670, and the Criminal Ordinance of Philip II for the Spanish Netherlands in 1570) and began to expand their judicial institutions to impose state justice throughout their territories. The expansion of state justice injected a measure of violence into European life through the corporal and capital punishments that the penology of the day employed, yet we will see this brutality eventually diminishing along with violent crime itself. But early modern authorities also exercised the growing power of the state more subtly than in simple, raw displays of brutality in public executions. Increasingly, the early modern state regulated its citizens' lives in a multitude of ways. The state issued ordinances and rules governing all manner of human activities, from tavern closure hours to sports, dress, and gender relations. Collectively, such regulatory power, backed at the end of our period by the growing police power of the state, gradually reshaped human behavior.

This was also an age of religious change. Historians of this change now increasingly consider that the first century and a half of our period was an era characterized not by two opposing religious movements – the Protestant Reformation and the Catholic phenomenon styled either the "Counter Reformation" or the "Catholic Reformation" – but of Protestant and Catholic expressions of essential religious reform. Both Catholic and Protestant communities engaged in a complex process,

[handwritten marginal note: Grand Jours – Louis XIV*]*

which many of the era's historians describe as "confessionalization," in which each solidified its dogma and institutions and also imposed discipline on its communicants. The Tridentine Catholic Church, Lutherans, and Calvinists, all sought with pastoral visits and institutions of ecclesiastical discipline to inculcate personal piety, respect for civil authority, and individual moral and ethical probity in their members. Historians increasingly recognize that this work of the early modern church complemented the mission of the state in pacifying society.

The process advanced by Church and state affected gender relations, too. Civil-law theory increasingly replicated the absolutist state in family legislation, erecting the husband and father as the domestic equivalent of the monarch. The scope of women's activities consequently became increasingly circumscribed, from the world of work (as Merry Wiesner has shown) to participation in recreational activities outside of the home.[3] Certainly all of these developments reinforced traditional gender roles to limit further women's participation in activities that might turn violent. But a concomitant of such attitudes that placed women under the legal authority of husband or father limited the legal liability of women in many violent acts. The principle of "coverture" in English law, for example, expressed the almost universal concept that the husband subsumed the wife as a legal entity and thus limited her liability for violent deeds.

Militarily, this was an age of especially sweeping change. The early modern period was one of almost constant west European warfare, and hostile forces imposed their violence on fearful civilian populations almost everywhere. But this was also an age of military revolution, in which warfare became technologically more advanced with the adoption of increasingly sophisticated projectile weapons, and as military forces became more professionalized, better disciplined, and less to be feared by peaceful civilians. The military was an important building block of the early modern state, too. At a most basic level, the state could employ troops to impose order on rebellious populations. But more importantly, the rising cost of the military weaponry and the new, standing, professional armies that employed it, forced the state to develop an institutional and fiscal infrastructure to support armed forces. Those structures sustained judicial, regulatory, and police agencies as well.

Finally, this was an age of great economic change. An expanding revolution in agricultural techniques, evident especially in English enclosures that forced many small farmers off the land, combined with a growing sixteenth-century population to produce a large, impoverished, and often

---

[3] Merry E. Wiesner, *Working Women in Renaissance Germany* (New Brunswick, NJ: Rutgers University Press, 1986).

rootless population. Additional economic dislocation increasingly over-
took artisans with the advance of protoindustrial techniques of organizing
work in the hands of less skilled workers. Although A. L. Beier has shown
that early modern officialdom probably overestimated the threat of such
persons, they did provide many recruits for bands of armed robbers.[4]

If our geographic boundaries can be easily defined, and our diachronic
parameters are revealed to be broad but comprehending a period increasingly well understood by historians, our topic itself, violence, is less easy
to grasp, and indeed poses several issues that we must address. The first of
these is one of definition. This volume manifestly will not address the military violence of war, civil war, and revolution as it affected opposing
forces in the many armed conflicts of this era. While we will chart the collateral violence inflicted by early modern armies on civilian populations
in their paths, our main focus will be on the more quotidian violence of a
civilian population that we will find far more violent than its twenty-
first-century counterpart. Much of the violence we will explore – such as
armed banditry, homicide and assault, rape, and riot – was criminalized,
but not infrequently we will find early modern judges dealing with such
offenses far differently than would the modern bench, reflecting very
different behavior standards in the early modern age. Those standards are
evident in another way, too. Some of the violence we will examine was not
criminalized in state law by early modern legislators. That fact is of tremendous significance for our understanding of the age and its violence,
and we will look, for example, at an apparently very high level of domestic
violence that received little or no official reprobation. Thus our survey
will include both violence proscribed by the law, and that omitted from
the statutes of our period.

Our topic, even when defined, however, remains a difficult one
because, in a sense, it is a moving target. This was quite clearly a violent
age, one in which, as a perceptive French historian wrote: "Like death,
like the cemetery which is at the center of the village, violence is at the
heart of life in the fifteenth, sixteenth, and seventeenth centuries." But the
"nasty, dirty, and violent" habits of Europeans that this historian identified were being transformed in our period.[5] Western Europeans were
becoming less violent, as a society increasingly governed by manners and
customs close to our own evolved in the early modern period. Thus our

[4] A. L. Beier, *Masterless Men: The Vagrancy Problem in England, 1560–1640* (London: Methuen, 1985), pp. 123–45.
[5] Robert Muchembled, "Anthropologie de la violence dans la France moderne (XVe–XVIIIe siècle)," *Revue de synthèse*, IVe sér., 108 (1987), p. 40. See also his *Popular Culture and Elite Culture in France, 1400–1750*, translated by Lydia G. Cochrane (Baton Rouge: Louisiana State University Press, 1985) and *L'invention de l'homme moderne: sensibilités, moeurs et comportements collectifs sous l'Ancien Régime* (Paris: Fayard, 1988).

task will be not only one of description of the forms of early modern violence, but also one of charting the evolution of those forms.

Historians and sociologists have long identified this evolution of western behavior, and have attempted to pose explanations of the process. Almost a century ago the German Max Weber, one of the early, great figures of modern social thought, warned of the "iron cage" created by an emerging rationalized and bureaucratized capitalist society that increasingly confined the actions of the individual. Modern capitalist society for Weber meant the growing imposition of discipline in all social phenomena, the army, industry, and the state, with its obvious impact on human behavior.[6]

But if Weber characterized the general evolution of modern society, few at first attempted to describe the processes by which this discipline was imposed. The constraints of traditional academic disciplines seem to have inhibited many scholars in undertaking such a task. Sociologists tend to be concerned with present problems, rather than historical trends; historians, with their individual periods of specialization, often fail to address general or long-term issues; and many philosophers lack sufficient foundation in history to undertake diachronic studies.

The scholars who did address these changes largely concurred with Weber that a process of imposing social discipline through new power dynamics marked the early modern period. The French philosopher Michel Foucault was one of the first modern scholars to offer a vision of the process. Identifying changes in punishment and enforcement of social norms with basic alterations in mentality occasioned by the rise of the bourgeois-capitalist state, he described an increasingly subtle, and devious, state repression of the individual. Foucault highlighted the disappearance of traditional chastisements of the bodies of criminals in brutal public capital and corporal punishments, and their replacement by confinement designed to remold the spirits of offenders. This "great confinement" dated from the late medieval period, and aimed to bend nonconformists of all sorts to society's norms in a growing institutional structure of asylums, hospitals, workhouses, and prisons. Indeed, Foucault's work traced the institutional expressions of confinement, from the evolution of madhouses from medieval lazar houses rendered obsolete by the disappearance of leprosy, to the birth of the modern

[6] Max Weber, *The Protestant Ethic and the Spirit of Capitalism*, translated by Talcott Parsons (London: Allen and Unwin, 1948), p. 181. While fairly standard among English-speaking scholars, Parsons's translation of *"ein stahlhartes Gehäuse"* as "iron cage" is not universally accepted.

penitentiary.[7] In what he termed his "archaeology of knowledge" Foucault found such institutions producing a society much more closely disciplined than that of the early years of our period of study.

But many scholars increasingly found Foucault's theories, little grounded in historical research, to be inadequate explanations of behavioral changes in western Europe in the early modern period. In Germany the historian Gerhard Oestreich also posed an explanation for behavioral changes reshaped by new power realities. Observing such problems of late medieval society as population growth and resulting subsistence crises, as well as the inability of spiritual institutions to regulate behavior and morals, Oestreich discerned the need for municipal authorities to provide enhanced policing of human behavior. In the face of real problems of public order, civic functionaries, responding according to need, not a systematic plan, began a process of social regulation. A new stage in this process, one styled "social discipline," was achieved when territorial governments assumed the controlling role in it. Guided in part by Neostoic philosophy associated with Justus Lipsius (1547–1606), governments first built disciplined armies and then, in the eighteenth century, bureaucracies capable of regulating much more of human life. The result, according to Oestreich, was massive empowerment of the state to control and regulate the behavior of its subjects.[8]

The chief scholar to move beyond the simple linkage of behavioral change with the growth of the early modern state institutions and processes of social discipline, however, was Norbert Elias. A social theoretician of very great influence today, Elias advanced an extraordinary account of the "civilizing process" of the early modern period in a book that gained scant recognition when first published on the eve of World War II.[9]

A German scholar with especially broad training, Elias studied medicine, philosophy, and psychology before completing graduate work in sociology. For Elias the "civilizing process" only partially involved the

---

[7] Michel Foucault, *Madness and Civilization: A History of Insanity in the Age of Reason*, translated by Richard Howard (New York: Pantheon Books, 1965); *The Birth of the Clinic: An Archaeology of Medical Perception*, translated by A. M. Sheridan Smith (New York: Pantheon Books, 1973); and *Discipline and Punish: The Birth of the Prison*, translated by Alan Sheridan (New York: Vintage Books, 1979).

[8] Gerhard Oestreich, "Strukturprobleme des europäischen Absolutismus," *Vierteljahreschrift für Wirtschafts- und Sozialgeschichte* 55 (1968), pp. 329–47, and *Neostoicism and the Early Modern State*, edited by Brigitta Oestreich and H. G. Koenigsberger, translated by David McLintock (Cambridge University Press, 1982).

[9] Published as *Über den Prozess der Zivilisation* in 1939, Norbert Elias's work is now available in translation: *The Civilizing Process*, vol. I, *The History of Manners*; vol. II, *Power and Civility*, translated by Edmund Jephcott (New York: Pantheon Books, 1978–82).

growth of state power for social control. Elias also described the civilizing process as "a specific transformation of human behavior," both of individuals and of groups; and he examined not only that behavior but also the social and psychological structures that reshaped it, beginning in the late medieval period. Elias described evolving patterns of conduct and inclination, drawing on such sources as normative texts like etiquette books, literary works, and art. And he traced the diffusion and internalization of new norms of behavior through society as new groups experienced heightened levels of psychological inhibition. Linked to this process was the evolution of modern social interdependency that, in late medieval court society as in modern business relationships, required self-control and deliberation in one's interpersonal relations.

This process of social and psychological transformation first affected the warlike, knightly order of late medieval society. Feudal warriors evolved by the sixteenth and seventeenth centuries into a court society in which one's standing depended not only on lineage but in large measure, too, on one's civility and cultural level. That development facilitated the civilizing process, for the pacification of the knightly order created a power vacuum in society that was filled by the state. As this increasingly centralized authority monopolized power, it was able to increase levels of peace and security to achieve a subtle effect identified by Elias:

> The monopoly organization of physical violence does not usually constrain the individual by a direct threat. A strongly predictable compulsion or pressure mediated in a variety of ways is constantly exerted on the individual. This operates to a considerable extent through the medium of his own reflection . . . in other words, it imposes on people a greater or lesser degree of self-control.[10]

Elias described a process of internalization of restraints that first affected the aristocracy, then spread through society. This was a process continuing over generations, leading eventually to a society less prone to violence as the "threshold of shame and embarrassment" attending the commission of violence rose. Most interestingly, the process Elias posited spread first to urban areas; contrary to their modern, violent image, the cities were the first zones pacified after the royal and princely courts. Historians also identified conscious, organized efforts by elites, beginning in the fifteenth century, aimed at raising popular behavioral standards. The seventeenth-century Compagnie du Saint-Sacrement in France, the Societies for the Reformation of Manners in England, and the eighteenth-century Dutch Society for the General Welfare (Maatshappij tot Nut von het Algemeen) attacked swearing, lewd behavior, gaming, and bawdy houses in an attempt to improve the level of popular conduct.

Elias recognized that the civilizing process was not marked by an

---

[10] Elias, *The Civilizing Process*, vol. II, p. 239.

ineluctable linear progression. The Holocaust that consumed many, including his own parents, during his lifetime was proof that war, revolution, and other events rendered the civilizing process a fragile one. Nonetheless, Elias provided a theoretical framework that has influenced much historical writing on the early modern period, including the present book.

The differing interpretations of these social thinkers, in addition to historians' findings on violence, indicate that in regard to human behavior, too, the early modern period on which we will focus was one of dynamic change. In the chapters that follow we will address numerous aspects of the problem of violence in the early modern period.

Perceptions of dangers are important in shaping individual and governmental responses to them. Often, as we suggested at the outset of this Introduction, perceptions do not accurately reflect reality. But perceptions must be a part of our historical study because what people of the past thought was occurring at a particular time was often more important than what (as scholars, exploiting archival evidence, now know) really was occurring. Such perceptions shape human action, especially when they reinforce a sense of endangerment. In Chapter 1 we will examine the perception of violence in early modern society through its representations in popular culture. Asking basic questions about society's fears and insecurities, we will analyze the perception of violence in early modern Europe as represented in popular literature and in other cultural forms. We will find that violence was never far from the consciousness of early modern Europeans.

In Chapters 2 and 3 we will focus on the modes of containing violence in early modern Europe. We start in Chapter 2 with an examination of arms possession among early modern Europeans and the largely ineffective efforts of the state to limit privately owned weapons and to establish its own monopoly of force. We will also assess the threat posed to civilians by the early modern army and the slow evolution of that force as an imperfect instrument for maintaining order among the state's subjects. In Chapter 3 we will focus on the practice of justice in early modern Europe, and we will discover the persistence of various modes of regulating disputes outside of the institutions of state justice. Such modes of resolution included duels that resembled medieval trial by combat, feuds, and various forms of subjudicial arbitration and accommodation. In the enforcement of state justice we will find police resources limited, if not nonexistent. The judicial institutions of the state often added considerably to the violent atmosphere of the first centuries of the early modern era by responding to violence with exemplary brutal punishments.

With Chapters 4, 5, 6, and 7 we will turn to the violence of the early modern era. We will find attitudes toward violence quite different from our own. Indeed, for men and women of the era we will see that violence was less a problem to be solved than an almost accepted aspect of inter-personal discourse. In Chapter 4 we will treat the violence individuals wrought on those whom they knew, addressing assault and homicide, domestic violence, rape, and infanticide. Chapter 5 presents a treatment of the highly ritualized violence of the early modern period in activities of youth groups, the popular festivals of the age, and the entertainments and sports that added particular violence to the life of the age. Chapter 6 offers an examination of the multifaceted repertoire of early modern popular protest. Armed collective action rooted in subsistence problems, issues of taxation, and religious differences all figure in this chapter. And finally, Chapter 7 discusses organized crime and the violence wrought by the smugglers and robbers who filled its ranks.

FURTHER READING

The constraints of space preclude a full bibliographic essay including works in all of the major western European languages. The following is a brief listing to provide a basis for further reading, and emphasizes works in English. A full biblio-graphic essay, including works in English, French, German, Italian, and Spanish is available at this website: http://uk.cambridge.org/resources/052159894X.

Elias, Norbert, *The Civilizing Process*, translated by Edmund Jephcott. 2 vols. (New York: Pantheon Books, 1978, 1982).
  The Court Society, translated by Edmund Jephcott (New York: Pantheon Books, 1983).
Foucault, Michel, *Madness and Civilization: A History of Insanity in the Age of Reason*, translated by Richard Howard (New York: Pantheon Books, 1965).
  The Birth of the Clinic: An Archaeology of Medical Perception, translated by A.M. Sheridan Smith (New York: Pantheon Books, 1973.
  Discipline and Punish: The Birth of the Prison, translated by Alan Sheridan (New York: Vintage Books, 1979).
Hsia, Ronnie Po-chia, *Social Discipline and the Reformation: Central Europe, 1550–1750* (New York: Routledge, 1989).
Muchembled, Robert, *L'invention de l'homme moderne: sensibilités, moeurs et com-portements* (Paris: Fayard, 1988).
Oestreich, Gerhard, *Neostoicism and the Early Modern State*, edited by Brigitta Oestreich and H. G. Koenigsberger, translated by David McLintock (Cambridge: Cambridge University Press, 1982).
Raeff, Marc, *The Well-Ordered Police State: Social and Institutional Change Through Law in the Germanies and Russia, 1600–1800* (New Haven: Yale University Press, 1983).
Shoemaker, Robert B., "Reforming the City: The Reformation of Manners Campaign in London, 1690–1738" in Lee Davison *et al.* (eds.), *Stilling the Grumbling Hive: The Response to Social and Economic Problems in England, 1689–1750*, pp. 99–120 (Stroud: Alan Sutton, 1992).

1   Representations of violence

Large numbers of soldiers filled the marketplace of Valence, France, on 26 May 1755 to maintain order at the public execution of a brutal smuggler. Carrying out the verdict of the Commission of Valence, a special court dealing only with smugglers, the public executioner bound Louis Mandrin to a structure in the "X" shape of the cross of Saint Andrew, broke his limbs with an iron bar, and displayed the dead man's remains on a wheel for spectators to see the results of his offenses.

The brief career that brought Mandrin to the gruesome fate of being broken on the wheel had been a violent and spectacular one. Born the son of a prosperous horse merchant in Saint-Etienne-de-Saint-Geoirs in southeastern France in 1725, Mandrin initially followed his father's trade, branching out into supplying the royal army in Italy in the War of the Austrian Succession (1740–48). The war's end, however, nullified Mandrin's supply contract, commercially ruined him, and embittered him toward the royal tax administrators, officials of the Ferme, or tax farm, with whom he had dealt as an army contractor. A resident of the border province of Dauphiné, Mandrin then turned to defying the tax regulations enforced by the Ferme by smuggling goods into France from nearby Switzerland and the neighboring Savoy region of the kingdom of Piedmont-Sardinia.

Such smuggling activities to avoid payment of taxes levied by governments on certain goods were common in border and coastal regions of early modern Europe, particularly where widespread poverty drove many to the trade in contraband simply to survive. In the relatively poor Dauphiné region, many engaged in smuggling tobacco, salt, and other products, their activities concealed from the authorities' detection by the province's rugged terrain and forests. The extent of the smuggling and its importance to the local economy, indeed, gave it a certain legitimacy in the view of the peasant population and thus made easy Mandrin's adoption of a trade patently illegal in the view of the state.

Mandrin quickly graduated in 1754 from petty smuggling to leadership of a band of 200–300 men drawn from the ranks of the economically marginal population of Dauphiné, including impoverished peasants, demobilized soldiers, and deserters. With such numbers, Mandrin could move large quantities of contraband tobacco, cotton textiles, and other products into France and sell them with impunity throughout the eastern and central regions of the country at low, tax-free prices. Those who opposed these activities, whether soldiers, tax officials, or civilians, often met violent ends at the hands of Mandrin's large band, and in one engagement his group killed fifty-three soldiers. Indeed, the group's strength permitted it briefly to occupy two sizeable towns, and, when opposed by overwhelming numbers, to escape across the border to Savoy.

The authorities viewed Mandrin as a serious threat, most especially because they feared he enjoyed widespread local popularity. A charismatic leader, Mandrin appeared to some to struggle against tax oppression and was rumored to leave the poor untroubled, almost a Robin Hood type in the public mind. Thus, French officials were willing to take risks to capture Mandrin, indeed to break international law. Acting on information from a traitor to Mandrin, French forces violated the border of Piedmont-Sardinia to capture the smuggler in early May 1755 and to spirit him back into France for trial.

These are the facts of the Mandrin case. They reveal him to have been one of the most notorious representatives of the numerous bands of armed robbers, military deserters, and smugglers who violently terrorized rural early modern Europe that we will examine in detail in Chapter 7. And he was the victim of the sort of grisly public execution that we will examine in Chapter 3. But of more immediate importance for us is the way Mandrin and his violent acts were represented to the public of his age. As we saw in the Introduction, the public's understanding of violence in our own era is founded not only on facts, but also on perceptions that can lead people to conclusions quite different from those based on empirical data. This was the case in the early modern era as well, and to understand whether the public in that period felt secure from violence or whether it believed violence was increasing in its midst, we must examine the information that reached it.

We may use the Mandrin case as an example. Only a tiny minority of the French public had experienced firsthand Mandrin's brutality. Knowledge of the smuggler's activities thus entered the consciousness of the vast majority of the French people in two secondhand fashions. The most reliable knowledge of any act of violence usually emerges from the investigation of the case and the presentation of the resulting evidence in court, if the act is prosecuted as a crime. Sometimes, in the courts of continental Europe in our period, torture even elicited evidence of a violent crime directly from the defendant. True, the public could witness the presentation of evidence only in English courtrooms; in France and other continental European countries, where Roman rather than common law jurisprudence prevailed, most criminal courts were closed to the public. But early modern tribunals, even on the continent, generated large quantities of printed matter that were posted or read publicly. These might be court decrees announcing sentences, printed legal briefs, or perhaps church decrees (called *monitoires* in France) that spelled out the basic facts of a case and called on Catholics, under threat of excommunication, to bring any evidence they might have to judicial authorities. All of these documents provided factual data on violence under judicial investigation to a public that had an active interest in the law's operation.

But the early modern public, like its modern counterpart, formed many of its perceptions of violence from other, less factual sources. Rumor, songs and popular entertainments, and the print media shaped its public perceptions, while folk traditions, such as beliefs in Robin Hood figures and a diabolical presence in the world, informed popular understanding of violence. Thus the early modern public's perception of violence sometimes differed substantially from the reality. Moreover, the number of accounts assailing the public could be vast. In the case of Mandrin, the historian Hans-Jürgen Lüsebrink studied the representations of the smuggler in popular literature and pictures published in the wake of his execution. He examined thirteen different narrative accounts of the smuggler's career, some with radically different portrayals of Mandrin's violence, as well as dramatic works, pamphlets, poems, and pictures of the criminal. Indeed, shortly after his execution the smuggler's story appeared in English and Italian versions, and some of the numerous printed accounts of Mandrin's career remained in print for almost a century.[1] Assessment of the impact of such texts on popular perception of violent crime requires analysis of how violence was represented to the early modern public.

From oral to print culture

The culture of early modern Europe remained largely an oral one; in most countries the majority of the population was illiterate and received its information by word of mouth or seeing, not by reading. Indeed, recent research on the history of reading suggests that even many literate

---

[1] Hans-Jürgen Lüsebrink, "Images et représentations sociales de la criminalité au XVIIIᵉ siècle: l'exemple de Mandrin," *Revue d'histoire moderne et contemporaine* 25 (1979), pp. 347–64, and *Kriminalität und Literatur im Frankreich des 18. Jahrhunderts. Literarische Formen, soziale Funktionen und Wissenkonstituenten von Kriminalitätsdarstellung im Zeitalter des Auflärung* (Munich and Vienna: R. Oldenberg Verlag, 1983).

members of socially elite groups read very narrowly, chiefly in religious texts. Thus for much of our period they, like their less privileged neighbors, probably received a large part of their news from nonprinted sources that they heard or saw. From the historian's point of view, this exchange of information is difficult to follow because it left no written record. But there are points at which we can glimpse the effect of spoken news and rumor on early modern Europeans, and the character of the reports may strike us as familiar.

People readily transmitted bad news by word of mouth, especially information indicating, correctly or incorrectly, that conditions were growing worse. Violence was a favorite theme. Thus the city marshal of London reported in 1718 on talk in the public houses:

Now is the general complaint of the taverns, the coffee-houses, the shop-keepers and others, that their customers are afraid when it is dark to come to their houses and shops for fear that their hats and wigs should be snitched from their heads or their swords taken from their sides or that they may be blinded, knocked down, cut or stabbed; nay the coaches cannot secure them, but they are likewise cut and robbed in the public streets, & c. By which means traffic of the City is much interrupted.[2]

But urban centers were not the only zones in early modern Europe in which we may discern rapid and widespread circulation of rumors of violence, true or not. As we will see in Chapters 2 and 7, wandering bands of armed robbers, military deserters, and other renegades violently threatened the security of rural Europe in our period, and the fears they generated could be inflated by rumors to create panics that historians have documented. Indeed, one of the best examples of this phenomenon occurred in France in the Great Fear of 1789. Widespread and unfounded rumors of "brigands" and soldiers roaming the countryside led to a panic in which peasants armed themselves for defense and, when the rumored attackers failed to appear, turned on the local landowning nobility in one of the opening acts of the Revolution.

Proverbs, a key part of this oral culture that helped to define the existence of early modern Europeans, also suggest a familiarity with violence. Thus an old Dutch proverb, which defined an age in which most men carried knives in order to cut their food, conveys to us ominous suggestions about the level of public order: "One-hundred Netherlanders, one-hundred knives."[3]

---

[2] Quoted in Ian A. Bell, *Literature and Crime in Augustan England* (London and New York: Routledge, 1991), pp. 13–14.

[3] A. T. Van Deursen, *Plain Lives in a Golden Age: Popular Culture, Religion and Society in Seventeenth-Century Holland,* translated by Maarten Ultee (Cambridge: Cambridge University Press, 1991), p. 110.

Even popular entertainments spread the message that early modern society was a violent one. In Sicily blind wandering minstrels, the *urvi*, often sang songs about brigands while accompanying themselves on violins, and such performing was common elsewhere as well. In fact, songs, which were easy to remember because their lines were rhymed, carried all manner of current news, including acts of violence. Indeed, historians have found evidence that many people committed large numbers of such songs to memory simply by hearing their repetition in public places set to familiar tunes, and many educated persons as well as the unlettered enjoyed such popular music.

Other entertainments gave more tangible forms to early modern violence. Street players, like the improvising members of Italy's companies of the Comedia dell'Arte, often portrayed violence. And in England, in the "Punch and Judy" puppet shows performed in the eighteenth century in streets, markets, and fairs, we find an entertainment form that drew a largely young-adult audience to witness levels of violence perhaps only matched by those in twenty-first-century cinema and television. A typical presentation featured Punch abusing his neighbor's dog with a stick, decapitating its owner, beating his own wife and child, and skewering the devil on his own trident. All of this was presented with slapstick, scatological humor, and sexual innuendo that caused the audience to laugh at high levels of violence. French audiences guffawed at fundamentally similar presentations of "Guignol."

In the sixteenth century, however, the oral culture coexisted with a new print culture that would eventually dominate western Europe. True, in our period the majority of Europeans were illiterate, with inhabitants of the north far more literate than those of the south, the wealthy and privileged far more likely to be able to read and write than the poor, and men more likely to be lettered than women, but that illiteracy did not totally impede the spread of print culture. It now seems clear that early modern Europeans were far more familiar with printed texts than historians earlier imagined. It is evident, for example, that the oral and the written overlapped in this society. Basic printed materials surrounded early modern Europeans in the form of decrees, announcements, advertising flyers, and even street signs. And the literate often read these to the unlettered. The act of reading aloud may not have been a conscious choice on the reader's part; many readers only read aloud, even when alone, a fact underlined by the sixteenth-century German employment of the same verb to mean "to read" and "to read aloud." In eighteenth-century Paris the unlettered could hear the news read at several public reading locations in return for payment of a small sum. A great deal of reading aloud went on in workplaces, religious assemblies, and social gatherings, and many of the texts we will analyze seem to have been designed for reading aloud because they open with phrases like "Listen . . ." and "As you are about to hear . . ."

In addition, the actual rate of reading ability may well have exceeded the rate of signatures, the traditional measure by which historians have attempted to gauge literacy. Access to education was certainly limited, but schooling was available, and a city such as Paris had more than 500 elementary schools in the late eighteenth century, many of them free. Research in England and France, moreover, suggests that some children attended these schools only long enough to learn to read. Reading was taught before writing, and teaching it was quicker and easier than writing, which required close instructional supervision. Indeed, many who could read but not write passed through no formal schooling at all. In Sweden, whose Lutheran faith demanded scriptural reading, home instruction and teaching by parish clergy had achieved almost universal literacy by the eighteenth century, a fact attested to by records of reading-comprehension examinations conducted by pastors under a church ordinance of 1686. But even as late as 1770 only 20 percent of Swedes could write.

If many early modern Europeans thus had direct or indirect access to printed materials, they found in such materials representations of violence that indicate that early modern publishers had already discovered that the more sensational the news of an act of violence, the better were sales of the press account. And a wide and evolving range of materials was available in the sixteenth, seventeenth, and eighteenth centuries. The materials to which we turn were all works designed for mass circulation and have sometimes been referred to as products of the "popular" press to suggest they addressed the lower orders of early modern society, participants in a culture some historians have characterized as increasingly separate and distinct from that of socially elite groups. But the work of such scholars as Roger Chartier and others has demonstrated that very little was written in this period exclusively for the lower orders of society, although elite texts might have been adapted in style and presentation for a popular readership.[4] Moreover, the presence of supposedly popular texts in the libraries of socially elite persons suggests a very wide readership and influence for many of the materials that we will examine.

[4] Roger Chartier, *The Cultural Uses of Print in Early Modern France*, translated by Lydia G. Cochrane (Princeton: Princeton University Press, 1987). See also Bernard Capp, "Popular Literature" in Barry Reay (ed.), *Popular Culture in Seventeenth-Century England* (New York: St. Martin's Press, 1985), pp. 198–243; and V. A. C. Gatrell, *The Hanging Tree: Execution and the English People, 1770–1868* (Oxford: Oxford University Press, 1994), pp. 127–33.

Forms of print materials

The first form of printed matter to gain wide circulation in our period was the broadsheet. Broadsheets dealt with all sorts of themes, but it was their focus on current events that made them the primary news source in much of sixteenth- and seventeenth-century western Europe. War, religious issues, witchcraft, crime, and violence, were all reported on these sheets, and broadsheets drew on familiar cultural forms to achieve wide diffusion in the sixteenth century.

Their format was a familiar one in the period, that of a sheet of paper printed on one side that looked much like the official proclamations that had been posted on the walls of European cities since the late Middle Ages. In England even the size of early broadsheets often replicated the nine-by-twelve-inch folio sheets of royal proclamations.

Broadsheets also deployed various other strategies to attract a public still largely wedded to the older, oral culture. Many of these sheets (called *Bilderbogen* in Germany, *pliegos sueltos* in Spain, and *canards* or *complaintes* in France) employed a series of pictures that scholars have likened to early comicbooks. Figure 1 illustrates one of the early German *Bilderbogen*, a sequence of pictures printed from woodblocks illustrating an act of violence from its inception to its final consequences. In the pictures Heinrich Rosenzweig, having been ruined at gambling, made a pact with the devil and brutally murdered his wife and children with a sword and ax. His punishment was painful. He was drawn to the place of execution in a cart while the executioner tore his flesh with hot pincers. Then the executioner broke his limbs and displayed Rosenzweig's remains on a wheel. Such sensational pictures tempted the unlettered to acquire these sheets, but for the literate a print message like that in Figure 1 often accompanied the picture. In the print message publishers often employed the song, another familiar cultural form that, as we have seen, had long been an element of news transmission in traditional oral culture. The following lines, excerpted from a ballad sung to a popular tune, *Bragandary Downe*, appeared on an English broadsheet of 1635 as *Murder upon Murder*. They recount the bloody careers of robbers Thomas Sherwood (alias "Country Tom") and Elizabeth Evans (alias "Canbery Bess").

> List Christians all unto my song,
> 'Twill move your hearts to pity,
> What bloody murders have been done,
> Of late about the city:
> We daily see the blood of Cain,
> Amongst us ever will remain.
> O murder, lust and murder,

Figure 1. Jacob Sing, *News of Heinrich Rosenzweig, Who Murdered His Wife and Six Children in Quedlinburg, Saxony, 2 January 1621*. Woodcut, c. 1621.

Is the foul stink of sin.
      . . .
Of the story now at hand,
The truth I will declare,
How God leaves man unto himself,
Of Satan then beware,
Thus doth Sherwood truly find,
He unto murder bent his mind.
O murder, lust and murder,
Is the foul stink of sin.

A man of honest parentage,
Trained up to husbandry,
But weary of that honest life,
To London he did hie:
Where to his dismal woeful fate,
He chose a quean[5] for his copesmate.[6]
O murder, lust and murder,
Is the foul stink of sin.

One Canbery Bess in Turnbull Street
On him did cast an eye,
And prayed him to give her some drink
As he was passing by;
O so too soon he gave consent,
And for the same doth now repent.
O murder, lust and murder,
Is the foul stink of sin.

For by alluring tempting baits,
She sotted so his mind,
That unto any villainy
This Sherwood was inclined,
His coin all spent he must have more,
For to content his filthy whore.
O murder, lust and murder,
Is the foul stink of sin.

Much mischief then by them was done,
In and about the city,
But still they escape unpunished
[Not known] more was the pity,
To deadly sins they then did fall,
Not only rob but murder all.
O murder, lust and murder,
Is the foul stink of sin.

---

[5] "Quean": prostitute.   [6] "Copesmate": colleague.

The first was M.[7] William Loe,
A gentleman of note,
And cruel Sherwood laid him low
With an inhuman stroke:
Nor birth nor blood they did regard,
Yet death for blood is their reward.
O murder, lust and murder,
Is the foul stink of sin.

. . .

The last that fell into their hands
Was M. Claxton he,
A gentleman of good descent
And well beloved truly,
Who walked unarmed by break of day,
In Holborn fields they did him slay.
O murder, lust and murder,
Is the foul stink of sin.

A scarlet coat from him they took,
New suit from top to toe,
His boots, hat, shirt they took from him,
Much money eke[8] also,
And left him in the fields so wide
And fled away and not descried.
O murder, lust and murder,
Is the foul stink of sin.

But mark the goodness of the Lord,
On the succeeding day,
That Sherwood with his trull[9] did think
Beyond sea take their way,
In Houndsditch were together tane,[10]
Selling the coat in the same lane.
O murder, lust and murder,
Is the foul stink of sin.

. . .

For these bad acts he now doth die,
Just judgment for his meed.[11]
All such ill-livers grant they may,
No worse nor better speed,
So shall England from crying sin,
Be ever freed, God's mercy win.
O murder, lust and murder,
Is the foul stink of sin.
Finis[12]

[7] "M.": master.   [8] "Eke": in addition.   [9] "Trull": prostitute.
[10] "Tane": taken, captured.   [11] "Meed": just reward.
[12] Reprinted in Joseph H. Marshburn and Alan R. Velie (eds.), *Blood and Knavery. A Collection of English Renaissance Pamphlets and Ballads of Crime and Sin* (Rutherford, Madison, and Teaneck: Fairleigh Dickinson University Press, 1973), pp. 66–73.

The song itself was an important marketing device for popular print materials that may also have provided a bridge between oral and written cultures for the ill educated. In Spain, in Madrid and the surrounding regions, a confraternity of blind peddlers monopolized the sales of much popular print matter from 1581 to 1836. Their sales methods appealed to both the literate and the unlettered, for these vendors, accompanied by a violin or guitar, sang from memory the songs and rhymes they sought to sell. And in Germany *Bänkelsänger*, itinerant street vendors, set up illustrations of the crimes of the condemned on execution days then sang and acted out the offenses while pointing to the appropriate pictures. They concluded their performances by selling print copies of their songs and rhymes to the crowd drawn by their show.

The use of songs on broadsheets persisted throughout our period, although, as we will see, other printed materials eventually replaced broadsheets as the chief source of news. Some broadsheet printers, having found a good story, printed it in song as long as it was marketable, and we find evidence of the enduring marketability of such songs in a French *canard* confiscated by the police in 1796. The *canard*, illustrated in Figure 2, is a celebration of the fantastic career of Poulailler, a robber executed ten years earlier, who allegedly stole from the rich and shared his spoils with the poor. The sixth stanza reads:

> Everyone says that this Poulailler
> Destroys no one
> When he stops them;
> And if you tell him your plight,
> He will have pity on you,
> And give you money.[13]

The *canard* further portrayed Poulailler as the leader of a band of some 500 men whose ability to elude the authorities suggested magical powers to disappear or metamorphose into nonhuman forms.

Broadsheets with prose texts also employed pictures to enhance sales of news stories. Some of the actions portrayed suggest that the author had heavily sensationalized the facts of the story or, worse, had created a work of fiction. One such account, luridly illustrated, allegedly came from Frankenstein in Silesia in 1606. Drawing on longstanding superstitions about the evil character of grave diggers, the broadsheet reported that eight grave diggers, two of whom were women, had killed a number of their neighbors with a poison powder applied to thresholds and door handles. These evil grave diggers then robbed houses, corpses, and churches, cut the fetuses from pregnant women to eat them, and had

---

[13] Archives Nationales de France, BB[18]748. Ministère de la Justice, Correspondance générale de la Division criminelle, Seine.

Figure 2. Anonymous, *New Song to the Tune of Meunière. The Famous Poulailler*. Centre historique des Archives nationales à Paris (BB[18] 748). Colored engraving, 1796.

sexual intercourse with bodies unearthed from the graveyard. In all, 1,500 people were said to have perished in the gruesome crimes for which the grave diggers were executed.[14]

While broadsheet publishers did use familiar forms to attract readers, they also adopted new techniques to assist sales. Many broadsheets had

[14] Illustrated in David Kunzle, *The Early Comic Strip: Narrative Strips and Picture Stories in the European Broadsheet, c. 1450–1825* (Berkeley: University of California Press, 1973), p. 171.

lurid or suggestive titles, like headlines, to attract customers, as those of a few English broadsheets illustrate: *The notorious robber's lamentation, or, Whitney's ditty in the gaol of Newgate* (1693); *A sad and true relation of the apprehension, trial and confession, condemnation and execution of two murtherers who killed a worthy knight* (1675); *The bloody-minded husband, or, the unfortunate wife* (1690); and *The Yorkshire tragedy* (c. 1685).

Pictures never disappeared from this sort of publication and, indeed, groupings of pictures developing an account of sensational events reached their greatest early modern development in the work of the English artist and engraver William Hogarth (1697–1764). In Hogarth's skillfully executed pictures, many of which were sold at modest prices, image overwhelmed text and portrayed much-sensationalized violence. The most graphic of Hogarth's illustrations of violence is the series of four engravings entitled *The Four Stages of Cruelty* that follow the career of Tom Nero.

In *The First Stage of Cruelty* the artist portrayed Nero as a child cruelly tormenting animals with his friends. *The Second Stage of Cruelty* showed Nero as an adult coachman abusing his overburdened horse, and *Cruelty in Perfection* (Figure 3) depicted a particularly heinous act of violence, Nero's murder of his lover, Ann Gill. A letter in the hand of one of those persons surrounding the captured Tom shows that Gill had robbed her employer to give the proceeds of the theft to Nero. Yet Gill is pregnant and, perhaps to avoid his responsibility for the child, Nero has cut her throat, and partially dismembered her. The picture evokes elements of the macabre later successfully employed by twentieth-century Hollywood, including the tombstone, a bat, the owl that is a stock character in modern horror films, a clock showing that the deed was done near the midnight witching hour, a skull and crossbones, a crescent moon with clouds, and an apparently haunted house with an escaping figure, to create an especially eerie view of this manifestation of Nero's violence. In the final frame in this series, *The Reward of Cruelty*, Hogarth depicted the dissection of the executed Nero by surgeons who allowed dogs to eat his heart and intestines. Eighteenth-century viewers of Hogarth's work must have felt themselves part of a brutal society indeed.

Pamphlets and small books were the second form of print material widely circulated in our period. In the late sixteenth century they became the most common form of cheap German texts, while in England, France, and the Dutch Republic these publications began to supplant broadsheets as leading sources of news in the course of the seventeenth century. Publishers often produced these works in the cheapest possible fashion, using inexpensive ink and low-quality paper in a production process that frequently employed secondhand, worn type for printing and

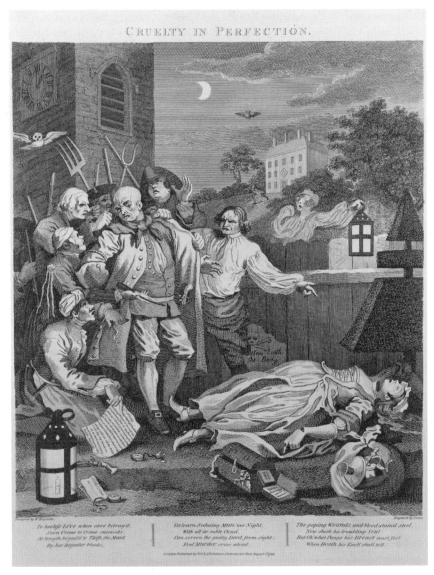

Figure 3. William Hogarth, *Cruelty in Perfection*. Engraving, 1751. From the Collection of the Patrick and Beatrice Heggarty Museum of Art, Marquette University, Milwaukee, Wisconsin.

recycled woodblocks for illustrations. But these works were longer than the broadsheet, and the added space permitted more detailed accounts of events that increasingly appeared in prose rather than rhymes or songs.

This kind of text circulated under a number of names. In England such pamphlets and small books were called "chapbooks" after the "chapmen," or peddlers, who marketed them. In Sweden they were called *Skillingtryck*, or "shilling literature," after the small coin required for their purchase, while in Spain they were known as *literatura de cordel* or *pliegos de cordel* after the cords on which vendors displayed them in markets, and German buyers acquired *Flugschriften*, or pamphlets. But the expression of this literary form most intensively studied by historians is the *Bibliothèque bleue* of France. So named because of the cheap blue paper covers of books in the series, the *Bibliothèque bleue* began as a publishing strategy by the Oudot family of printers in Troyes about 1600 to offer a series of cheap books, in a uniform format, adapted from existing texts for a mass audience.

In whatever language, these pamphlets and small books grew out of printed broadsheets. Publishers printed four pages on broadsheet folio pages, then folded and cut the sheets to create a multipage booklet. Several such sheets might then be sewn together to produce booklets ranging from eight to more than 100 pages. Thus the term *canard* in French designated both illustrated broadsheets and booklets in our period, and the themes of the pamphlets and small books often duplicated those of the broadsheets.

These works offered practical advice on manners and farming matters, as well as works of popular religion, fairytales, romances, and stories of legendary heroes. Publishers of pamphlets and little books, like those of broadsheets, also realized that tales of the monstrous, supernatural, catastrophic, criminal, and violent always yielded many sales: literature on rogues engaged in crime and aberrant behavior proved a consistently good seller for publishers of these texts. Also especially attractive to readers were works developed out of the popular Spanish picaresque fiction of the sixteenth and seventeenth centuries in which their narrators recounted their experiences in the underworlds of thieves, cheats, and gypsies.

If tales of petty crime and trickery sold, so, too, did those of more spectacular and violent events, and these figured prominently in the corpus of printers in every western country. The more spectacular the violence, either because of its brutality or because of the unusual character of the perpetrator, the better. Particularly saleable were accounts of armed robbers and smugglers, including: the Guilleri brothers, Mandrin, and Cartouche in France; Robin Hood, James Hind, and Dick Turpin in

England; Diego Corrientes in Spain; and Christian Käsebier and Schinderhannes in Germany.

Much of this literature also recounted the exploits of those who committed violent deeds, culminating in a final act of violence in the public corporal and capital punishments they endured. Indeed, when an execution occurred, street vendors, like the *Bänkelsänger*, usually hawked the stories and alleged confessions of the condemned individuals in pamphlets near the gallows. The market leader in this genre for much of the eighteenth century was *The Ordinary of Newgate, His Account of the Behaviour, Confession, and Dying Words of the Malefactors who were Executed at Tyburn*. First offered in broadsheet form in the late seventeenth century, and then after 1712 as a pamphlet, this publication by the chaplain of London's Newgate prison recounted the careers, trials, and sometimes the confessions and last words of criminals. But such texts appeared almost everywhere in western Europe on days of execution.

As we have seen with broadsheets, the titles of pamphlets and booklets often sensationalized their tales to aid sales. Thus an English pamphlet of 1703 bore this graphic title: *An Account of a most Barbarous and Bloody Murther Committed on Sunday Last by Mr James Smith . . . on the Body of one Mr Cluff . . . With an Account of how he mangled his Body in a most Barbarous manner, Cut off his Left Hand, and stabb'd him in several places of the Body, leaving him Dead upon the Place, with other particulars relating to the occasion of that Inhuman Action*. And bold print on Dutch seventeenth-century booklets cried out such messages as "Horrible murder happened at Delft!" as well as "Son murders his father and mother!" and urged readers to "Come and read how three students in Kloppenburg raped two girls and murdered four!"[15]

This approach to events resembles the techniques employed by modern newspaper editors to sell their journals, and it is to the newspaper that we now turn. The modern European newspaper emerged in the seventeenth century from occasional broadsheet announcements of news and from manuscript newsletters, like the *avvisi* of Rome, that were the work of scribes who functioned increasingly like journalists. At first regularity of publication was problematical. Nevertheless, weeklies appeared widely in the seventeenth century. London led, with its first weeklies, the *Corante* (1621) and the *Weekly News* (1622). Paris followed with the weekly *Gazette* in 1631, then Florence (1636), Rome (1637), and Madrid (1661) acquired their equivalents. The daily subsequently emerged, too, with the Leipzig *Einkommende Zeitung* in 1660, and London's *Daily Courant* in 1702. Other countries acquired dailies rather later; Spain's

---

[15] Quoted in Van Deursen, *Plain Lives in a Golden Age*, pp. 147–48.

Diario Noticioso began publication in 1758, and Paris received its first daily only in 1777. As communications improved, and the price of paper fell in the later part of our period, newspapers grew in number and circulation.

Early newspapers lacked modern means for newsgathering, and salaried reporters were seldom part of the process. Some newspapers even relied on news sent in by subscribers and thus mingled a great deal of rumor with "hard" news. As with other print forms of the era, editors often sensationalized violence to attract buyers. In England some journals, including *Applebee's Original Weekly Journal*, even specialized in crime reporting by the early decades of the eighteenth century.

The circulation of early modern broadsheets, pamphlets, and newspapers is difficult to gauge by the methods historians have long applied to study sales of expensive, bound books. Printers of broadsheets and pamphlets kept few of the records that publishers and booksellers kept of book buyers. Moreover, in this age before modern copyright laws, one publisher's successful text might be pirated and issued by many other printers to enjoy especially wide circulation. And inventories of property at the deaths of the owners of these cheap texts generally fail to mention such popular works, either because inventory compilers regarded them as lacking value or because the texts failed to endure, having supplied the needs of a society requiring paper for various purposes. Nevertheless, we can get some idea of the circulation of these texts by extrapolating from other pertinent evidence.

We know that the bookstore was a rarity in much of western Europe, and that it was largely unknown in Scandinavia prior to the nineteenth century. Hence peddlers or hawkers in the streets and marketplaces sold the vast bulk of this mass literature. Drawn from the ranks of the disadvantaged – such as residents of poor, mountainous regions of France, Italy and Switzerland, or the members of the confraternity of the blind who had a monopoly of sales of the *pliegos de cordel* in Madrid – these peddlers seem to have been ubiquitous.

Indeed, everything we know about the peddlers of pamphlets and small books suggests that they were part of a business undertaking increasingly targeting a mass market, at first in the cities but later on a wider scale. Peddlers were numerous, with some 2,500 paying a £4 licensing fee in England in 1696 and many additional chapmen probably evading payment.

Prices for their print wares were low, and falling throughout our period as paper prices decreased. In sixteenth- and seventeenth-century England broadsheet ballads sold for a penny, the cost of a pot of ale or admission to standing room in the pit of the Globe Theater. Small chapbooks and pamphlets sold for two or three pence in the middle of the seventeenth century in England when building workers earned twelve pence per day. In Germany small books sold for the modest sum of three to six *pfennigs* in the seventeenth century, while in France in the same period the *Bibliothèque bleue* volumes sold for about the price of a pound of bread.

The scattered records of publishers also suggest the growth of a mass market for cheap print in our period. The case of England is instructive. In the 1660s as many as 400,000 almanacs appeared annually, enough for every third family in the kingdom, and while 3,000 ballad titles received publication licenses in the 1550–1700 period, many more circulated without licenses. French records also suggest mass marketing. When Etienne Garnier, who had bought the Oudot publishing house, died in 1789, his firm had on hand 443,069 volumes awaiting sale. In Italy the Remondini family of Bassano del Grappa ran one of Europe's largest publishing firms by the eighteenth century, integrating all aspects of mass literature production in one operation, from paper making to distribution through the employment of 2,000 peddlers.

Newspapers sold chiefly to subscribers in the early modern period, but their impact on the public was increasing dramatically by the eighteenth century. By the 1780s Germany's 151 newspapers had a circulation of approximately 300,000 subscribers and England's fifty provincial journals reached 400,000 subscribers per year. And newspapers were accessible to far more than these individual subscribers. They sometimes were read aloud to groups and they often were available to readers in coffeehouses and other such establishments. In addition, many individuals pooled their resources to buy a subscription to a paper that circulated through the group. Thus individual copies of newspapers reached many more readers than just the subscriber.

Themes of violence

In the early modern period, as today, violence had a double effect on those who were not its victims. Of course, it at once shocked and repelled people by its brutality. But it also fascinated many because it so contradicted religious precepts and social norms.

In catering to that fascination, however, early modern publishers had to function within certain constraints. Violence can be politically dangerous when it is directed against authority and socially subversive when it is portrayed positively. At an early stage both oral and print representations of violence came under the regulation of governments that in every early modern European state operated some form of censorship. In the British

Isles the venerable Robin Hood legend, to which the noble practice of robbing the rich to aid the poor seems to have been added only in the seventeenth century, soon ran into official condemnation. When brawling representations of Robin and Little John began to appear in festivities like the May Games, in 1555 the Scottish parliament forbade celebrations including the men of Sherwood Forest and decreed banishment as the penalty for those playing such roles. City ordinances in Nuremberg, Germany, one of the great centers of early modern German printing, rigidly controlled print materials. Forbidden there in the sixteenth century were broadsheets describing not only crimes and punishments but also those dealing with other sensations like miracles. And in France the Old Regime police, just like their Revolutionary-era counterparts, were watchful for dangerous texts like the *canard* portraying Poulailler as a noble bandit.

This was a religious age, and both popular and elite literature reflected Christian thought and precept throughout much of the early modern period. Consequently, the popular-press accounts of violence often took on a didactic character, showing how minor sins inevitably led to more egregious ones. Executions took on the aspect of religious rites for many in this period, too, and the real or alleged last words of repentant sinners appear frequently in broadsheets, pamphlets, and early newspapers, stating a religious message. And when a condemned person died without spiritually edifying expressions of repentance, authors piously commented that they presented the criminal's behavior only as a warning of how not to behave.

Recognizing that the religious sensibilities of the age and the fear of penalties by the authorities charged with censoring the press affected the representation of violence in print matter, historians have long debated the reliability of reports of crime and violence in popular literature. Some scholars have argued for the historical reliability of this literature as a reflection of real violence because of the wealth of factual detail it sometimes contained. Other scholars have correctly noted the stereotypical characters and situations that they find in much of this literature. Observing the frequency with which Robin Hood types appear among armed robbers, the almost universal incidence of gallows repentance among the condemned, and other stereotypes, some historians have suggested that popular literature contains little that is factually reliable. And many students of popular literature have wondered about its veracity because it so frequently offered such sensationalized details that some tales of violence seem to have been concocted by their authors simply to attract readers.

Historians have been able to check the accuracy of some early print accounts of violence by comparing these texts against police and judicial records. Their findings are ambiguous. The sales leader in eighteenth-century crime and punishment reports, the *Account* of the Ordinary of Newgate, seems to have been accurate in its reporting, despite some embellishment of criminals' stories and confessions by the chaplain. We cannot say the same for other print materials focusing on crimes ending in executions. In print materials describing executions, the vast majority of the condemned died for homicide. But murder was not the most frequent capital offense, at least in England where statistics from court records have been compared to the numbers of murderers in popular literature. Indeed, three-quarters of sixteenth- and seventeenth-century executions in some English jurisdictions were for mundane crimes against property, not murder. Thus much of the literature of violence grossly misrepresented the real nature of English offenses, at least.

If popular literature focused on offenses that were unrepresentative of all crimes, many authors also took considerable liberties with the truth in describing homicidal violence. The song of Poulailler, to which we referred earlier, reveals just how far an author might deviate from the facts of a case to present a titillating, and saleable, story. Far from being an eighteenth-century Gallic Robin Hood at the head of a band of some 500 followers, Poulailler was a common thief. "Poulailler" is a nickname meaning "the chicken man," and it suggests his mundane crime specialty. Beginning with the theft of poultry and livestock, Poulailler had only just graduated to armed burglary by the time of his arrest. His band, moreover, numbered five persons, not 500, and he little resembled his characterization in the *canard*.

Our purpose here, however, is not to enter the debate on the historical reliability of these texts; factually correct or not, these texts were familiar to a broad public and the stereotypical nature of much of what they offered that public is what interests us. First, recurring stereotypical representations made these works intelligible to their consumers. Readers' previous knowledge of themes, characters, texts, and frequently reprinted illustrations allowed them to comprehend new texts incorporating familiar elements.

Second, and most importantly because this literature addressed a broad market whose sensibilities it wished not to offend, the thematic and situational stereotypes we find in the literature tell us much about the attitudes and assumptions of its audience. We will find little in this literature challenging the traditional religious, political, and social order. Thus in religiously and socially conservative Spain the literature in the *pliegos de cordel* portrayed violence and vengeance while using such accounts to uphold traditional Catholic principles and to offer the reader "a school of good habits" drawn from lessons based on the criminal's career.[16] In fact, sixteenth- and seventeenth-century Spanish broadsheets often portrayed the character flaws that propelled an individual into a life of crime. The same fundamentally conservative message appeared in the very different religious atmospheres of England and the Dutch Republic. In this regard, we will find instructive the kinds of violence portrayed in the mass press, and the attitudes about society, including women, revealed in them.

Two stock forms of violence dominated much of early modern crime reporting: armed robbery and murder. Both offered endless possibilities for sensationalizing violence to titillate the public and, since both robbers and murderers incurred capital punishment everywhere, these criminals offered the additional opportunity of a moral lesson in the act of execution.

Armed robbery on the roads, as we will see in Chapter 7, flourished in early modern Europe. The heyday of its representation was the eighteenth century, when broadside, pamphlet, and newspaper accounts of armed robbery abounded. The figure whom the English called the highwayman, the Scots the reiver, the Germans the *Strassenraüber*, the Italians the *bandito*, and the Spanish the *bandolero* represented just the sort of exotic figure that interested early modern Europeans. The robber appeared in three stereotypical guises in popular texts in which the individuality of these criminals disappeared.

One common stereotype of the armed robber was that of a repulsive and brutish figure. In representations of the brutish robber the reader encountered a surfeit of violence, and no moral ambiguities. The bandit was clearly evil, the authorities good, and the fatal end of the lawbreaker fully justified. A bandit epitomizing this type was Sawney Beane, who was reported to have inhabited a Scottish cave with his family for twenty-five years in the early seventeenth century. He and his relations robbed and killed travelers and ate the flesh of their victims until the forces of James VI captured and executed them.

Another form in which the armed robber appeared was that of a buffoon. As a literary device, this stereotype offered attractive possibilities. Two saleable elements, humor and violence, might be melded, again without morally gray elements because the robber clearly merited his fate. Such a figure was Patrick Flemming, an Irish robber portrayed in various English-language publications as a rather brutal armed bandit and as a prankster who humiliated priests and others with obscene tricks.

The most popular portrayal of armed robbers, however, was that of the "noble bandit," a latterday Robin Hood who, like the Spaniard Diego

---

[16] Joaquin Marco, *Literatura popular en España en los siglos XVIII y XIX (una aproximación a los pliegos de cordel)*, 2 vols. (Madrid: Taurus, Ediciones, 1977), 1, pp. 89–90.

Corrientes, robbed from the rich to aid the poor: "Diego Corrientes, the robber of Andalucia/Who took from the rich and helped the poor."[17] Publishers of eighteenth-century mass-circulation literature everywhere enriched themselves with this theme, whether it was applied to Diego Corrientes and Joán Serralonga (Spain), Angiolillo (Naples), James Hind and Dick Turpin (England), Rob Roy (Scotland), or Mandrin and Cartouche (France). In many of the tales of these figures, individual characteristics disappeared, along with truth and accuracy, as authors used stock elements in their descriptions of robbers' careers. Many of these elements are those identified by Eric Hobsbawm in his study of bandit myths.[18] In these tales the noble bandit began his career not through a crime, but as a consequence of his victimization by some act of injustice, like that allegedly suffered by Mandrin. Launched on a career of armed robbery, the noble bandit fought injustice, often by robbing the rich of ill-gotten wealth to aid the poor. Authors frequently portrayed the noble bandit killing only for revenge or self-defense, and if he survived, his community honored him, even if his activities had been technically illegal. The noble bandit also emerged in these tales as loyal to the king, directing his activities only against those who oppressed the humble, and thus the English highwayman James Hind, ever loyal to Charles I, allegedly preyed only on the monarch's parliamentary opposition. In many of these stories the noble robbers allegedly possessed various magical powers to make themselves invisible, or invulnerable, like Poulailler. If the noble bandit did die, it was because he had been betrayed.

But the "noble bandit" theme was a risky one for authors. Certainly the noble aspect of the robber was attractive to buyers, but such portrayals of essentially violent lawbreakers risked official condemnation. In the case of Mandrin, for example, the officials of the Ferme almost entirely suppressed literature portraying the smuggler remotely positively. Indeed, the authorities instead circulated a specially commissioned, condemnatory *Histoire de Louis Mandrin depuis la naissance jusqu'à sa mort* (*History of Louis Mandrin's Life from Birth to his Death*). Hence accounts of noble bandits include elements to placate the authorities and to support the economic, social, and political status quo. Noble bandits rarely attacked institutions; rather, they concentrated their attacks on evil or proud people. A few of them mended their ways and retired from their trades, but those who did not gave ample proof of the basic evil that underlay their aid to the poor. Some final act of brutality on the part of the bandit

---

[17] Quoted in Peter Burke, *Popular Culture in Early Modern Europe* (New York: Harper and Row, 1978), p. 166.

[18] Eric J. Hobsbawm, *Bandits*, revised ed. (New York: Pantheon Books, 1981), pp. 42–43.

might prove this, like a tale of Mandrin trampling a pregnant woman with his horse, but ultimate proof of evil was execution of the bandit.

Tales of murder were a popular form of this literature, too, and the more sensational, it seems, the better. Nothing remained out of bounds in murder stories, even the murder of children. Among such tales are that of the Anabaptist Mary Campion who allegedly cut off her child's head to prevent its infant baptism by her Presbyterian husband in seventeenth-century England. A similarly repellent crime appeared in rhyme form in a German pamphlet of 1551 describing a woman who hacked her four children to death with an ax while her husband was at work. In this rhyme a child begs vainly for mercy:

> He said, "O dearest mother mine,
> Spare me, I'll do whate'er thou'lt say:
> I'll carry for thee from today
> The water the whole winter through.
> Oh please don't kill me! Spare me, do!"

> But no plea helped, it was in vain;
> The Devil did her will maintain.
> She struck him with the self-same dread
> As if it were a cabbage head.[19]

Narratives of murders and armed robberies might concentrate solely on the details of the crime itself, but the criminal biography or autobiography was an especially favored form, and the *Account* of the Ordinary of Newgate was one of the best-known expressions of this sort of popular literature. The biography or autobiography drew on the narrative form of the picaresque to recreate in prose or rhyme a titillating crime account under the guise of the Christian spiritual journey from creation to temptation, fall, and redemption.

In this scenario, the potentially violent robber or murderer was usually born into one of two settings. Most commonly the guilty person was born to poor but honest parents, origins that emphasized the danger that anyone might fall into evil ways. Thus the French eighteenth-century bandit Nivet was allegedly born to a crippled wool carder in Caen who was honest and hardworking, though poor. According to the *Bibliothèque bleue* volume on *La vie de Nivet, dit Fanfaron* (*The Life of Nivet, nicknamed Fanfaron*), evil companions then led Nivet into crime. Less commonly, the offender was born amid portents of the evil to come; implicit in such accounts were the actions of diabolical forces. Indeed, the author of one popular account claimed that the smuggler Mandrin was born with the

---

[19] Joy Wiltenburg, *Disorderly Women and Female Power in the Street Literature of Early Modern England and Germany* (Charlottesville: University Press of Virginia, 1992), p. 228.

monstrous likeness of a goat, with teeth and a thick coat of hair. Trouble ensued immediately; no one could nurse him because of his teeth, and three of the cows that were able to suckle him died owing to his bites. He turned to thievery at a young age, beat a priest to death at age fifteen, and went on to become the brutal smuggler we encountered earlier.

A pact with the devil, bad company, greed, and even pride helped early modern authors explain violence. Indeed, one author alleged pride was the cause of violence in his story of a sixteenth-century German secretary who responded to his master's reprimanding cuff by dismembering the man. But supernatural elements marked accounts of violence well into the seventeenth century, and sometimes allegedly aided in the apprehension of criminals. In fact, an apparent miracle occurred in *The Most Cruel and Bloody Murther Committed by an Innkeeper's Wife, called Annis Dell and her sonne George Dell, Foure yeeres since . . .* published in England in 1606. In the pamphlet thieves killed the parents and brother of Elizabeth James and then cut out her tongue to prevent her giving testimony against them. Elizabeth wandered about from London to Hertfordshire for four years until she miraculously regained her power of speech and named the criminals.

Drawn to violent behavior by a variety of causes and captured perhaps with the aid of divine forces, the individual offender then achieved redemption in much of this literature. The criminal hereby demonstrated the mercy of God and provided a moral lesson to obscure the gratuitous violence of popular literature. This might be an admonition by the condemned from the scaffold that others not follow his path, like that attributed to James Selby in 1691:

> All you that come to see my fatal end
> Unto my dying words I pray attend
> Let my misfortune now a warning be
> To ev'ry one of high and low degree.[20]

The moral message also might be in the form of a full religious conversion on the eve of execution. Even the murdering German mother of the 1551 pamphlet, after a suicide attempt, repented:

> Th'eternal God then lent his grace,
> That by God's word improved was she,
> And then converted blessedly,
> And earnestly did yield her soul to God.[21]

---

[20] Quoted in James A. Sharpe, "The People and the Law" in Reay (ed.), *Popular Culture in Seventeenth-Century England*, p. 258.
[21] Quoted in Wiltenburg, *Disorderly Women and Female Power*, p. 229.

In Spain Diego Corrientes, "the generous bandit," came to be portrayed in some popular literature in almost religious terms. Noting that he, like Christ himself, suffered betrayal by an associate, some authors went so far as to remind readers that the authorities brought Corrientes to Seville on a Sunday and executed him there on Friday of the same week, a chronological sequence duplicating that of the last days of Jesus. And whatever his guilt, at his execution by quartering on 30 March 1781 Corrientes was repentant. He died with these words, according to one of the *pliegos de cordel*:

> Farewell, miserable world,
> I am finished with you.
> Protect me holy Mother,
> As I surrender my soul to you here.
>
> Here I die for my guilt,
> Disgraced unfortunate
> Asking God to forgive
> The guilt of Diego Corrientes.[22]

Violence involving women appeared in popular literature, too, informed by a body of ideas about females widely accepted in the early modern period. From the Old Testament both Jewish and Christian societies early derived a vision of male superiority to women. The most widely known account of the Creation portrayed Eve, formed from Adam's rib, succumbing to temptation in the Garden of Eden, the original sin in Christian doctrine that led to their mutual fall. Thus much religious thought portrayed women as passionate, unreasoning, and potentially violent individuals, the source of earthly sin, whose evil natures could be kept under control only by male domination. This essential misogyny persisted throughout the medieval period and, despite debate on the status of women opened during the Renaissance and the somewhat enlarged spiritual role accorded women by many Protestant reformers, the subordinate status of women remained the norm embraced by most western thinkers through much of our period. Indeed, the customary and written laws of most western European countries accorded husbands the right to enforce this subordination with physical violence.

The subservient wife was thus an ideal for many early modern authors, and popular-print materials often employed violent themes to show the maintenance of domestic order based on this subservience. German authors and printers particularly seem to have excelled in portraying brutal and bloody domestic violence. Figure 4 illustrates the apparently casual attitude toward a husband's violent "discipline" of his wife as

[22] Quoted in Marco, *Literatura popular*, 2, p. 449.

Figure 4. Anonymous, *The Power of Manhood*. Undated woodcut.

depicted on a German broadsheet. The following lines, drawn from a mid-sixteenth-century ditty entitled *Song of How One Should Beat Bad Women*, also portray such domestic violence:

> Her body be sure well pound
> With a strong hazel rod;
> Strike her head till it turns round,
> And kick her in the gut.
> With blows be every zealous,
> Yet see you don't her kill.

Thus shouldst thou thy wife punish
If you wilt have her tame;
Car'st thou about thy honour
Then must thou beat her lame
Of hand and foot also
So she can't run away.
Thus must thou beat and damp her
So to no priest she'll scamper;
Then first she'll thee obey.[23]

In their quest to present the sensational and therefore saleable, authors of broadsheets, pamphlets, and early newspaper crime reports frequently concentrated on acts of violence in which women acted out their passionate natures by transcending their subservient roles as wives and mothers. The most sensational act of such female rebellion was a woman's murder of her husband, an offense considered so grave in the early modern period that it was called petty treason in England and, until the late eighteenth century, was punishable there by burning.

Historically, as we will see in Chapter Four, the most common form of domestic violence in this period was the husband's attack on his wife. Nevertheless, accounts of murders of husbands were especially numerous for much of our period. Perhaps this was because the period's religious and political turmoil made authors very concerned about all acts of rebellion, or perhaps their focus on husband beating was simply the result of authors' searches for sensational and saleable subjects. In either case, authors presented this violence carefully, offering readers a wealth of sensational crime details followed by the murderers' gallows repentances or authors' statements that the crime should be a warning "to be always on guard against passions."[24]

Frequently, illicit love, an act of rebellion against the marital bond itself, was at the root of husbands' murders. One such, the murder of John Brewen by his wife, Anne, in 1590 elicited at least two pamphlets and four ballads. According to popular English authors, two goldsmiths, John Brewen and John Parker, had courted Anne. She allegedly loved Parker, but had accepted gifts from Brewen, who demanded of Anne either the return of the gifts or her hand in marriage. Since she no longer had the former, she felt trapped into the latter. Three days after the wedding Parker supplied her with poison, the classic weapon of the woman in popular thought because she could use it in her trusted role in food preparation. Anne prepared some "sugar sopples" laced with poison, and

[23] Wiltenburg, *Disorderly Women and Female Power*, 2, p. 121.
[24] *Lettres amoureuses de la dame Lescombat et du Sieur Mongeot ou l'histoire de leurs criminels amours*, reprinted in Hans-Jürgen Lüsebrink (ed.), *Histoires curieuses et véritables de Cartouche et de Mandrin* (Paris: Editions Montalba, 1984), p. 324.

Brewen died after eating them. The authorities soon discovered the conspiracy and executed the lovers, Anne suffering burning, the penalty for petty treason portrayed on the cover of one of the pamphlets.

Women could express their rebellion against their husbands in other, nonlethal, ways, too. They might verbally abuse and strike their husbands, for instance. The English called this practice "scolding" and it was widely regarded in early modern Europe as a wifely transgression of the female role of subservience that rendered husbands of such women effectively cuckolds. Another way a woman might violently transgress her traditional role was to kill her newborn infant, a crime frequently imputed to women pregnant out of wedlock in an age that made few provisions for unmarried mothers and their offspring. One German verse from about 1650 recounted the career of the daughter of honorable, but indulgent, parents:

> But she was much too brazen,
> And full of malice, too.
> This made them let her have her will
> In all that she desired
> Thus into shame she fell.

The girl's parents sent her into service in a city at the age of fifteen, and her problems grew worse:

> There long she played the wanton
> In secret, no one knew;
> And vaunted still her honesty.
> And thus she did her sinning
> Ever deceitfully.

The young woman became pregnant, delivered her baby, and threw it into a privy to die. She moved to another town where she was unknown, continued her promiscuous ways, again became pregnant, delivered the baby, and left it to be killed by a hog. A third pregnancy ended in a monstrous birth that the verse's author interpreted as evidence of divine disapproval of the young woman's sins, and the resulting detection led to execution with hot oil poured into her mouth and the removal of one breast. The ballad, whose chief concern seems to have been discipline of wanton women, rather than infanticide, concluded with advice to parents in dealing with their children: "And take them under the rod/While they can still be bent."[25] Indeed, children, like women in general, were seen as passionate, naturally unruly, and in need of discipline, if necessary by male violence, to maintain order in the household and society.

The international conflicts of the late sixteenth and the seventeenth

---

[25] Wiltenburg, *Disorderly Women and Female Power*, pp. 236–37.

centuries led to frequent portrayals, in many formats, of the violence of warfare, and most particularly of the violence of soldiers against civilians. As with representations of other forms of violence, accuracy of reporting was not necessarily the goal in accounts of soldiers' actions. Certainly sensationalism in the interest of good sales for print products was a primary consideration in presentation of the actions of military men, but we must also recognize that early modern rulers already understood the power of the press to mold opinion. Thus in France the war ministry largely dictated the contents of the state-sponsored *Gazette* in the 1680s and 1690s in order to place French actions in the best possible light. Nevertheless, negative print representations of combatants were ubiquitous in wartime, and accounts of murder, rape, burning, and looting flourished in the popular press. In one early seventeenth-century Walloon dialogue, forces in Dutch employ killed the father of the main character, Weri Clabå, and raped his sister in an account that begins:

> It was Wednesday at the dinner hour
> When a mass of Mansfeld's soldiers came.
> Not demanding lodging or food,
> They arrived enraged at the hearth
> To steal and sack
> Without saying a word, not even "to the death" or "on guard."[26]

Soldiers of the Thirty Years' War figured notably in Germany's greatest seventeenth-century novel, the tale of Simplicius Simplicissimus, by Grimmelshausen. In this work the author described marauding soldiers plundering the home of the protagonist and then torturing the peasants to force them to reveal the hiding places of their valuables:

Then they began to take the flints from their pistols and to put the peasants' thumbs in their places. They tortured the poor devils as if they had wanted to burn witches. They even put one of the captured peasants into the bake oven and went after him with fire, even though he had not yet said anything to them. They put a rope around the neck of another man and twisted it up with a club till blood squirted out of his mouth, nose and ears. In short, each soldier had his own tactic to torment peasants, just as each peasant had his own special suffering.[27]

Engravings adorning broadsheets, or sold separately, also portrayed the wars of the late sixteenth and early seventeenth centuries, and as copperplates replaced woodblocks for the production of these works, they appeared in increasing numbers. The works of many engravers depicted

---

[26] Quoted in Myron P. Gutmann, *War and Rural Life in the Early Modern Low Countries* (Princeton: Princeton University Press, 1980), p. 33.

[27] Hans Jakob Christoffel von Grimmelshausen, *An Unabridged Translation of Simplicius Simplicissimus*, translated by Monte Adair (Lanham, MD: University Press of America, 1986), p. 10.

military themes, but perhaps the most realistic work on war was that of Jacques Callot in his series *Miseries and Misfortunes of War* (1633). In the eighteen engravings of this group, the artist illustrated the manifold brutalities of war, from battle itself to the looting and atrocities of soldiers, the brigandage and banditry of the freebooters who followed in the wake of armies, and the bloody punishments that awaited some of those offenders.

Perceptions

It is extremely difficult to trace the impact on popular opinion of these representations of violence in the popular press. The different groups in early modern society certainly derived somewhat varied meanings from these texts. We also lack any sort of precise gauge of that opinion, such as the modern polls we drew on in the Introduction, but historical researchers do provide us with some insight into the impact of these accounts. They detect the evolution in eighteenth-century England and France of aspects of public opinion regarding violence and crime that are familiar to modern North Americans and Europeans. In these countries, with their relatively high rates of urban literacy and growing press output, rising concern about individual security, fueled by the popular press, could take on the aspect of modern crime panics. So in a century in which the incidence of violence was in general decline, press accounts of violence that were often inaccurate, sensationalized, stereotyped, or even fabricated, affected public perceptions of events. The early modern press, just like the modern media, could create a perception of rising violence. And, as we have seen, perceptions, not factual knowledge, shaped responses to crime. The resulting fear could lead to panic or sometimes ill-considered changes in public policy and law to deal with the perceived rise in violence.

The basic elements of public opinion sound familiar to us. Public opinion increasingly linked crime and violence with urban life. As we will see, this was an incorrect, though not illogical, assumption. Cities were the centers of publishing and it was within their confines that everyone who could see or hear encountered the broadsheets, ballads, pamphlets, and newspapers describing all manner of offenses. Thus, even in the seventeenth century, the diary of Londoner Samuel Pepys for 1664 showed the insecurities of many a modern urban householder:

And so home, weary; and not being very well, I betimes to bed. And there fell into a most mighty sweat in the night, about 11 a-clock; and there, knowing what money I have in the house and hearing a noise, I begin to sweat worse and worse, till I melted almost to water. I rung, and could not in half an hour make either of the wenches hear me; and this made me fear the more, lest they might be gag'd . . .

At last Jane rose and then I understand it was only the dog wants a lodging and so made a noyse.[28]

Despite the mundane explanation of the noises Pepys heard during the night, peace of mind seemed to have eluded him. Less than a year later he recorded his fears about noises on his roof and the intentions of a woman and two men loitering near his door.

The public perception of an omnipresent and growing crime problem endured, so that a century later even publications for relatively sophisticated English readers included listings of crimes, and *The Gentleman's Magazine* for October 1783, noted:

Eleven malefactors were carried from Newgate and executed at Tyburn. It is really a melancholy reflection on the police of this country that, notwithstanding the boasted levity of our laws, more people are cut off annually by the hands of the executioner than in all Europe besides. The papers are filled with little else but robberies and villainies of one kind or other, not confined in a manner, as formerly, to the metropolis, but practically all over the country, where the gaols are full of felons.[29]

Portrayals of armed robbers and other criminals also created the impression for many early modern Europeans that their society harbored a criminal subculture. Popular printed works often disclosed the distinctive vocabularies allegedly employed by dangerous elements that convinced many lawabiding people that criminals were a breed apart from them. Indeed, there were works purporting to be vocabularies of criminal language on the market.[30] Thus the criminal cant described in English works, the *argot* recounted in French popular literature, and the *Rotwelsch* vocabulary ascribed to German bandits all contributed to fears of violence and crime at the hands of members of a dangerous subculture.

Indeed, the press seems to have played an enduring role in creating fears of violence and crime. Songs and verses publicized on broadsheets entered the oral culture of the age, to reappear periodically. Louis-Sébastien Mercier, an eighteenth-century French author who knew Paris well, noted: "A parricide, a poisoner, an assassin, on the morrow of their executions, even on the same day, songs appear composed by the singers of the Pont-Neuf, which are sung at all the crossroads . . . they thus extolled Desrues and his song reappears from time to time, like a theater restages an old and memorable play."[31] Particularly interesting crime

---

[28] Robert Latham and William Matthews (eds.), *The Diary of Samuel Pepys*, 11 vols., (Berkeley: University of California Press, 1971), 5, p. 201.

[29] *The Gentleman's Magazine*, October 1783, p. 891.

[30] *Le Jargon ou Langage de l'argo réformé comme il est à présent en usage . . .* (1629) is an example of this genre.

[31] Louis-Sébastien Mercier, *Tableau de Paris, nouvelle édition*, 12 vols. (Amsterdam, 1782–1788), 10, pp. 255–56. Desrues was a poisoner executed in Paris in May 1777.

accounts were repeated orally and in print, contributing to a mythology of insecurity. Thus, as we have noted already, Poulailler's armed robberies were still being recounted in printed rhymes a decade after the criminal's execution. And the partially apocryphal memoirs of the eighteenth-century French glass worker, Jacques-Louis Ménétra, include events that had become part of the common storehouse of crime knowledge through the popular press, but which Ménétra could not have witnessed. For example, he recounted seeing Mandrin seven years after the smuggler's execution. And Ménétra drew on a broadsheet account of a killing that had been circulating in France since at least 1618 to describe an innkeeper's murder and robbery of his own son who had returned home, unrecognized, after twenty years in the army.[32]

Given this enduring popular memory of crime, very little reporting of new acts of violence in the expanding eighteenth-century newspaper press was required to produce fear and even panic in the public. Hence, when the editors of a new English provincial newspaper, the *Chelmsford Chronicle*, sought to fill unsold advertising space and perhaps sell more copies by giving heightened publicity to a series of highway armed robberies in 1763 in Colchester, there was an immediate local response. The newspaper daily reported this response, further heightening local fears with its accounts of locals arming themselves and of families leaving markets earlier than usual to travel home in groups. Soon local authorities were arresting, without any evidence of guilt, strangers and persons dressed in the white smocks alleged to have been worn by the armed robbers in response to a public convinced it faced a wave of armed robberies.

The reaction of Colchester officials to their constituents' fears, in what must be seen as a classic crime panic born of the media, reminds us again that perceptions of violent activity – whatever the reality – can affect the law and its operation. Thus the English Murder Act of 1752 sought to deter homicide by making the death penalty for it more fearsome. This legislation sought "some further terror and peculiar mark of Infamy" by ordering the dissection of the bodies of hanged murderers for medical instruction, the fate of Hogarth's Tom Nero. The rationale for such legislation, which sparked riots by the friends and kin of the executed, was that murder was "more frequently perpetrated than formerly and particularly in the metropolis."[33]

In actual fact, the long-term trend in English violence at this time

---

[32] Jacques-Louis Ménétra, *Journal of My Life*, edited by Daniel Roche, translated by Arthur Goldhammer (New York: Columbia University Press, 1986), pp. ix, 83, 104.

[33] Quoted in J. M. Beattie, *Crime and the Courts in England, 1660–1800* (Princeton: Princeton University Press, 1986), p. 78.

seems to have been downward, but with the perceptions we have noted widespread in early modern society it is no wonder that Pepys had trouble sleeping. He perceived his world to be a very dangerous place, and, just as today, early modern developments in law and judicial practice reflected this public perception of widespread, violent threats to personal safety. Undoubtedly contributing to such concerns was the widespread presence of arms in this society that we will examine in Chapter 2.

FURTHER READING

Bell, Ian A., *Literature and Crime in Augustan England* (London and New York: Routledge, 1991).

Catty, Jocelyn, *Writing Rape, Writing Women in Early Modern England* (New York: St. Martin's Press, 1999).

Chartier, Roger, *The Cultural Uses of Print in Early Modern France*, translated by Lydia G. Cochrane (Princeton: Princeton University Press, 1987).

Egmond, Florike, "The Noble and Ignoble Bandit: Changing Literary Representations of West European Robbers," *Ethnologia Europaea* 17 (1987), pp. 139–56.

Judges, Arthur V. (ed.), *The Elizabethan Underworld* (New York: E. P. Dutton, 1930).

King, Peter, "Newspaper Reporting, Prosecution Practice and Perceptions of Urban Crime: The Colchester Crime Wave of 1765," *Continuity and Change* 2 (1987), pp. 423–54.

Kunzle, David, *The Early Comic Strip: Narrative Strips and Picture Stories in the European Broadsheet, c. 1450–1825* (Berkeley: University of California Press, 1973).

Malcolmson, Robert W., *Popular Recreations in English Society, 1700–1850* (Cambridge: Cambridge University Press, 1973).

Marshburn, Joseph H. and Velie, Alan R. (eds.), *Blood and Knavery: A Collection of English Renaissance Pamphlets and Ballads of Crime and Sin* (Rutherford, Madison, and Teaneck: Fairleigh Dickinson University Press, 1973).

Rawlings, Philip, *Drunks, Whores and Idle Apprentices: Criminal Biographies of the Eighteenth Century* (London: Routledge, 1992).

Sharpe, James A., *Crime and Law in English Satirical Prints, 1600–1832* (Cambridge: Chadwyck-Healey, 1986).

Spufford, Margaret, *Small Books and Pleasant Histories: Popular Fiction and Its Readership in Seventeenth-Century England* (Cambridge: Cambridge University Press, 1985).

Twitchell, James B., *Preposterous Violence: Fables of Aggression in Modern Culture* (Oxford: Oxford University Press, 1989).

Wiltenburg, Joy, *Disorderly Women and Female Power in the Street Literature of Early Modern England and Germany* (Charlottesville: University Press of Virginia, 1992).

2   States, arms, and armies

As we saw in the Introduction, historians advance a number of hypotheses on how violence was increasingly brought under control in early modern western Europe. But whether they write of a "civilizing process," "social disciplining," or control of individuals through a "great confinement," all concur that the developing state institutions were of importance in this process.

Violence is a central concern of every modern state. The security necessary for effective government is impossible to achieve as long as there is a widespread capacity among individual citizens to wreak violence on one another or on the state's agents. And political authority itself ultimately rests on the state's ability to maintain its laws with force or the threat of force. Indeed, most of us regard as legitimate only such force as is exercised by the state or that its laws permit. Thus the modern state seeks to monopolize violence in the hands of its officials and, in identifying the importance of this process, Max Weber wrote: "The claim of the modern state to monopolize the use of force is as essential to it as is its character of compulsory jurisdiction and continued operation."[1]

In our period, from 1500 to 1800, state control of violence was tenuous at best. Almost all early modern states lacked the centralized police agencies with which their modern counterparts regulate violence among their citizens. They relied on an inadequate range of local police operatives, which we will survey in Chapter 3, to deal with daily problems, and they depended on their armies to counter the most serious threats to domestic order. But early modern armies, while growing in size, were highly flawed instruments for such duty. The very nature of the age's warfare, and structural inadequacies of the state's apparatus of military discipline, finance, and supply, meant that armies inflicted much violence even on friendly and passive civilians. Consequently, most early modern Europeans feared and hated soldiers. Ominously, they also retained

[1] Max Weber, *Economy and Society: An Outline of Interpretive Sociology*, edited by Guenther Roth and Claus Wittich, translated by Ephraim Fischoff *et al.* (Berkeley and Los Angeles: University of California Press, 1978), p. 56.

significant levels of armaments with which to express that hatred and, as we will see in subsequent chapters, to inflict violence on each other and sustain a brutal popular justice. In this chapter we will examine that capacity of civilians to inflict armed violence, the violence of the early modern army, and the role of that force in imposing some degree of security in the face of civilian armaments.

Arms

In 1500, at the beginning of our period, nowhere did the state monopolize the instruments of violence. Of greatest immediate danger to the state's tenuous control of its internal affairs were the noblemen of every realm. Individually, they bore swords as evidence of their status and often used such weapons violently to settle personal scores in the duels that we will examine in Chapter 3. But the magnates among them posed the ultimate threat to the order of the state. Their castles provided them with fortified bases beyond the authority of the central government, and these citadels often housed substantial personal arsenals.

The military capacity of many great aristocrats, as measured by the size of their personal arsenals, was formidable. Robert Dudley, earl of Leicester, seems to have possessed the largest sixteenth-century English military establishment, maintaining his own gunpowder maker as well as firearms and other weapons sufficient to equip 200 cavalrymen and 500 infantrymen. The subjects of the Spanish monarchy included such aristocrats as the duke of Grandía, the greatest Valencian magnate of his age, whose private arsenal in 1564 could supply 50 men-at-arms and 600 harquebusiers, and the duke of Medina-Sidonia who possessed 42 cannon in the early seventeenth century.

The danger of such arsenals, of course, was that they would be used to equip small private armies to challenge royal power and to maintain the traditional political, judicial, and social positions of aristocrats. These traditional roles of aristocrats were under challenge everywhere in the early modern period. On the one hand, the inflationary spiral of sixteenth-century prices sapped the income of seigneurs reliant on fixed feudal dues, while on the other hand, the centralizing state, backed by new military technologies that we will shortly examine, eroded the nobility's traditional governmental and judicial prerogatives. The result was the violence of armed revolt that has been closely studied for the 1560–1660 period, and noble-led conflict and banditry that assumed several forms.

At the start of our period, great aristocrats everywhere maintained armed men. English aristocrats armed their servants, tenants, and clients and clothed them in livery (that is, uniforms bearing their coats of arms) to field bodies of armed men quite military in appearance. And they occasionally used such forces, as in 1589 when Sir Thomas Langton and eighty men-at-arms attacked Thomas Houghton at Lea Hall in Lancashire and killed Houghton. But English magnates came under increasing royal pressure to disband such forces.

The first Tudor monarch, Henry VII (r. 1485–1509), initiated a number of acts to limit the armed retinues of noblemen and to confine livery and maintenance of such men to those aristocrats most loyal to the king. These regulations at first achieved little; the crown lacked a standing army in this period and, ultimately, had to rely in part on the armed retainers of its noblemen in time of war. Only in the reign of Elizabeth I (1558–1603) did the practice of maintaining armed retainers begin to break down. Legal prohibitions continued, but the queen also cut her reliance on the nobility for armed men by developing an alternative force in a better-trained militia. In addition, she used the crown's patronage to draw gentry away from clientage to magnates. Changing cultural norms, which we have associated with an early modern "civilizing process" that inculcated in aristocrats the ideals of courtly behavior, also contributed to a decline in aristocratic bellicosity. Thus, in a slow and essentially peaceful process, the armed retainers of noble English households diminished greatly in number by the mid-seventeenth century.

On the European continent many noblemen assembled bands of armed men and, as a continuation of their tradition of private warfare, pursued feuds with their enemies. Indeed, many aristocrats considered such recourse to violence one of their legitimate privileges. In the rural French province of the Périgord in the sixteenth and seventeenth centuries noblemen commonly regulated their disputes by force, assembling armed men who even attacked the castles of neighbors with whom they were in dispute. In the sixteenth-century western Friuli of the Venetian Terraferma local aristocrats like Alessandro Montica assembled armed bands of servants, relatives, and unemployed professional soldiers, called *bravi*, to scourge their enemies. Indeed, one Venetian official wrote: "They make a trade in men, bringing in strangers to kill now this, now that person for money, at the request of others."[2] In Spain's Valencia many aristocrats employed bands of common criminals to wreak violence on their enemies. And in sixteenth-century Germany knights like Franz von Sickingen headed sufficient forces at times to affect decisively the

---

[2] Quoted in Nicholas S. Davidson, "An Armed Band and the Local Community in the Venetian Terraferma in the Sixteenth Century" in Gherardo Ortalli (ed.), *Bande armate, banditi, banditismo e repressione di giustizia negli stati di antico regime* (Rome: Jouvence, 1986), pp. 421–22.

political life of the Empire. Lesser German aristocrats carried on almost constant feuding, well into the sixteenth century.

Recourse to armed bands was a noble tactic in retaining local positions of social and political prominence, too. Valencian magnates used intimidating armed bands to influence the selection process for local officials in the *insaculocia*, the drawing of new officials' names from a sack. Armed bands, functioning like Anton Blok has shown the latterday Sicilian Mafia operating, kept peasants under seigneurial control and allowed a financially stressed nobility to extract more than their legal due in France, Italy, Valencia, and elsewhere.[3] Indeed, in France suppression of such extortion was a goal of special tribunals like the Grands Jours de Poitiers in 1634 and the Grands Jours d'Auvergne in 1665–66.

Finally, some nobles turned to outright banditry, engaging in highway robbery and other crimes. Such nobles were particularly numerous in Italy and Spain, and, while many needed money, some may also have chosen the activities as a protest against the encroachments of early modern states on noble prerogatives. This seems to have been the origin of the banditry of Alfonso Piccolomini, duke of Monte Marciano, who fiercely opposed the inquiry of Pope Gregory XIII (1572–85) into feudal property titles in the Papal States that aimed at raising revenue for the papacy by extracting long-unpaid dues. Piccolomini launched a thirteen-year career in brigandage that did not end until his capture and execution in 1591. Piccolomini's band attacked shipments of papal tax revenues and merchant convoys and received support and shelter from many nobles in Romagna and the Marches, including his relatives, the powerful Orsini family. Indeed, at times in the late sixteenth century the papacy feared a bandit descent on Rome itself.

Under the Spanish monarchy noble banditry flourished in Catalonia, Aragon, Valencia, and in the region of Jaén in the sixteenth and seventeenth centuries. The decrees of a sixteenth-century Valencian viceroy offering pardon terms to the "nobles, knights, gentry, and citizens, and all the other bandits and their supporters" suggest its extent.[4] And in Catalonia the most famous bandit of the seventeenth century, immortalized in *Don Quixote*, was Perot Rocaguinarda, an aristocratic highway robber who operated from 1602 until 1611, when he received royal pardon in return for military service.

Even in a country like France with a growing central authority, breakdowns in royal authority during the religious wars of the sixteenth

---

[3] Anton Blok, *The Mafia of a Sicilian Village, 1860–1960: A Study of Violent Peasant Entrepreneurs* (New York: Harper and Row, 1974).

[4] Quoted in Henry Kamen, "Public Authority and Popular Crime: Banditry in Valencia, 1660–1714," *Journal of European Economic History* 3 (1974), p. 655.

century and in the first five decades of the seventeenth led to noble banditry. In Champagne a group of noblemen committed robberies and thefts accompanied by murders, beatings, and rapes in the 1570s, while in Brittany a former member of the Catholic League, La Fontenelle, led a robber band until 1602. In the Périgord the chevalier de la Hitte stole receipts of the royal tax known as the *taille* on the Bordeaux highway in 1623. Numerous other country gentlemen of the southwest in the 1620s and 1630s retained armed men in their castles for less spectacular robbery that led to the deaths of some in armed showdowns with the authorities, or on the executioner's block. Noble bandits also operated in the eastern provinces of Burgundy and Franche-Comté, and in neighboring Lorraine, at the end of the Thirty Years' War. But perhaps the most famous French noble bandit was a gentleman operating in western France, especially Bas-Poitou, under the name Guilleri at the end of the religious wars. He extorted money from peasants and as a highwayman hung signs along roadways expressing his policy: "Peace to gentlemen, death to provosts and archers [the police] and the purse from merchants." Captured living under the guise of a merchant, Guilleri died on the wheel at La Rochelle in 1608.

Such noble armed robbery and private warfare waged by nobles did not flourish everywhere, however; it was not a great problem, for example, in the Low Countries, where the aristocracy lacked a strong military tradition. And even where this sort of armed violence did occur, the danger posed by armed bands led by nobles with military training mandated decisive action to control such activities. In France legal action like the Grands Jours d'Auvergne and the growth of the royal army under Louis XIV brought noblemen under control. Much the same process occurred in Spain in the early eighteenth century when the monarchy used the opportunity offered by its repression of anti-French revolts during the War of the Spanish Succession to revoke provincial privileges in areas like Valencia and greatly to expand central governmental authority. Everywhere, too, evolving concepts of personal honor increasingly made the duel, which we will examine in Chapter 3, the favored alternative to private warfare in defending aristocratic honor. Thus such noble armed violence was on the wane both in England and on the continent by the late seventeenth century.

Commoners also had the potential to inflict violence, however, because many of them bore arms, too. Like many of their social superiors, commoners routinely carried knives, either to use in their work or to cut their food in an age in which publicans seldom accommodated their guests' needs for cutlery. Many of them also possessed longbows and crossbows, used for both hunting and warfare through much of the seventeenth

century. Moreover, the recurring warfare of the era left a large quantity of
early modern military surplus in civilian hands in the form of pikes,
maces, swords, battleaxes, and other weapons. Ominously, as advances in
military technology made firearms relatively cheaper and more portable,
the possession of guns became more diffuse as well. But even when such
lethal weaponry was unavailable, less specialized implements could serve
the violent ends of common people. Walking sticks, peasant staffs, and
cudgels could all inflict considerable harm, especially when the owners of
such blunt weapons had the foresight to drive spikes through the tips of
their implements in advance of an affray.

Indicative of the extent of arms possession among the general population at the very outset of our period is an inventory made by the officials of
Troyes, France, in 1475. Fearing an attack on a vulnerable frontier
municipality of some 15,000 inhabitants, these city officials sought to
count private arms in order to plan for their town's defense. Their survey
of some 2,400 households turned up: 1,894 pieces of armor, ranging
from complete suits to individual helmets and coats of mail; 287 crossbows; 37 longbows; 2,436 blunt or pointed weapons, including javelins,
halberds, and battle hammers; 547 primitive muskets (culverins); and 5
privately owned cannon. When we consider that this inventory omitted
the knives and swords of the citizenry as well as the arms of the seventy
archers who guarded the city, the impression that Troyes fairly bristled
with weaponry is inescapable. Private arms were common elsewhere, too.
Knife fights were common in the Dutch Republic throughout the early
modern period, and in Valencia in 1692 two-thirds of all the cases heard
by the criminal court judge Don Vicente de Cordona y Milár involved
firearms.

Private armament was especially widespread in early modern England.
In that country, with a longstanding tradition of entrusting defense to a
militia, rather than a standing army, possession of weapons by commoners was a duty for much of our period. Indeed, in the Assize of Arms in
1181 Henry II confirmed earlier Anglo-Saxon practices by requiring
freemen to maintain arms for the defense of the realm. Almost four centuries later, similar defense concerns prompted Henry VIII (r. 1509–47)
to require that his subjects maintain longbows and arrows for defense.
Englishmen had additional reason to maintain arms, because the crown
also required that they assist in law enforcement. As early as the thirteenth century, the crown required householders to serve in municipal
night watches, to join the "hue and cry" in the aid of sheriffs and constables apprehending criminals, and to counter riots and other disorders
by serving in the *posse comitatus*, the body of citizens that local officials
could call up in such emergencies.

Everywhere officials at every level of government recognized the inherent danger of such widespread possession of weaponry, and early on sought to limit arms in private hands through outright bans on them or through systems of licensing. These strategies, individually or in combination, had little effect. The French monarchy's effort to ban arms began in 1287 with a decree that limited pointed weapons in Paris. The crown expanded the scope of its ban in 1487 with a decree forbidding its subjects to bear "bows, crossbows, halberds, pikes, swords, daggers, and other invasive weapons."[5] Nevertheless, their subjects' armaments forced French kings repeatedly to issue arms restrictions during the last three centuries of the monarchy's existence.

Provincial and municipal officials elsewhere also failed at arms control. In Florence Duke Cosimo I de' Medici, coming to power in 1537 after the Strozzi conspiracy and the murder of Duke Alessandro de' Medici, hastened to impose both a weapons ban and a system of licensing. The duke banned crossbows and other offensive weapons and ordered the guards at the city's gates to examine those entering Florence for such implements. The duke also required licenses for swords, daggers, guns, and even chainmail jackets. Nevertheless, weapons remained so common in the city that sixteenth-century Florentines assumed that all unarmed men were priests.

The same lack of success in arms regulation was the case in the Low Countries. In the Dutch Republic repeated bans failed to separate men from their knives. The states of Holland banned knives from taverns unsuccessfully in 1589, while some twenty-five years on the municipal government of The Hague in 1616 met similar failure in keeping rapiers, daggers, muskets, pistols, and other weapons out of servants' hands. In the Spanish Netherlands Philip II of Spain also vainly banned the bearing of pointed knives in 1589. The Spanish monarch also failed to force compliance with an ordinance designed to keep peace at social gatherings by requiring all in attendance at weddings, dances, and other celebrations to lay down swords, knives, and other weapons before taking part in the festivities.

All early modern states recognized the special danger of short firearms and pistols because they were easily concealable. The development of wheel-lock firearms, which did not require a fuse, made control of such weapons all the more imperative, and virtually every major western European state also attempted to control concealable guns less than about 2 ft (65 cm) in length. Such regulations seldom achieved more than

---

[5] Ordinance of Sainte-Catharine-du-Mont-de-Rouen, 25 November 1487, in François-André Isambert et al. (eds.), Recueil des anciennes lois françaises, depuis l'an 420 jusqu'à la Révolution de 1789, 29 vols., (Paris: Belin-Le Prieur, 1821–33), 11, p. 170.

passing success. Venice, for example, struggled with the early modern profusion of firearms as the Council of Ten unsuccessfully tried a succession of gun-control policies in the sixteenth century. Thus in 1533 the Council decreed death and confiscation of property as penalties for anyone using a firearm against another. Then the Council tried a licensing system for a while, ordered a complete ban on harquebuses in 1596, and returned to licensing in 1608. None of these policies seems to have had much effect on the spread of firearms.

Agents of the French monarchy attempted one of the most comprehensive efforts to deprive civilians of firearms in the early modern period. In the years from 1759 to 1772 the military governor of the Guyenne in southwestern France, fearing that the region's large Protestant minority might link up with the British during the Seven Years' War, ordered disarmament of all male commoners in the region. The governor assigned the rural police, the Maréchaussée, to the task, and encouraged the policemen's efforts with a bounty for each confiscated gun. They disarmed 7,335 persons, roughly 2 percent of the entire male population of the region by 1772. Nevertheless, within a year police officials complained that the effort appeared to have had no effect on the level of possession of civilian arms.[6]

In England, too, the crown repeatedly sought with scant success to regulate arms in the hands of those it considered a threat to order. Henry VIII for a time forbade persons with annual incomes of less than £300 from owning handguns and crossbows. The Militia Act of 1662 authorized arms searches in the homes of persons deemed dangerous to the realm's security. And, in spite of the Bill of Rights' assurance in 1689 of the privilege of the crown's Protestant subjects to maintain weapons, various parliamentary game acts in the late seventeenth and eighteenth centuries, including the Waltham Black Act of 1723, sought to limit arms under the guise of restricting hunting to the privileged. A brilliant commentator on much of this legislation, Sir William Blackstone (1723–80), recognized that the full intent of such laws was much more than the proclaimed goals of land improvement, game preservation, and the prevention of agricultural laborers wasting their time on hunting. He noted that the other objective of such laws was "prevention of popular insurrections and resistance to government by disarming the bulk of the people."[7]

---

[6] See Julius R. Ruff, *Crime, Justice and Public Order in Old Regime France: The Sénéchaussées of Libourne and Bazas, 1696–1789* (London: Croom Helm, 1984), p. 147, for the records of this effort.

[7] Sir William Blackstone, *Commentaries on the Laws of England*, 4 vols., (1765–69, reprint, Chicago: University of Chicago Press, 1979), 2, p. 411.

The failure of most early modern authorities to limit arms effectively, and the consequent ready availability of weapons, sustained a high level of interpersonal violence that we will examine in subsequent chapters. At the beginning of our period the state relied chiefly on the army to contain the violence of its subjects. But that force was of limited effectiveness, in part because it was a source of considerable violence itself.

Military violence

The period from 1500 to 1800 was one of almost continuous warfare, in which the size of armies grew dramatically. But our subject is not the violence of the battlefields of this age; rather, we will consider the violence inherent in the relationship between growing numbers of soldiers and the civilian population. To do so we must briefly examine the nature of the early modern army.

Warfare was changing radically in Europe by the sixteenth century owing to the late medieval introduction of projectile weapons like the crossbow and longbow, artillery, and portable firearms. Weapons whose projectiles were capable of piercing armor rendered the traditional feudal levy of armored knights militarily obsolete. They also demanded increasingly skilled infantry operations that exceeded the capabilities of medieval militias and forced almost all governments to maintain at least the skilled cores of standing armies from one campaign season to the next. Moreover, military engineers responded to primitive artillery by designing a low, defensive brick fortification, the *trace italienne*, which withstood cannonshot far better than high, stone castle walls and forced attacking armies into lengthy siege operations.

Armies were growing larger, too. Successful siege warfare required large forces, for an attacker not only had to maintain pressure on the defenders of a fortified place, but also had to guard against attack by a relieving force. The nature of sixteenth-century conflicts mandated larger armies as well. The Habsburg–Valois conflict, like many others of the age, was fought on more than one front, and army sizes grew accordingly. Whereas the French monarch maintained 20,000 men under arms in 1451 in the last stages of the Hundred Years' War, that king fielded forces totaling more than 350,000 in 1710 in the midst of the War of Spanish Succession.

Weaponry, like the new artillery, and the growing manpower of armies imposed fiscal and administrative burdens on the state that few early modern governments could sustain easily, despite war imposts that sparked tax revolts and borrowing that pushed some monarchs into bankruptcy. The heavy burden of early modern warfare is evident in its share of royal budgets: 75 percent of England's in 1689–1713; 74 percent of France's in 1689–97; and 68 percent of Piedmont-Sardinia's in 1734–40. Even expenditures of such magnitude, however, failed to fund fully the requirements of early modern armies. That failure was most evident in the areas of recruitment, supply, pay, and housing.

In recruitment few governments could fund the administrative machinery to meet their manpower needs completely. Recruitment efforts amounted to a mixed bag that often produced less than reliable soldiers. In the sixteenth and seventeenth centuries every state relied to some extent on military contractors, known as *condottieri* in Italy, who supplied companies and even whole armies of mercenary troops from a variety of national backgrounds for services to the highest bidder. Even when this contract system disappeared, many states still employed whole regiments of mercenary foreigners. In our period only Sweden, and later Prussia, extensively conscripted national armies, but every government did some recruiting of volunteers in its territories, attracting largely young unmarried men of limited resources by means of enlistment bonuses and the promise of pay. Enlistment bonuses varied with manpower availability, and the record from France suggests the link between poverty and a man's voluntary decision to join the army. Bonuses increased at harvest time, when unskilled labor was in demand and well paid, and reached their greatest amounts in years of prosperity and high rates of civilian employment like 1706. At other times, like the disastrous famine winters of 1693–94 and 1709–10, recruits signed up without the enticement of a bonus, perhaps seeing in the military life a chance for simple survival.

The sobriquets on the rolls of a regiment raised in North Holland in the 1570s for service in the Dutch war for independence from Spain also suggest the nature of the soldiery: Without Money, Seldom Rich, Gambled-Away, Spoiled-Early, Big Thirst, and Unwashed. Thus as late as the 1780s the French war minister, the comte de Saint-Germain commented: "It would undoubtedly be desirable if we could create an army of dependable and specially selected men of the best type. But in order to make up an army we must not destroy the nation; it would be destructive to a nation if it were deprived of its best elements. As things are, the army must inevitably consist of the scum of the people and of all those for whom society has no use."[8]

When enlistment payments yielded insufficient manpower for the army, officials resorted to impressing unwilling soldiers. In times of greatest need governments, including those of England, Genoa, and Spain,

---

[8] Quoted in M. S. Anderson, *War and Society in Europe of the Old Regime, 1618–1789* (London: Fontana Press, 1988), p. 163.

reluctantly forced prisoners into service. Other states impressed individual subjects into service, and France and Piedmont-Sardinia integrated into regular military operations unwilling peasant militias customarily reserved for home defense. Not surprisingly, there were difficulties in retaining the services of men recruited by force. As late as the eighteenth century, English officers sometimes moved recruits to their units in irons to prevent escape, and large numbers of French, Piedmontese, and Spanish militiamen and regular army recruits avoided active service by flight.

Supply, too, was a major problem for the early modern army. A seventeenth-century army of 60,000 men required daily 45 tons of bread, 40,000 gallons of beer, and the meat of 200–300 cattle for its men, as well as 90 tons of fodder for its horses; transportation of these quantities of food, let alone of artillery and equipment, was clearly beyond the logistical capacity of the sixteenth- and seventeenth-century state. Armies had therefore long expected soldiers to live off the land, although by the late sixteenth century many of them attempted to force soldiers to buy their own food and to supply their own equipment, and even ammunition. When stationed near large population centers astride major trade routes, troops might find such a practice workable, but in the field it was impossible. In the countryside quantities of food sufficient for an army were often unavailable in one place, so foraging parties ranged widely and simply seized what they needed from peasants.

Even had supplies been available, early modern military pay was unreliable at best. Royal fiscal regimes, notably that of Spain, broke down under the strain of raising revenue sufficient for the expense of modern war, and soldiers went unpaid for months and years as a consequence. Some troops in the Spanish Army of Flanders, for example, claimed pay arrears of 100 months in 1594; 15,000 Swiss mercenaries in French service received no pay at all in the period 1639–48; English parliamentary forces were due £2,000,000 in backpay in 1647; and one English regiment in 1713 was still due £198,000 in salary dating to the siege of Londonderry in 1689. Even when backpay reached the troops, they were often the victims of unscrupulous officers who charged them usurious rates for loans they had advanced the men between paydays, and who also docked men's pay of exorbitant sums for equipment and services. And sixteenth- and seventeenth-century soldiers also had other claims on their pay when it did arrive; many soldiers campaigned with their wives, kept women, and children in the long caravans that followed the armies. As a result, the relatively low wages of fighting men seldom provided for their needs, and sixteenth- and early seventeenth-century soldiers often took what they required from peasant producers. Armies chiefly campaigned in the months from March to October when food and fodder were available to support soldiers, their horses, and camp followers. As we will see, this practice of living off the civilian population perpetuated a consistently violent relationship between soldiers and resisting peasants for much of our period. There had been efforts to curb such pillage since the fourteenth century, but they could have little effect until pay and supply became more regular, as they did in the seventeenth and early eighteenth centuries.

Lack of pay created other potentially violent situations, too. Voltaire is said to have commented acerbically "No money, no Swiss," of the Swiss mercenaries who were so numerous in early modern armies, and lack of pay must certainly have contributed to the high desertion rate experienced by most armies. In the French army during the War of the Spanish Succession perhaps one man in four deserted, while 8,500 men illegally left the ranks of Saxon infantry units enlisting 20,000 in 1717–28. Such desertion freed men from all military controls, and many took up violent activities like armed robbery in bands of freebooters who traveled in the wake of all armies.

Mutiny was another response to unpaid military wages. The search for booty to compensate for lack of pay drove mutinous Imperial troops to sack Rome in 1527. The Spanish Army of Flanders pillaged Antwerp in 1576 for the same reason, and that force experienced a total of forty-six mutinies between 1572 and 1607. Parliamentary inability to pay English troops in 1646 and 1647 generated mutinies, too, and in 1638 French troops, mistrusting the government's ability to pay them, refused to obey orders to cross the Rhine to begin a German campaign until they had received an advance on their pay.

Mutinies could be extremely dangerous to civilians, although in the Spanish Army of Flanders and among German forces in the Thirty Years' War these affairs had a certain organization. Mutineers elected leaders and drafted demands that always sought backpay for the men and pardons for their chiefs, and sometimes more. They would back their demands by seizing a defensible town from which they could forcibly extract subsistence: the seizure and sack of Antwerp by the Army of Flanders mutineers cost that city the destruction of some 1,000 houses and the deaths of 8,000 citizens. Restoration of discipline, of course, required pay by the authorities, but large sums of money were difficult for early modern states to raise. Hence towns remained in the grasp of mutineers for extended periods; in the most lengthy mutiny of the Army of Flanders, mutineers held Hoogstraten in the Spanish Netherlands from 1602 to 1605.

Hungry and unpaid soldiers, mutineers, and freebooters certainly looted civilian property out of necessity. But the violent actions that we have seen figuring so prominently in early modern popular-print material had an additional cause: looting also originated in European military custom. In medieval practice the enemy was not only the opposing lord and his army, but all of his subjects as well. Thus looting of the farms, towns, and properties subject to an enemy ruler was an accepted act of war, a practice that was taken for granted by soldiers and civilians alike. The Italian mercenary armies of the fifteenth and sixteenth centuries, for example, maintained military pioneers, the *guastatori* ("devastators"), whose mission was not only to build fortifications but also to strike at the civilian population by destroying crops, vines, and olive trees – devastation that could cripple a region's agriculture for years. Three centuries later, commanders still sought to cripple their foes' warmaking capabilities and will to resist by systematically destroying crops, livestock, and towns in their homelands or operational zones. Perhaps the most devastating such destruction of our period took place in the Palatinate of western Germany, a natural area for staging attacks on France. To prevent such a use of the Palatinate, French troops under Marshal Turenne devastated the region in 1674, and the impending War of the League of Augsburg prompted Louis XIV of France to order devastation of the Palatinate again in the winter of 1688–89. This later act was one of systematic destruction, based on a map of target sites prepared by the war ministry, and the French destroyed many of the significant towns in the region, including Worms, Spier, Bingen, and Oppenheim. In Mannheim, the capital of the Palatinate, the French not only destroyed the city but also executed citizens who returned to the ruins.

Looting and violence also occurred whenever an army took an enemy city. By the seventeenth and eighteenth centuries, however, certain rules generally applied to the capture of cities. Besieging commanders called on cities to surrender and announced that, in the event of failure to do so, all civilians within the walls would be treated as enemies when the city fell. If surrender followed this announcement, the city was supposed not to be looted, but such behavior was extremely difficult to prevent. If the city fell only after assault by the besieging forces, looting with violence against civilians for three days was a widely observed practice. The case of Magdeburg in Germany perhaps most clearly exemplified the levels of violence that the sack of a city could reach. When that Protestant city fell to assault by Imperial troops on 20 May 1631, fires were started that destroyed much of the city, and perhaps as many as 25,000 people, 85 percent of the city's population, perished amid the flames and pillage. Another great postsiege slaughter occurred at Maastricht in the Dutch Republic; when the Spanish captured that city in 1579 perhaps a third of the civilian population died in its sack. Such looting of a major city could be a handsome reward for the troops; Oliver Cromwell's soldiers sent sixty shiploads of booty home to England after their sack of Dundee during the Scottish campaign in 1651.

Faced with such common actions by soldiers, the most vulnerable victims, the peasants, had three possible responses to military violence. Passive acquiescence to soldiers' demands for food and money was one possible response, but it presented certain dangers. Force and violence always underlay soldiers' demands, especially the threat of execution or burning of property if demands were not met, a practice called *brands-chatting* in Flemish, literally extortion by threat of fire. Peasants suspected of hiding possessions might also be tortured or killed. Grimmelshausen described such acts in *Simplicius Simplicissimus*, and Callot's *Miseries and Misfortunes of War* engravings, which we also discussed in Chapter 1, showed soldiers roasting a peasant on a spit, presumably to extract information on hidden property from him. Moreover, soldiers could even strip bare a cooperative area. In the county of Hohenlohe occupying Imperial troops developed a system of peasant payments in cooperation with local authorities early in the Thirty Years' War. But army demands quickly escalated, then the Swedes arrived with their own demands, and by 1634, when the war's exigencies combined with famine and disease, peasants in one village, Bächlingen, were reduced to eating dogs, cats, bark from trees, and stubble in the fields. Pillage of nonresisting populations occurred even in the eighteenth century when discipline had improved. Thus in 1709 Dutch troops occupying Rumegis in the Spanish Netherlands killed villagers, raped women, and stole livestock. When they left the town, the *curé* reported: "We found only the walls were left. Not a door, not a window, not a pane of glass, not a piece of metal, and, what is worse, not a single bundle of straw."[9] Even the most obliging civilians could become victims of soldiers' violence; in Bapaume, near Arras, France, a householder lodging six Imperial soldiers in 1640 found himself in a brawl because he had served one group of the men *tarte au fromage* and the other *flan*.

A second course of action open to rural residents was to flee their homes before the advance of troops. Peasants devised warning systems of troop movements, and sought refuge in nearby fortified towns where they had often stockpiled food supplies. But this could be very disruptive of personal lives: the diary of one shoemaker in Neenstettin, Germany, described his thirty flights to nearby Ulm during the Thirty Years' War.

[9] Quoted in Frank Tallet, *War and Society in Early-Modern Europe, 1495–1715* (London and New York: Routledge, 1992), p. 149.

The historian of a century's conflict in the Netherlands estimated that 175,000 residents fled their homes in that area between 1540 and 1630. And in central Germany one Franconian official wrote to his ruler in 1645: "None of your subjects are here; they have all gone to Nuremberg, Schwabach and Lichtenau with every bit of their possessions down to goods worth scarcely a kreuzer."[10] Flight entailed signal risks: crops and livestock remained untended, and soldiers were apt to burn everything that was not portable.

Peasants, however, were not just victims of violence. A third response open to them was resistance fueled by the hatred many of them felt for soldiers. Figure 5 is the work of a Flemish artist, David Vinckboons (1576–1632), who was very familiar with the violence of war in the Low Countries. The picture was one of a pair of paintings by the artist. The first, *Peasant Sorrow*, showed gluttonous, bullying soldiers gorging themselves at the expense of a peasant household. The second, *Peasant Joy*, reproduced in Figure 5, shows the tables turned as the peasants drive the soldiers from their home. The painting obviously displays the role reversal so celebrated in early modern popular culture, but its meaning is ambiguous. Amid the crisis of war the artist portrayed no one as clearly good or evil. The soldiers were gluttons and bullies, but not murderers, while the peasants' bared teeth make them virtual beasts, not far above the level of their dog.

The peasant hatred of soldiers captured by Vinckboons revealed itself in countless acts of violence. Peasants often concentrated their wrath on isolated soldiers. Thus peasants slew Spanish and Italian stragglers from the Bavarian army in 1622 near Nuremberg; individual Swedes fell victim to peasant wrath after their defeat at Bamberg in 1631; and Piedmontese peasants killed men separated from Imperial forces in 1705. Drunken and wounded soldiers especially were vulnerable to peasant violence, and German peasants reportedly buried alive Russian wounded after the Battle of Zorndorf in 1758. Sometimes, too, rural residents organized their resistance. In Overijssel province in the Dutch Republic armed peasants fortified their villages and rallied against soldiers under a banner bearing a broken eggshell and sword embodying the Netherlandish saying "Better half an egg than an empty shell." Other Dutchmen formed Huisliedengilde, or self-defense groups. And during the Civil War in England Midlands and West Country villagers organized to resist soldiers under standards inscribed: "If you offer to plunder or take our cattle, be assured we will bid you battle."

[10] Quoted in Geoffrey Parker *et al.*, *The Thirty Years' War*, 2nd ed., (London and New York: Routledge, 1997), p. 191.

Figure 5. David Vinckboons, *Peasant Joy*. Oil on canvas. Rijksmuseum, Amsterdam.

Contemporaries were shocked by the cost of early modern soldiers' depredations upon civilians. The Italian historian and statesman Francesco Guicciardini (1483–1540) wrote of his homeland, which had become a battlefield for not only Italian forces but also those of France and the Spanish monarchy, that everywhere one "saw nothing but scenes of infinite slaughter, plunder and destruction of multitudes of towns and cities, attended with the licentiousness of soldiers no less destructive to friends than foes."[11] Other early modern observers reported that, in the wake of soldiers' devastations, wolf packs reappeared in the southern Netherlands in the 1590s and that a dozen communities in lower Alsace had disappeared in the seventeenth-century wars.

Primitive population estimates also painted a grim picture of soldiers' impact on civilians, as samples of such data from several particularly war-ravaged regions suggest. In northern Italy the population of Pavia was more than halved from 16,000 in 1500 to 7,000 in 1529. In the Netherlands rural areas around Courtrai and Ypres were almost abandoned by the late 1580s, and the populations of the provinces of Brabant, Flanders, and Hainaut dropped by 25 to 50 percent. In France the population of Rouen diminished by a quarter during the religious wars, while authorities reported population losses of 20 percent in the Paris basin in the 1630–50 period of the Thirty Years' War and the Fronde revolt. But it was Germany that reported the most horrendous losses. Parts of the country, including Mecklenburg, Pomerania, and Württemberg, suffered population losses of more than 50 percent during the Thirty Years' War, prompting scholars well into the twentieth century to conclude from these examples that warfare was a demographic disaster for Germany.

Only recently has modern historical demography given us a more accurate picture of such early modern population losses. We now know, for example, that not all of the population decreases shown on local records represented deaths. Some of the losses, instead, represented population transfers as people fled permanently to safer or more religiously hospitable regions. Thus Middleburg in the northern Netherlands acquired 1,174 new men and their families in 1580–91, most of them Protestants fleeing Spanish forces in the south; and peasants everywhere similarly fled for sanctuary behind city walls.

Careful modern population research has also revealed that war's damages were not uniform, especially in Germany. The losses in Mecklenburg, Pomerania, and Württemberg were great, but other parts of the country, such as the northwest, suffered little loss. As a result, when

---

[11] Quoted in J. R. Hale, *War and Society in Renaissance Europe, 1450–1620* (New York: St. Martin's Press, 1985), p. 179.

estimating Germany's losses historians now seek a wider statistical base than data from the sites of the most glaring military brutality. The outcome is that modern scholars now estimate Germany's seventeenth-century population loss at about 15 or 20 percent of the prewar population, a loss that some scholars estimate the country had recouped by 1700.

Twentieth-century studies of early modern local burial records permit historians to understand better the fates of those who did die. Direct violence by soldiers was not the chief cause of death among them, in most areas. Civilians died in the greatest numbers when war coincided with, and aggravated, other disasters, especially famine and epidemic disease. Myron Gutmann's study of the population of the economically vital Basse-Meuse district around Liège demonstrated that war worsened the effects of famine and that the vulnerable young and old among malnourished populations fell easy victims to disease spread by the armies, including dysentery, influenza, pulmonary ailments, and typhus. In addition, the recurrence of bubonic plague cost many lives. But, like many epidemic diseases that civilians linked to the movement of armies, it especially reflected environmental factors. All of these diseases were most virulent in one part of the year, the months from August through to October when arduous agricultural work weakened farmers and hot weather spoiled existing food supplies before the new harvest was gathered.[12] Loss of life at the hands of early modern soldiers, therefore, was considerable in our period, but nowhere near as great as contemporaries believed it to have been.

Looting and its attendant violence were not the only depredations visited on civilians by soldiers. Billeting was a further problem for sixteenth- and seventeenth-century Europeans. Soldiers of the new standing armies had to be housed over the winter, when they seldom fought, and sixteenth- and seventeenth-century governments, lacking the means to build barracks, quartered soldiers on civilian populations. Armies on campaign also sometimes billeted troops in civilian homes. Householders feared and resented such quartering, because its cost could be great, and governments began to provide some reimbursement for these expenses only late in our period. Householders owed soldiers the *utensile*, that is, usually a fire, bedding, candles, cooking utensils, and salt. But the soldiers' arms provided them with the force to take much more from resistant householders if they chose. And if soldiers were from a foreign army, civilian losses of life and property could be great. Suggestive of the problem is a Spanish colloquial response to bad behavior: "Where do you think you are, the Netherlands?" ("¿Estamos qui o en Flande?").

---

[12] Myron P. Gutmann, *War and Rural Life in the Early Modern Low Countries* (Princeton: Princeton University Press, 1980), pp. 151–73.

Even garrison duty by soldiers led to problems for civilians. The record of the French Guards garrisoned in Paris in the seventeenth and eighteenth centuries may serve as an example of the victimization of citizens by their garrison troops. Until the 1760s the government provided no barracks for these units, and the soldiers lived in the community. Moreover, since military wages were inadequate, many guardsmen took various low-skill civilian employments, or sought illegal gain in a variety of ways, especially contrabanding and petty thefts.

Military regulations required the guardsmen to leave only their guns at the guardhouse; they retained their swords and often went about armed with these weapons. Thus members of the French Guards frequently engaged in fatal tavern brawls with other soldiers and citizens, like that of 30 December 1765 in which a guardsman employed as a sawyer killed a Nanterre butcher in a fight, cutting his throat and methodically mutilating his body. There is also evidence that some soldiers engaged in more organized violence, undertaking contract killing of civilians' enemies for pay. And when the authorities arrested the Parisian robber Louis-Dominique Cartouche, the head of a large armed band, 30 guardsmen fled the city, 150 sought transfers to non-Parisian regiments, and 33 eventually stood trial in the case in 1721. When the authorities two decades later broke up another armed band, that of Raffiat, sixteen soldiers, eleven of whom were French Guards, went on trial. Only after the mid-eighteenth century did the behavior of the Parisian garrison begin to improve, thanks to better policing, more careful screening out of criminals among recruits, and construction of barracks.

A number of seventeenth- and eighteenth-century developments in both military tactics and civilian administration slowly enabled governments better to control and supply their forces and to begin to contain military violence against civilians. In the area of tactics the Dutch commander Maurice of Nassau (1567–1625) was the earliest exponent of a revolutionary method of employing the new infantry firepower on the battlefield. Abandoning the squares of pikemen that had dominated much of fifteenth- and sixteenth-century warfare, Maurice arranged his musketeers in ranks trained to shoot successively as units so as to maintain a constant fire on the enemy. Such tactics were quite expensive to implement; they required intensive drill, the mastering of which demanded the employment of many more noncommissioned officers than in the past. Such officers also upheld discipline by preventing much desertion of trained men from the ranks.

Maurice's tactical innovations were widely imitated, especially his version of the articles of war laying down the code of conduct every general sought to impose on his troops; his *Artikelbrief* of 1590 found emulators particularly in the Swedish army of Gustavus Adolphus and the New Model Army of the English parliament. The articles of war thus evolving typically made mutiny, desertion, pillage, and rape capital offenses because such activities destroyed the discipline required of these new forces. At the same time armies created officers (called variously provosts, advocates, *barrachels*, and *écoulètes*) charged especially with imposing discipline through a system of military justice. The discipline these officers stood for took years to impose, but it was evident in some armies from the mid-seventeenth century.

Governments also began to address the pay and supply problems that underlay many breakdowns in military discipline and violence toward civilians. The Spanish Army of Flanders, so plagued by pay problems, led the way in this regard. Spain contracted with private suppliers to make large quantities of food available at specified intervals along the "Spanish Road," the overland route by which her forces moved from the Mediterranean to the Netherlands, to prevent plunder along the route. And most importantly, Spanish officials contracted with *proveedores de viveres* to feed troops once they reached their destination, and with other suppliers to clothe the Army of Flanders. To facilitate supply the army also increasingly standardized arms and clothing, deducting the value of these supplies from soldiers' pay when they eventually reached the men. All of these steps assured that soldiers' needs were met much more reliably than in the past. Significantly, mutinies diminished when this system was in place, and many states imitated Spain. In Germany during the Thirty Years' War the Swedish under Gustavus Adolphus established supply depots at strategic points on the army's line of march. The French also established supply depots on key lines of march and along the eastern frontiers, as well as a system of contractual suppliers (*munitionnaires*) to the army and officials to supervise military supplies and other administrative matters (*intendants d'armée*).

But not all rulers possessed the foresight of Gustavus Adolphus or the resources and growing administrative infrastructure of the French monarchy. Therefore many armies, including that of France when it moved beyond its depots, continued to live off the land well into the eighteenth century. In such case, armies increasingly used a system pioneered by the Spanish Army of Flanders in the 1570s and perfected during the Thirty Years' War. Known by its German name, *Kontributionssystem*, it aimed to limit soldiers' pillage of a region, and thus to maintain the area's productivity and ability to feed an army. In this system armies extracted regular payments in money or kind from a region under threat of force. The process often grew to be quite orderly, with written agreement between army commanders and local officials, and the costs sometimes apportioned between residents using local tax rolls. In return for the *Kontributions*, occupying commanders promised to safeguard the region from violence by their soldiers. Indeed, out of pure self-interest commanders recognized that failure to prevent troops from pillaging the countryside in search of food was counterproductive. Such arrangements, of course, did not entirely end violence to civilians; little in war always occurs completely as planned. Nor did such orders always meet everyone's needs. Sometimes armies' demands exceeded a locale's ability to pay, and soldiers resorted to seizing forcibly what they wished or took hostages to assure final payment – as did the Swedes in 1631 when they evacuated Munich with a third of their *Kontribution* unpaid. Sometimes, too, an army might be driven from an area after it had collected what it needed, only to be replaced by its opponents with fresh demands on civilians. The system could thus still be extremely costly for inhabitants and have long-term consequences, due to the period's recurring warfare. In the prosperous Basse-Meuse region the cost of *Kontributions* doubled – and sometimes tripled – the normal levels of taxes in the 1690s, a burden from which the area nonetheless recovered eventually. In economically less strong areas, like Nördlingen in Germany, early modern military exactions contributed to long-term decline.

Such high costs for civilians notwithstanding, improved supply and pay procedures and stricter discipline not only contained military damage to civilians by the early eighteenth century, but also greatly diminished the incidence of mutinies and desertion. Improvement even occurred in the problems of military housing. Construction of barracks, begun by the Venetians in the 1570s and the Army of Flanders in 1609, went forward slowly but started to alleviate some of the conflict between civilians and soldiers over billeting. Some towns even expended local revenues to fund the building of barracks or to acquire housing for military use in order to prevent billeting of soldiers in civilian residences. But, as always, discipline remained a problem, and one French ordinance of 1719 required a wall 10 ft (3 m) high around barracks.

Even as military discipline, pay, supply, and housing improved, however, the relationship between civilians and soldiers remained fraught with violence. The freeing of soldiers from their military obligations, whether as a result of cessation of hostilities, or of separation from the service due to wounds or age, created problems of violence and public order in the early modern period. Soldiers came mainly from the ranks of those without skills or resources, and they rarely fitted easily back into civilian life as a result. Moreover, many were young men without roots or families, the very group criminologists tell us are most prone to crime in any society. As for those who became too old or too sick to serve, the few institutions to assist them, like the Hôtel des Invalides (completed 1676) in Paris and the Royal Hospital for Soldiers at Chelsea (completed 1692) in London, were inadequate to help large numbers of veterans, who consequently might turn to crime, too.

In an age without government assistance in the transition to civilian life, most of these unskilled men joined the ranks of the poor, a group their more prosperous contemporaries saw – with some justification – as a breeding ground for crime. The Venetian senate averred in 1599 that for garrison duties foreign mercenaries served the republic better than native troops because when a war ended they would return home, taking their criminal habits with them. One German historian found many ex-soldiers moved directly from the ranks to crime. Thus rates of many offenses, including armed robbery, increased with demobilization, and Sir Thomas More (1478–1535) probably summed up the view of most propertied people of his age aptly when he wrote: "Robbers do not make the least active soldiers, nor do soldiers make the most listless robbers; so well do these two pursuits agree."[13]

Demobilized troops posed another threat, too. They were apt to linger around the capital, sometimes demanding backpay and always threatening public order. Elizabethan legislation in England ordered demobilized soldiers to return home directly or face incarceration, while French royal ordinances of 1518, 1523, 1525, 1537, and 1561 threatened death (vainly) for soldiers who failed to go home immediately after service. The danger posed to public order by masses of demobilized soldiers roaming around a capital is summed up by a report to the London Common Council on 25 September 1550 regarding troops returning from France after the Treaty of Boulogne and other soldiers released by the peace from garrisons in the north and east. The report noted of these men: "that they cannot work, nor will not work, and if they cannot obtain living at the King's hands in consideration that they have long served the King's highness and the King his father, . . . they will appoint themselves in several companies in London . . . and thereupon set upon the citizens and their houses and take there such booties and spoil . . . they can lay hand upon."[14]

Several decades later, in 1589, London authorities prevented the looting of Saint Bartholomew's Fair by 500 soldiers returned from an unsuccessful expedition to Portugal only by calling up 2,000 militiamen. Still later, in France, the monarchy launched major police actions around Paris in 1644, 1655, 1657, and 1660 to round up unemployed persons, especially ex-soldiers.

[13] Thomas More, *Utopia*, edited by Edward Surtz and J. H. Hexter, vol. 4 of *The Complete Works of St. Thomas More*, 15 vols., (New Haven: Yale University Press, 1963), p. 63.
[14] Quoted in Hale, *War and Society in Renaissance Europe*, p. 88.

Recruited from crime-prone elements of the populace, the sixteenth- and early seventeenth-century army was often a threat to the safety of civilians it encountered. But by the mid-seventeenth century the wanton brutality of such forces was diminishing. Military codes, like that of Maurice of Nassau, began to limit the impact of troops on noncombatants. And certainly, as we have seen, improved military discipline, pay, supply, and housing also hastened the process of restricting the destruction wrought by soldiers. In consequence, soldiers could be used to some limited effect by their rulers to maintain internal order in their states.

Armies and internal order

The army constituted the only instrument of large-scale coercion available to states in which, as we will see, police services were nonexistent or in their infancy. But we will also find that military power proved to be a highly imperfect instrument for achieving the three chief goals assigned to it by rulers attempting to assure the internal order of their states. Such rulers employed armies to curb the armed might of the aristocracy and of provinces whose independent tendencies noblemen might exploit. They also deployed troops as their only real weapon against collective violence. And by careful location of barracks they sought to impose a secondary duty on soldiers as a form of police.

The military capabilities of the aristocracy assumed particularly threatening form when they supported provincial or sectarian opposition to central government. Outside of England and the urbanized and commercial Dutch Republic, aristocrats and their armed retainers yielded chiefly in response to force. France is the classic example of this, a country in which in 1600 noble magnates still possessed considerable military capacity. Moreover, many leading aristocrats were Huguenots, as French Protestants were called. Rejecting the official Catholic faith, these men had been leaders in the religious wars of the sixteenth century and stood ready to take up arms again for their faith. In such an uprising they could draw on the additional military resources of Protestant cities in the south of the country. Endowed by the Edict of Nantes (1598) with the right to maintain fortifications and garrisons to defend themselves after the end of the religious wars, these cities, including Alès, La Rochelle, Montpellier, Montauban, and Nîmes, constituted a "state within a state."

The French monarchy took a first step to curb aristocratic capacity for private violence in the reign of Henri IV (r. 1589–1610), the king who had ended the religious wars and sought to establish confessional peace with the Edict of Nantes. In 1604 Henri ordered one of his ministers, the duc de Sully, to draw up an inventory of private armament, and the next year, declaring that "to us alone belongs the right to possess artillery," he ordered cannon to be removed from a number of aristocratic châteaux.[15]

In the next reign, that of Louis XIII (r. 1610–43), the king and his able minister Cardinal Richelieu moved against both the nobility and the Huguenots. In response to a Huguenot revolt in 1621–22, the king led the royal army against the Protestant strongholds, capturing one of the greatest, Montpellier. In the resulting peace agreement the Huguenots lost the right to fortify some eighty places. A second Huguenot rebellion in 1627–29 resulted in a victory for royal arms in the siege of La Rochelle. The resulting Peace of Alès, which confirmed Protestants' rights to worship in their faith, required in return the destruction of their remaining fortifications, a process Richelieu oversaw with the royal army.

Reduction of Protestant fortifications, however, was part of a more general policy, for in the same year as the Peace of Alès the monarchy announced that it would also seek the destruction of noble fortifications in the kingdom's interior. The last nonfrontier fortifications did not come down until the reign of Louis XIV (1643–1715) and the crown was still seizing privately held artillery in the kingdom's interior in the 1660s, and it was only military might, or its threat, that made possible these actions so fundamental to the crown's monopoly of force.

The revolt of the Fronde (1648–52) revealed that even these tactics had not bound the aristocracy unreservedly to the crown. Much else was required for that; the nobility's complete pacification took the rest of the seventeenth century. Inculcation of the ideals of courtly society so central to Elias's "civilizing process" supported this process, but the crown also bound aristocrats to itself through links of clientage and outright purchases of loyalty through awards of honors, offices, and privileges.

In the Spanish kingdom the existence of religious and cultural minorities in an intolerant age complicated the process of forcibly disarming the nobility and curbing the historic separatism of provinces with whose causes aristocrats sometimes allied. In Valencia the monarchy brought the grandees' military might under control in several ways in the late sixteenth and seventeenth centuries. Fear of continuing resistance to Catholic rule led in 1563 to the disarmament of the Moriscos, the people of Muslim heritage who provided the bulk of the grandees' armed retainers. The crown further enhanced its military authority in the region in 1596 with the creation of a militia under royally appointed officers that sustained a dual military and legal offensive against aristocrats employing violence. Even such efforts, however, could not completely control violence in Valencia. Elimination of noble armed retainers removed from

[15] Quoted in Anderson, *War and Society in Europe of the Old Regime*, p. 31.

rural life private forces that had controlled much petty violence. Indeed, one grandee complained at the disarming of the Moriscos: "We rode out to right wrongs with these people, which we cannot do if the Moriscos are disarmed."[16] Banditry flourished as a consequence.

On the Bourbon accession to the Spanish throne, the new monarch further consolidated royal authority. When Aragon, Catalonia, and Valencia rose up against Philip V (r. 1700–46) and made common cause with his foreign enemies in the War of the Spanish Succession, the king responded with military force. After a lengthy siege of Barcelona ended the last resistance in 1714, the king abolished all of the old liberties of the rebellious provinces and imposed a centralized and essentially military regime on them. Under the Nueva Planta of 1716 Captain-Generals, selected from among senior military officers, took over much of provincial administration. In other states, too, including Piedmont-Sardinia, Prussia, and even many of the smaller German states, the army sustained the efforts of rulers to control the capacity of overpowerful subjects to commit violence.

Yet rulers also faced civil disorder from their more modest subjects, and they used the military against rebellion and riots in default of modern police forces with specialized crowd-control training. Rebellions against rising tax burdens and increasing feudal dues and rents for peasants, as well as riots over food shortages, or labor, religious, and political issues all threatened the security of early modern Europeans, as we will see in detail in Chapter 6. Governments' only possible response to such threats was to employ their increasingly large armies against civilians, because any sizeable assembly of them was beyond the capacity of local officials to control.

Use of the army against large-scale rebellions and widespread rioting could require considerable manpower. In France, where peasant rebellions recurred through the seventeenth century, the crown employed some 10,000 troops, many of them foreign mercenaries, against the Nu-Pieds of Normandy in 1639 and some 20,000 soldiers against a Breton peasant rebellion in 1675. A century later the monarchy still had recourse to the army, mobilizing 25,000 soldiers to suppress the violence of the Flour War of 1775. In eighteenth-century England one military historian estimated that infantry units spent an eighth of their time on various kinds of police work, including crowd control, and cavalry units a fifth of their time. To quell the Gordon Riots of 1780 in London the government required the services of 15,000 troops. And the Spanish monarchy had employed large numbers of soldiers to curb riots in Madrid in 1766.

[16] Quoted in James Casey, *The Kingdom of Valencia in the Seventeenth Century* (Cambridge: Cambridge University Press, 1979), p. 209.

If the military was the only weapon the state could wield against rebellion and riot, it was a weapon with considerable limitations for such employment. First, the early modern army could never achieve the omnipresence of modern police services, even when, as we will see, early modern states dispersed their soldiers fairly widely through the construction of barracks. Communication and transport remained poor, and troops often took days to arrive at danger points. While local authorities awaited troops' arrival, violence and destruction might escalate considerably, as happened during the Gordon Riots. These began on 2 June 1780, yet troops were not available in sufficient quantity to have much effect until 8 June. Before soldiers were able to restore order, crowds liberated the inmates of London's Newgate, Fleet, and New Bridewell prisons and damaged persons and property throughout the metropolis.

A second problem with the deployment of troops against civilian crowds is that troops were seldom prepared for such duty. Early modern armies had no training in crowd-control techniques, and they bore only muskets, bayonets, and swords – the lethal weaponry of the battlefield. Often such weaponry intimidated crowd members, and they dispersed without a violent confrontation. But when this failed to happen, and soldiers opened fire, the loss of life could be considerable; in London's Gordon Riots, soldiers killed an estimated 285 people and wounded 173 others.

Finally, there were occasional legal problems that impeded the use of troops against civilians. In France the high court for much of the country, the Parlement of Paris, long contested the crown's right to deploy force in the capital. But the use of troops was especially fraught with legal complexity in England. Common law required that everyone had the duty to suppress a riot, traditionally defined as any assembly of three or more persons that might cause another to fear a breach of the peace. The circumstances of the assembly defined its gravity, and while the law treated most riots as felonies, serious ruptures of the peace could be prosecuted as treason – literally, war against the king. In 1715 parliament sought better to protect the kingdom's order with the passage of the Riot Act, an ordinance that remained in effect until 1967. The Act defined the "heinous offense" of riot as an assembly of twelve or more people for violence against the crown's authority. The rioters were guilty of capital felony if they did not disperse within one hour of a magistrate reading the proclamation to disband included in the Act. The same charge applied if rioters destroyed churches, residences, or farm buildings. The Act further called for all persons to aid in breaking up riots and absolved them of any civil or criminal liability that they might incur in the process.

Parliament passed the Riot Act under the threat of Jacobite resistance to the new Hanoverian monarch, George I (r. 1714–27). The Act was not intended to contradict common law, but to give magistrates added power in dealing with unrest. But the Act was badly drafted and widely misunderstood. Some believed that it superseded common law tradition and that crowds could only be dispersed one hour after the reading of the proclamation, and then only on the express orders of a magistrate. Others attempted to reaffirm the common law principle that restricted those dispersing rioters to the very minimum force necessary to achieve that end. Caught in the midst of the law's ambiguities were the soldiers. On the one hand, they had to obey military commands to open fire under threat of court martial for disobedience. On the other hand, they could be tried for murder for using "undue" force. Often juries that included the friends and relatives of soldiers' victims decided such cases. Nevertheless, for much of the eighteenth century British authorities provided no clarification of the law, and individual soldiers often chose to fire over rioters' heads.

The construction of barracks in scattered locations made the employment of troops in controlling riots, and in other police work, a little easier, although, as we noted earlier, transportation problems still slowed the movement of troops. Officials in many countries sited barracks to facilitate the use of troops for local police work. As prime minister, William Pitt (1759–1806) sponsored a program of English barracks construction in the 1790s. When questioned about them in the House of Commons, he readily pointed out that the government located barracks in certain areas, such as manufacturing cities with labor unrest, as a police measure.

A military presence in population centers enabled civilian authorities increasingly to employ soldiers for routine police work, including patrolling streets, conveying prisoners, and making arrests. Thus the French Guards units did armed nightly street patrols in Paris after 1742. Public safety probably improved as a result of these patrols and other such measures, but these assignments for the troops had a cost. Police work can be quite destructive of military morale, which depends, in part, on the separation of soldiers from civilians to foster discipline and *esprit de corps*. Police assignments were not popular with the army; the French Guards complained repeatedly about patrol duties, and in the French army as a whole officers routinely refused to command troops under the orders of magistrates. Morale in the French Guards reflected this dissatisfaction, and the Guards and other garrison units became so enmeshed in civilian life that they were unreliable in crises. In 1788 troops in Rennes and Grenoble refused to open fire on rioters, and in Paris in July 1789 not only did the French Guards refuse to fire on unruly crowds, they joined them.

In our period of study the discipline of the early modern army improved and the army was employed to some effect in containing violence. But the persistence of private arms among European civilians and the inadequacy of the army as a police mechanism demanded a more comprehensive institutional structure for containing violence. As we will see in Chapter 3, by the eighteenth century the states of early modern western Europe developed a foundation for that structure by perfecting their bureaucratic machinery, and beginning the creation of comprehensive police agencies. We will find that such developments also contributed to the diminution of private violence.

FURTHER READING

Anderson, M. S., *War and Society in Europe of the Old Regime, 1618–1789* (London: Fontana Press, 1988).
Babington, Anthony, *Military Intervention in Britain: From the Gordon Riots to the Gibraltar Incident* (London: Routledge, 1990).
Bercé, Yves-Marie, *History of Peasant Revolts: The Social Roots of Rebellion in Early Modern France,* translated by Amanda Whitmore (Ithaca: Cornell University Press, 1990).
Emsley, Clive, "The Military and Popular Disorder in England, 1790–1801," *Journal of the Society for Army Historical Research* 61 (1983), pp. 10–21, 96–112.
Hale, J. R., *War and Society in Renaissance Europe, 1450–1620* (New York: St. Martin's Press, 1985).
Kamen, Henry, "Public Authority and Popular Crime: Banditry in Valencia, 1660–1714," *Journal of European Economic History* 3 (1974), pp. 654–87.
Lynne, John, "How War Fed War: The Tax of Violence and Contributions during the *Grand Siècle*," *Journal of Modern History* 65 (1993), pp. 286–310.
Malcolm, Joyce Lee, *To Keep and Bear Arms: The Origins of an Anglo-American Right* (Cambridge, MA: Harvard University Press, 1994).
Mallett, Michael E., *Mercenaries and their Masters in Renaissance Italy* (Totowa, NJ: Rowman and Littlefield, 1974).
Parker, Geoffrey, *The Army of Flanders and the Spanish Road, 1567–1659: The Logistics of Spanish Victory and Defeat in the Low Countries' Wars* (Cambridge: Cambridge University Press, 1972).
The Military Revolution: Military Innovation and the Rise of the West, 1500–1800, 2nd ed. (Cambridge: Cambridge University Press, 1996).
Redlich, Fritz, *De Praeda Militari: Looting and Booty, 1500–1815* (Wiesbaden: Franz Steiner Verlag, 1956).
The German Military Enterpriser and His Work Force. A Study in European Economic and Social History, 2 vols. (Wiesbaden: Franz Steiner Verlag, 1964–65).
Reynolds, Elaine, *Before the Bobbies: The Night Watch and Police Reform in Metropolitan London, 1720–1830* (Stanford: Stanford University Press, 1998).

Roberts, Michael, "The Military Revolution" in Michael Roberts (ed.), *Essays in Swedish History* (Minneapolis: University of Minnesota Press, 1967), pp. 195–225.

Stone, Lawrence, *The Crisis of the Aristocracy, 1558–1641* (Oxford: Oxford University Press, 1965).

Tallett, Frank, *War and Society in Early-Modern Europe, 1495–1715* (London: Routledge, 1992).

Tilly, Charles, "War Making and State Making as Organized Crime" in Peter B. Evans, Dietrich Rueschemeyer, and Theda Skocpol (eds.), *Bringing the State Back In* (Cambridge: Cambridge University Press, 1985).

Zmora, Hillay, *State and Nobility in Early Modern Germany: The Knightly Feud in Franconia, 1440–1567* (Cambridge: Cambridge University Press, 1998).

3　Justice

The widespread possession of arms in early modern western Europe, and the presence there of ill-disciplined armed forces, meant that the tensions and conflicts of that society often erupted into violence. We will explore the character of that violence in subsequent chapters, but before doing so we must examine the means by which early modern society sought to contain violence by resolving its conflicts. We will find paradoxically that many of this society's modes of conflict resolution only contributed to the violent tenor of the age.

For conflict resolution, whether in the form of some sort of compromise settlement between opposing parties or in a judicial finding of guilt and assignment of a penalty to one party, societies typically look to their mechanisms of justice. "Justice" to us implies the existence of formal courts of law, staffed by legal professionals and sustained by police forces and penal institutions that enforce laws formally drafted by state authorities. While such a system of state justice existed in our period of study, it coexisted with another mode of dispute resolution. There persisted everywhere a plethora of customs and practices, quite distinct from those associated with state law, infrajudicial modes of conflict resolution functioning below the level of state justice, often with little or no reference to it.

The persistence of infrajudicial modes of conflict resolution, the origins of some of which date to the customs of the Germanic tribes that overwhelmed ancient Rome, reflected the fact that early modern Europe was still in the midst of what many legal historians style the "judicial revolution."[1] They employ this term to describe the progressive extension of state criminal law to supplant infrajudicial means of conflict resolution. In continental western Europe the judicial revolution spelled the eventual triumph of procedure based on Roman and canon jurisprudence over

---

[1] The "judicial revolution" is a term employed most provocatively by Bruce Lenman and Geoffrey Parker, "The State, the Community and the Criminal Law in Early Modern Europe" in V. A. C. Gatrell, Bruce Lenman, and Geoffrey Parker (eds.), *Crime and the Law: The Social History of Crime in Western Europe since 1500* (London: Europa, 1980), pp. 11–48.

older customs. In England the extension of the authority of the crown's courts functioning in the common law tradition proceeded even more rapidly than on the continent. Well underway everywhere by 1500, the extension of state law substituted punishments for the private vengeance and restitutions that were characteristic of older practices. We should not assume, however – as many historians have until quite recently – that the increasing expansion of the judicial institutions of the early modern state inexorably triumphed over older or local traditions. Rather, the weakness of early modern police and military resources, and the solidarity of local communities in the face of unwanted incursions of outside authority that we will explore in Chapter 6, meant that such an extension of judicial power could not have occurred without the cooperation of many of those subject to it.

The slow success of the judicial revolution and the state justice that it represented was charged with significance in several regards. Symbolically, the state's control of justice and its public infliction of punishment demonstrated the existence of a power claiming superiority to both individuals and local institutions. This was of great importance because the fragility of developing state institutions, at least during the first century or two of our period, meant that "everything was built less on a reality of absolute power than on the rhetorical power of images and rituals."[2] There was practical significance to the extension of state judicial authority, too. Territorially, judicial institutions and the police forces that supported them pushed the state's authority to its farthest frontiers and reasserted central government control in rebellious areas. And politically, justice displayed the pretensions of the early modern state to a monopoly of violence. Overall, the judicial revolution began to create the conditions that we have seen Oestreich and other historians singling out as essential to the process of social disciplining.

Some historians also perceive another result of the growing power and stability of the early modern state represented by the new jurisprudence. As state power became more secure later in our period, and perhaps as the civilizing processes identified by Norbert Elias increasingly affected elite behavior, judicial institutions began to limit their violence and to experiment with a new and less brutal penology.

Our survey of the modes employed by western Europeans to regulate their disputes must open, however, with a consideration of actions outside of the institutions of state justice. Throughout early modern western Europe infrajudicial modes of resolving disputes represented

---

[2] Denis Crouzet, "Désir de mort et puissance absolue, de Charles VIII à Henri IV," *Revue de synthèse* 112 (1991), p. 424.

widely used alternatives to state justice when the latter was unavailable, its costs prohibitively high, or simply when individuals or the community believed that nonjudicial action could better resolve disputes. As we will see, recourse to infrajudicial means of conflict resolution did not preclude later appeal to formal tribunals, of state or local authorities, but infrajudicial practices had their own informal agents and unwritten rules.

Vengeance, honor, and violence

The most primal response of the individual to violent offenses like homicide, assault, rape, and extreme insults is the search of the victim or his or her kin for vengeance. To be victimized by such offenses certainly meant suffering physical, material, or emotional damage, but for early modern Europeans such suffering was compounded by damage to personal honor, a jealously guarded attribute.

Honor embraces the value one places on oneself, but even more importantly it also represents the esteem in which society holds one. The qualities early modern society attributed to a person of honor assumed different forms for men and women. In addition, many historians discern some evolution in concepts of male honor during the early modern period. Aristocratic men still linked personal honor to chivalric, martial ideals of bravery and loyalty, as well as to a lineage representing membership of a respected family. In Spain concern about lineage also focused on establishing the family's status as Old Catholics, that is, neither Jews nor Moriscos (those of Muslim heritage). In the early part of our period honor also involved for many men a concomitant of physical strength, sexual potency. To impugn a man's masculinity by alleging, for example, that he was a cuckold offended honor in many parts of Europe. Such concerns still defined honor for many nonaristocratic men, but for most bourgeois males and working men, honor increasingly revolved around a reputation for honesty and professional competence.

Female honor was highly sexualized, and in the main rested upon a woman's reputation for modesty, marital fidelity, and moral probity in general. Female honor intersected that of males when someone questioned a woman's possession of these qualities; such a challenge required defense of the female's honor by husband, father, or brothers.

Indeed, defense of honor was a key concern for all early modern Europeans, aristocrats as well as commoners. Individuals therefore took great personal offense at physical assault, because any attack on an individual represented a lack of respect, and therefore diminished the honor of the victim. But there was constant potential for conflict, too, in those ceremonies that define social life with their acts of deference and tokens of respect expressed in words, gestures, and even facial expressions. Defense of personal honor meant that each individual attempted to extract as much respect as he could from another while according that person the bare minimum in return. Thus words could provide offense. A direct insult – for example, calling a woman "whore" – was the clearest form of spoken offense, but even verbal subtleties caused problems, as in employing the familiar *tu* ("you") in French instead of the more formal *vous* in addressing another. Facial expressions, or refusal to remove one's hat in the presence of another could also be very provocative acts. Even property damage assumed exaggerated gravity as, by extension, it diminished the honor of its owner.

This great concern for personal honor was characteristic of all early modern Europeans. In cities as well as villages where, as a lieutenant of police of eighteenth-century Paris wrote, men and women lived "in one another's almost constant presence," any unanswered assault on an individual's honor could lead to a permanent loss of social standing.[3] Such a loss might be felt by generations of the victim's descendants in daily relations with their neighbors, and not just by the victim himself. Throughout western Europe we can discern the value that this society placed on honor in our period. One sixteenth-century French jurist considered honor as important as life itself: "A loss of property or patrimony is always reparable in one way or another, but never a loss of *honor* or *life*."[4] A sixteenth-century guild member opened his criminal court defense in Reutlingen in Germany by noting "every goodman is obligated to defend to his last breath his honor as his most valuable possession."[5] And the seventeenth-century Spanish dramatist Tirso de Molina (*c.* 1584–1648) wrote of assaults:

> A Spaniard never postpones
> Death for whomever maltreats him,
> Nor delays his revenge.[6]

Social conventions in early modern society demanded that individuals personally defend their honor when offended. For an individual to leave unanswered an offense to honor was to be further shamed, to appear cowardly, and seemingly to accept the validity of an insult. To attempt such

---

[3] Jean Charles Pierre Lenoir, "Mémoires," quoted in Philippe Ariès and Georges Duby, *A History of Private Life*, vol. 3, *The Passions of the Renaissance*, edited by Roger Chartier, translated by Arthur Goldhammer (Cambridge, MA: Harvard University Press, 1989), p. 580.

[4] Jean de Mille, *Pratique criminelle* (reprinted, Paris: Les Marmousets, 1983), p. 37.

[5] Quoted in Richard Martin Allen, "Crime and Punishment in Sixteenth-Century Reutlingen" (Ph.D. dissertation, University of Virginia, 1980), p. 98.

[6] Quoted in Bartholomé Bennassar, *Valladolid au siècle d'or. Une ville de Castille et sa campagne au XVIᵉ siècle* (The Hague: Mouton, 1967), p. 537.

defense in state courts might only compound damage to a victim's honor; that course of action demonstrated impotence in the face of an affront while giving the offense greater publicity. Such conventions propelled early modern Europeans of all social strata to seek violent redress of their grievances.

The duel

In the early modern period aristocrats frequently resorted to the duel to regulate matters of honor, an act defined by one of its chief modern historians as "a fight between two or several individuals (but always with equal numbers on either side), equally armed, for the purpose of proving either the truth of a disputed question or the valour, courage and honour of each combatant." This historian goes on to note the quasi-judicial character of such a fight: "The encounter must be decided or accepted jointly by both parties and must respect certain formal rules, be they tacit, oral or written, which will give it the weight of a legal proceeding, at least in the eyes of the two adversaries."[7]

The dueling evolved from the judicial duel, an outgrowth of medieval trial by combat that eventually became quite formalized for aristocrats, with formal treatises appearing on the subject. In the judicial duel aristocrats regulated their disagreements, after formal challenges, with combat on a site designated by the prince and attended by him, his officials, and an audience. The judicial duel was already something of an anachronism when it occurred for the last time in France in 1547. In that year a conflict between two courtiers, François de Vivonne, seigneur de la Châtaigneraye, and Guy Chabot, comte de Jarnac, resulted in a judicial duel with swords before the king, Henri II. La Châtaigneraye, a favorite of the king, perished in that combat, and Henri II, while not formally abolishing judicial duels, never again granted a field for such an encounter. The king's exit from the judicial duel deprived it of royal sanction in France and set the stage there for increasing recourse to unsanctioned, and therefore unlimited, duels. The Italians pioneered this sort of dueling, and aristocrats choosing such means to settle their disagreements employed relatively new Italian techniques of fencing with rapiers; they justified their actions with a body of writings portraying dueling as evidence of the aristocratic quality of valor and refusal to duel as confirmation of cowardice.

European aristocrats dueled widely in our period, but the practice seems to have flourished most in Italy, Spain, and especially France.

---

[7] François Billacois, *The Duel: Its Rise and Fall in Early Modern France*, edited and translated by Trista Selous (New Haven: Yale University Press, 1990), p. 5.

DUEL FAMEUX ENTRE LE CHEVALIER DE GUISE, ET LE BARON DE LUZ

Figure 6. Anonymous, *The Famous Duel between the chevalier de Guise and the baron de Luz*. Engraving, *c.* 1613. Bibliothèque nationale de France (Cabinet des Estampes), Paris.

Deprived of official sanction, and, as we will see, increasingly illegal, dueling procedure became quite simple. It commenced with an oral or written challenge that stated the offense that had provoked the duel, and culminated in a fight between the disputants, assisted by seconds. The formal challenge, which was sometimes published, and the presence of seconds underline the enduring sense among aristocrats that duels perpetuated the search for justice evident in the earlier tradition of trial by combat and the judicial duel. The weaponry employed in such combat was typically the weapon of the aristocracy, the sword or rapier illustrated in Figure 6. However, the pistol was increasingly the weapon of choice later in our period.

Figure 6 illustrates the duel between two French courtiers in 1613. The conflict began with the efforts of the baron de Luz, a confidant of Marie de' Medici, the queen mother, to arrange a marriage between the children of two aristocratic families. Fearing loss of position at court if the marriage occurred, the aristocratic Guise family opposed the match, and the chevalier de Guise cut down the baron de Luz one day in a fight in the street. The son of the baron de Luz soon sought revenge, writing to Guise a challenge that epitomized aristocratic notions of honor: "I ask you to do me the honor to see you with sword in hand to give satisfaction for the death of my father. My respect for your courage leads me to hope that you will not use your station to avoid that which your honor requires of you."[8] Guise, of course, took up the challenge, and the young baron de Luz met the fate of his father.

These highly ritualized confrontations unfortunately left relatively few of such records. Historians, therefore, cannot estimate the actual number of duels; we must rely instead on appraisals of the duelists' contemporaries. Such unverifiable estimates for France place the annual number of duel victims in the early seventeenth century at anywhere between about 300 and almost 500 men – figures that, if nothing else, suggest to us how common early modern Frenchmen believed dueling to be.

Although the roots of these lethal confrontations between aristocrats were deceptively complex, the limited written records of the challenges yield references to disputes over women, office, legal cases, inheritances, precedence, and other matters. What these conflicts really seem to have represented was the culmination of longstanding differences between the two parties that finally came to a head over some relatively minor provocation, which one party chose to view as an affront. Occasionally, the rancor that underlay a duel had festered for a long while. This was the case with the Spaniard Don Juan de Fiueroa who published a challenge to Don García de Avila in 1631 alleging that the latter had offended his elderly father in 1627. In his challenge Fiueroa justified his delay in confronting his enemy with the claim that García de Avila had avoided him by holing up in a castle surrounded by armed retainers.

The lethal violence of the duel increasingly became an object of ecclesiastical and state condemnation in our period. Representing the unregulated power of according life or death, and the danger of decease without spiritual preparation, the duel forced the Church to take action. It was seen as a practice akin to the trial by ordeal, from which the Fourth Lateran Council had withdrawn clerical sanction in 1215. Therefore the last session of the Council of Trent in 1563 condemned both judicial duels and the less formal confrontations we have examined. Even the French Church, which never formally accepted the decrees of the Council of Trent, opposed dueling after 1614. Individual rulers also condemned duels, often as acts of *lèse-majesté*, because private vengeance subverted the very law of which the monarch was guarantor. Indeed, in

---

[8] Quoted in François Billacois, *Le duel dans la société française dans les XVIᵉ-XVIIIᵉ siècles. Essai de psychologie historique* (Paris: Editions de l'Ecole des hautes études en sciences sociales, 1986), p. 461.

France, where dueling had been illegal since 1602, the king declared in an edict of 1643 restating the prohibition: "We cannot think without horror of this detestable crime that completely violates the respect due us as sovereign and the obedience due God as creator and judge."[9]

Most other rulers also sought to end the duel. In the Iberian Peninsula the Council of Toledo forbade the judicial duel as early as 1473, and in 1480 Queen Isabella outlawed the duel in all forms in Castile. James I of England condemned dueling in a proclamation of 1613, and Emperor Matthias forbade dueling in Germany in 1617. But rendering the practice illegal did not end it, and dueling continued, in part because many of the enforcers of antidueling regulations shared the values of those they were policing. Henri IV of France, for example, even while forbidding dueling, was always indulgent in pardoning those violating his ordinances.

We find more stringent state enforcement of laws against dueling only after the first decades of the seventeenth century, as central government power grew in many states. The most famous campaign against dueling was that pursued in France by Louis XIII (r. 1610–43) and his chief minister, Cardinal Richelieu. This campaign began in the face of a flagrant violation of antidueling laws. François de Montmorency, comte de Bouteville, an inveterate duelist who had killed twenty-two opponents, dueled once again in the most public of places, the Place Royale in Paris, and was sentenced to death in 1627. Ignoring pleas for his pardon, the crown executed the young man, committing itself more firmly to its antidueling campaign. Other states followed the French lead, prosecuting the early modern state's drive to monopolize force, and the number of duels decreased in the face of state and ecclesiastical condemnation. A growing literature on courtly behavior contributed to this decline. So, too, did the slow evolution of institutions for the peaceful adjudication of aristocratic disputes of honor, reflecting the courtly values of the civilizing process. In France the monarchy created the Tribunal du point d'honneur, directed by the marshals of France, to regulate such disputes. And the archducal rulers of the Spanish Netherlands, in forbidding duels in 1610, ordered that "everyone who feels his honor and reputation grievously offended by another bring his complaint to us."[10] Although dueling did not entirely disappear – in the nineteenth century it enjoyed a minor vogue among some aristocrats, German students, and bourgeois with aristocratic pretensions – its heyday was ending.

[9] Quoted in Jacques Lorgnier, *Maréchaussée, histoire d'une révolution judiciaire*, vol. 2, *Quand le gendarme juge* (Paris: L'Harmattan, 1994), p. 224.
[10] Quoted in Marie-Sylvie Dupont-Bouchat and Xavier Rousseaux, "Le prix de sang: sang et justice du XIVᵉ au XVIIIᵉ siècle," *Mentalités* 1 (1988), p. 53.

Feuds

Aristocrats and commoners alike carried on other forms of direct action
that, like dueling, represented the search for private vengeance that all law
codes seek to channel and contain. Individual men certainly responded
violently to murder, assault, or offenses to their honor, or that of their
womenfolk. Far more dangerous in many ways, however, was feuding.
This involved a rallying of the kinsmen and allies of an injured party to
inflict physical reprisals on an individual, and often his clan and clients,
for an act resulting in death, injury, or an offense to honor. A feud, in fact,
represented a state of private war that could recur for generations, and
this form of conflict flourished especially in periods during which the
agencies of state law were weak or in areas where they were inaccessible.

This sort of warfare had been particularly widespread in the medieval
age, and was even recognized in medieval law codes that at the same time
tried to contain the impulse to vengeance. The statutes of Faenza, Italy, of
1410 stated: "We order and we decree that if anyone shall be offended in
his person, and still exact vengeance on another than he who offended
him, so that he shall die, and he shall fall into the power of the commune,
his head shall be cut off."[11] But by our period states employed their
growing power to forbid private vengeance entirely. As early as the thirteenth century, the rapid growth of judicial institutions in England made
it possible for litigation increasingly to replace the blood feud, and the
growth of state authority elsewhere confined it more and more to areas
where normal legal processes were weak or unavailable. Thus in our
period, after 1500, most feuding flourished in isolated upland regions,
like the Gévaudan in France and the Highlands of Scotland, or along the
Mediterranean littoral, in Friuli, Liguria, and Valencia, and on the islands
of Corsica, Sardinia, and Sicily. Indeed, in some of these areas the
problem of feuding endures today.

Historians and anthropologists have discovered that, in even the most
primitive societies, these vendettas often proceeded according to elaborate unwritten rules in which the basic issue was the maintenance of
honor. In many places only certain offenses merited a bloody reprisal. In
Corsica, for example, the shedding of blood by homicide or the killing of
livestock demanded blood. So, too, did sexual dishonor, which could be
effaced only by the blood of the offender. The violation of property boundaries, however, typically did not require blood, unless accompanied by
destruction of fences or walls. The same unwritten rules that set the basis

---

[11] Quoted in John Larner, "Order and Disorder in Romagna, 1450–1500" in Lauro
Martines (ed.), *Violence and Civil Disorder in Italian Cities, 1200–1500* (Berkeley:
University of California Press, 1972), p. 68.

for feuds often specified the level of consanguinity with an offender that made an individual a potential victim. And, in some regions, including Languedoc and Corsica, residents expected some sort of formal announcement of a feud, almost a declaration of private war. Such rules also placed limits on the level of violence, and provided some basis for settlement when blood had repaid blood.

Historians' studies of feuds suggest, too, that they often involved not a society's poorest members but its leading families who rallied kinsmen as well as clients for their causes. Feuding, after all, required resources that the poorest elements in society usually lack. Anthropological studies, like those of Max Gluckman, also suggest that feuds, while violent, seldom totally engulfed a society in violence. Persons involved in feuding factions have multilateral links of kinship and clientage that limit a feud's expansion. Spreading conflict inevitably confronts participants with the need to choose allegiances as they find the conflict of their kinsmen or patrons extending to include as enemies persons or groups to whom they also owe loyalty through bonds of intermarriage or clientage. This situation of conflicting loyalty mandates "peace in the feud," in Gluckman's phrase, that is, pressure to contain violence within limits or to settle disagreements.[12]

Functioning according to such rules, feuds were common in our period. They could often be mundane affairs characterized by localized property damage or injuries, but some feuds could result in a large number of deaths. Edward Muir charted the brutal culmination of a feud between the aristocratic Zambarlano and Strumiero factions in Friuli in 1511.[13] Events came to a head in the city of Udine, during Carnival, a time that we will see in Chapter 5 was particularly propitious for violence. The leaders of the Zambarlani exploited popular resentment of local noblemen to incite three days of rioting and looting during which they liquidated fifty of the Strumieri. This violence eventually spread beyond the city into the countryside in Renaissance Italy's most costly peasant revolt against the seigneurial system.

The bitterness of this feud was especially evident in the treatment of the remains of the Strumieri dead. Their opponents certainly drew on the mockery that we will find characteristic of Carnival by throwing corpses into latrines or wells, but they also deliberately dishonored their victims. The Zambarlani dismembered corpses, leaving them unburied, to be consumed by dogs or pigs, and such denial of the rites of Christian burial precluded eternal salvation. Making "dogmeat" of victims was part of

[12] Max Gluckman, "The Peace in the Feud" in Max Gluckman, *Custom and Conflict in Africa* (Glencoe, IL: The Free Press, 1955), pp. 1–26.
[13] Edward Muir, *Mad Blood Stirring: Vendetta and Factions in Friuli during the Renaissance* (Baltimore: The Johns Hopkins University Press, 1993).

vendetta ritual in this region, and one of the leaders of the Zambarlani, Antonio Savorgnan, slain with a massive head wound by his victims' relatives six months later, was similarly left to have his brains consumed by a large dog. All such desecration fueled the bitterness of feuds, and we will see a measure of it reproduced in the rites of state justice.

Infrajudicial accommodation

The enduring nature of feuds, of course, is their principal danger. Every offense must receive a like response, or one party will be in a position of inferiority to its adversary. Violence could thereby extend over generations, flaring up after years of apparent peace as the youth of a family achieved the physical maturity to resume the fight. Thus early on all societies devised modes of resolving offenses infrajudicially, that is, without reference to state courts, before they led to bloody feuds. Because of the mutual illwill of the parties involved in conflicts, a respected mediator often arranged such accommodations. And in western Europe, at least from the time of the German invasions of the fourth and fifth centuries, mediation generally involved some payment by the offender to assuage the honor of the victim's kin. The German tribes called this *wergild*, and they predicated the precise amount of a payment on the value of the loss. A killer paid a sum appropriate to the status, gender, and age of his victim; someone who had maimed another paid the value of the lost limb, for example.

Such settlements might be worked out verbally, but increasingly they took the form of written agreements that allow historians to examine a process that remained essentially the same for centuries: an apology and a payment made in return for forgiveness and peace. In many areas there existed remarkable consensus as to the relative value of damages; thus in sixteenth-century Valladolid a woman's virginity and her life were equal in monetary terms, although the precise value of either varied according to the woman's social status. Procedures of settlement were regularized, too, and major feuds like that between the Zambarlani and Strumieri might be ended in agreements that resembled treaties. That Friulian feud ended with a solemn ecclesiastical ceremony in 1568 in which a large part of the Venetian aristocracy witnessed the leaders of the factions exchange a kiss of friendship.

Arrangements to settle disputes peacefully were difficult to work out at times, in part because they meant an admission of culpability on the part of the assailant, but also because they did not have to be accepted by the kin of the victim. Nevertheless, they established a practice for containing violence that persisted throughout our period, even as the institutions of state justice grew. Indeed, the threat of dragging to court all the principals in one of these conflicts seems often to have hastened a mediated private settlement in lieu of a trial. Litigation could prove damaging in the ultimate verdict that judges might reach. But the special fear of many was the cost of litigation. An early modern print popular in both France and Germany portrayed a lawyer uttering the words "I eat all." And an old French proverb recognized the value of a private settlement in place of a trial: "A bad agreement is better than a good legal proceeding."

Early modern criminal justice largely depended on the private plaintiff to press charges. In England, the country with perhaps the most comprehensive system of state justice, prosecution depended entirely on the initiative – and the purse – of the private plaintiff for much of our period. In Roman law countries like France, with royal prosecutors, limited funds permitted the crown to prosecute only the most serious crimes at royal expense. The rest (75 percent of all cases in local courts like the Sénéchaussées of Libourne and Bazas in the eighteenth century) came to trial at the expense of the crime victim or his kin. Court records in France, Spain, and other continental countries bear eloquent witness to the consequence of this in the large number of cases in which plaintiffs summarily dropped charges after an initial hearing allowed them to force a settlement out of court. For instance, in the Montes of Toledo in the seventeenth century more than half of privately initiated trials ended not in verdicts but in private settlements. Two French historians, in recognizing this process, concluded that their early modern countrymen, like most western Europeans of our period, "play[ed] justice like a musician plays an instrument."[14]

These private settlements thus persisted into our period, despite the growth of state justice. In some areas, like early modern Scotland, the crown actually encouraged these mediated settlements in place of costly and disruptive trials, although the growing power of the state ruled out these compromises for the most serious cases. Called *accommodements* in France, *amistads* in Spain, *paci e tregue* in Florence, and *Sühnevertragen* in Germany, these settlements required that both parties wished a settlement of the dispute. When the conflicting parties were of equal social standing, a process of direct negotiation might ensue. But when the parties were unequal, as when one was of lower social station, a minor, of diminished mental capacity, or simply deemed lacking in honor, the services of an arbitrator might be employed, and, in some cases, that individual could even impose a settlement, like a judge.

---

[14] François Billacois and Hugues Neveux, "Porter plainte: stratégies villageoises et institutions judiciares en Ile-de-France (XVIIᶜ-XVIIIᶜ siècles)," *Droit et cultures* 19 (1990), p. 8.

To function in such a fashion arbitrators required considerable respect, and a number of figures might fulfill the role. Of primary importance were religious leaders, because Christian doctrine forbids private vengeance. Thus parish priests, Protestant pastors, and Calvinist governing boards of laymen and clerics called consistories all tried to mediate disputes. The extent of their efforts may be gauged by the fact that fully a third of all the Protestant adults of Layrac-en-Brulhois, France, were summoned to explain their behavior to the local consistory and to seek reconciliation in various interpersonal conflicts in 1602–07. Other religious figures might also fulfill this arbitrating role; in the Cantabria region of northern Spain religious brotherhoods often mediated, while in the seventeenth-century Tuscan countryside around Altopascio itinerant preachers settled numerous disputes.

Disinterested locally prominent laymen might also mediate. In France or Spain such figures included local seigneurs. In the Highlands of early modern Scotland panels drawn from equal numbers of gentry from the clans of the aggrieved and offending parties, presided over by a local chieftain, could actually render binding decisions of reparations. But on the European continent notaries increasingly functioned as mediators. With their legal backgrounds and often considerable social standing, these men arbitrated disputes and received disputants' signatures on written settlements that became part of their permanent records.

Many jurisdictions established another type of mediator; official arbitrators of nonlethal violence appeared in the thirteenth and fourteenth centuries, at the outset of the judicial revolution when state justice was weak. These officials typically collected a fee for their services. Called *apaiseurs* or *juges de sang* in Francophone areas, or *peysmaekers* by Flemings, these officials operated widely in the early years of our period in such diverse jurisdictions as Brussels, Bologna, Douai, Ghent, rural Liguria, Lille, Nuremberg, Venice, and Zurich. Although the growing institutions of state justice eventually superseded the functions of these officials, they typically arranged compensation and could punish refusals to settle.

Mediators of all types settled many human conflicts in our period. Nicole Castan's research on the Parlement of Toulouse in the eighteenth century suggests the range of disputes thus amicably settled in this way; property disputes (including issues of fraud, contract violation, boundaries, and theft), sexual transgressions as serious as rape, and verbal and physical attack were all arbitrated.[15] But the state, as we have seen,

---

[15] Nicole Castan, "The Arbitration of Disputes under the 'Ancien Régime'" in John Bossy (ed.), *Disputes and Settlements: Law and Human Relations in the West* (Cambridge: Cambridge University Press, 1983), pp. 219–60.

increasingly legislated many kinds of offenses into its courts; by the late eighteenth century recourse to arbitration was universally on the wane owing to the growth of state justice.

There were, however, other ways in which early modern Europeans could resolve conflicts without mediation but still short of formal legal proceedings. There existed a battery of nonstate tribunals that some scholars have called a system of "parajustice." Church institutions, both Catholic and Protestant, in the sixteenth and seventeenth centuries exercised considerable oversight of their communicants' activities. Their proclaimed aim was to correct, but they did punish, often through their own courts, often informed of parishioners' activities by pastoral visits and laymen who reported on the morality and disputes of their neighbors. Church discipline might include admonition, penance, exclusion from sacraments, or excommunication; referral of continued misbehavior to state justice was also a possibility. In some countries church courts retained primary criminal jurisdiction over all those engaged in their work, laymen and clergy alike. The Inquisition in Spain thus judged independently of state courts the large number of individuals it employed.

Professional organizations, too, had the power to regulate the behavior of their members and to discipline them. Guilds reproved their members for business dishonesty and for practices like ostentatious dress and drinking that might lead to financial ruin. In some jurisdictions they also had the authority to fine their members for criminal behavior.

The rural community and the urban neighborhood alike were in many ways self-regulating. Threatened by repeated thefts or assaults, for example, neighbors responded collectively at times with very selective and violent justice to discipline their own. Local thieves might be beaten in the street by a crowd of enraged citizens, and in Amsterdam the practice of *maling*, in which neighbors seized a thief, beat him, and tossed him in a canal, long flourished. Crowds similarly beat pickpockets in England and France, and in some parts of rural France neighbors shamed notorious thieves by shaving half their head.

But early modern communities were self-disciplining only up to a point. Community members readily turned over to representatives of state justice both outsiders and locals whose behavior transcended the limits of their neighbors' tolerance. We now know that early modern Europeans, including even the peasant majority, knew the law and used it for their interests. Historians have noted especially the relative legal sophistication of this population in regard to the civil law, and have found that peasants from Iberia to northern Germany used the courts to contest property issues and the pretensions of their seigneurs.

Even so, the early modern state did not quickly substitute its criminal law for private vengeance and settlements. Early modern Europeans reserved state criminal law for those problems that could not be resolved in the modes we have discussed. The law could be expensive, as we have suggested, and it could also be brutal. Indeed, one sixteenth-century English jurist advised the crown that, in his opinion, less than one felon in five came to trial because: "most commonly the most simple country man and woman . . . [is] of the opinion that they would not procure any man's death for all the goods in the world."[16] Thus they prosecuted crimes only selectively, most commonly reporting offenses by outsiders in their communities and crimes by locals that exceeded the bounds of toleration by their repetition or particularly brutal nature. And conviction of offenders came only after a number of decisions by members of a community: by the plaintiff to come forward; by witnesses to testify; and, in England, Valencia, and Sweden, by juries to indict and convict.

Selective as this recourse to state justice may have been, however, it was one increasingly chosen by western Europeans by the eighteenth century. People made the choice to go to state law not, as historians long assumed, because the absolutist state everywhere empowered its institutions. Rather, they made this choice because the state, an institution still relatively weak, was winning the cooperation of those people whom the English call "the middling sort." These were the people who served as village elders in Germany and constables and jurymen in England, and made state law function at the grassroots level.

The last century of our period, especially, brought growing prosperity to such people and caused them increasingly to identify with the behavioral standards of the governing classes affected by the civilizing process. In both large states like France and smaller political entities like Württemberg they were more and more willing to work with the agencies of state law. Such cooperation was essential to this law for, as we will see, many of its official agencies, such as the police, were weak or nonexistent.

Police

The modern policeman is the embodiment of the state's claim to monopolize both the use of force among its citizens and the administration of justice. Charged with preserving public order against all threats, while at the same time pursuing proactive policies against crime and violence, police agencies are central to the functioning of the modern state. In our period, however, police agencies were weak, largely as a result of the

---

[16] Edward Hext to Lord Burghley, quoted in Lenman and Parker, "The State, the Community and the Criminal Law in Early Modern Europe" in Gatrell, Lenman, and Parker, *Crime and the Law*, p. 46.

inability of the early modern state to commit sufficient resources to them. Only late in our period did some states manage to enhance their police services, and the weakness of most countries' policing provides at least partial explanation for the persistence of infrajudicial modes of conflict resolution as well as the dependence of every police institution on the cooperation of those it regulated. The inadequacy of early modern policing was evident in both rural and urban areas.

France was the only western European country to attempt a centrally administered national system of rural policing in our period. The force known as the Maréchaussée originated in the thirteenth or fourteenth century as a military police unit. By the sixteenth century it had evolved into a uniformed rural police force with its own courts, pursuing and judging a growing number of offenses, while still hunting deserters as part of its original duty. The monarchy slowly enlarged the force, creating Maréchaussée outposts in key provincial cities, but throughout our period the force's troopers were numerically inadequate to their extensive responsibilities. They did make occasional forays from their outposts into the countryside, but an officer in Aurillac in the 1640s noted that his company remained in its quarters in the face of reports of armed robbers in its vicinity, "not having dared to journey there because we lack the strength to deal with the armed rebels stealing on highways and at fairs."[17] Morale and discipline were not of the highest order, either, perhaps because of low, irregular rates of pay that forced many troopers to take secondary employment.

In 1720 the French crown thoroughly reformed the Maréchaussée, enlarging it to provide one company for each *généralité*, or administrative zone, of the country and dividing each company into brigades of four or five men stationed at outposts throughout rural France. The reformed force, still not well paid, retained its police and judicial powers, and the crown charged it with routine patrols of the countryside. By 1789 the force had grown to 4,114 officers and men. That number led many foreign travelers to laud France as the best-policed nation in western Europe, but the force still lacked sufficient manpower to police a large country with regular mounted patrols. Residents of rural hamlets might have been fortunate to see the blue uniform of the police once a year.

Because of such numerical weakness, the French police had to rely on the cooperation of those they policed, and many of their arrests were of vagrants and notorious thieves turned over to them by local inhabitants. Historians of French policing have found that the force garnered growing

---

[17] Quoted in Iain A. Cameron, "The Police of Eighteenth-Century France," *European Studies Quarterly* 7 (1977), p. 48.

grassroots support in arresting such pariahs in the rural community, and that consequently the *cahiers* for the Estates General of 1789 widely demanded enhanced policing. Indeed, with the Revolution of 1789, the force, deprived of its judicial power, doubled in the number of its effectives and continued as the Gendarmerie Nationale. But citizen support for police action was always calculated. When the police moved against members of the rural community itself, local support could turn to violent opposition, as two troopers found in Saint-Sulpice-des-Faleyrens in the rural Bordelais in 1754. When they attempted to end a game of pétanque by revelers at a local festival that violated Sabbath ordinances, a mob of some 700 people turned on the policemen and pursued them through the town. Repeatedly denied refuge by householders, one policeman died at the hands of the crowd and the other was severely wounded.

The only other attempts at large-scale rural policing originated in the Spanish kingdom. In their Iberian territories, the Catholic monarchs in the late fifteenth century encouraged the expansion of local militias into the Santa Hermandad, the Holy Brotherhood, a confederation of locally financed forces that, like the Maréchaussée, had both police and judicial power over certain offenses. Uniformed and armed initially with crossbows, these forces had jurisdiction over rural crimes of arson, murder, rape, robbery, and rebellion, and eventually acquired some urban authority as well. Yet these forces were not particularly effective. They were never numerous, their funding was local, and the crown never forged them into a force for centralizing its authority. Moreover, the organization operated only in Andalusia, Castile, Galicia, and Léon; it did not patrol Aragon, the Basque provinces, and Catalonia. Thus in the early modern period Spanish travelers, shepherds, and many peasants carried arms for self-defense, landowners hired private guards, and merchants traveled in caravans with armed guards. But the Santa Hermandad endured until its replacement in 1835 by the Guardia Civil.

The Spanish crown also attempted such rural policing in its territories in the Netherlands. As early as 1517, a force with both police and judicial competence in certain crimes, not unlike the Maréchaussée, operated in the county of Artois and it continued to do so until that area passed to France in 1659. Similar police bodies appeared in the course of the seventeenth and eighteenth centuries in Flanders and the Namurois. But the limited manpower of these forces and their lack of central direction hampered their effectiveness, too.

Most of the rest of rural western Europe lacked even this level of policing. Law enforcement rested in the hands of judges and constables of local courts. Thus the court of Bergen op Zoom, complaining in 1700 about the problem of theft in the rural Brabant province of the Dutch

Republic, probably voiced an almost universal sentiment in noting: "there is no more protection than the law itself."[18]

Deprived of adequate police resources, judicial officials relied on the cooperation of those they judged to enforce the law. They depended on crime victims or their kin to take the lead by prosecuting offenders, and often for much more, including apprehension of criminals by participation in the "hue and cry" in England and some German jurisdictions.

The legal institutions themselves had limited staffing and efficacy. In France seigneurial courts and a rather extensive system of royal courts of first instance, the *bailliages* and *sénéchaussées*, sought to enforce order with small staffs of process-servers and bailiffs. Elsewhere, legal services were less comprehensive and professional. In England, the Dutch Republic, western Germany, and Sweden, the lower-court judges and the officers who assisted them were local men, usually without legal education, who served limited terms for little or no remuneration. The justice of the peace in England, the judge of the Dutch *schepenbanken*, the *länsman* in Sweden, and the Schultheiss in Württemberg were all legal amateurs endowed with judicial authority during their terms of office. Aiding them were local residents serving temporarily as law-enforcement officers, such as the constable in England, or the *baljuw*, *ruwaard*, or *drossard* in the Dutch Republic. Their administration of justice, of course, reflected their positions; they had to execute their duties in a way acceptable to their neighbors, or community life would have been untenable for them when they left their offices.

The English parish constable, unpaid and serving only a one-year term of office, epitomized the problems of this style of amateur law enforcement. These men had to be able to live and do business in their communities after their terms expired. At the same time, however, the growing power of the national government required them to enforce ever-greater numbers of regulations. To prevent their alienation from the community, they sometimes exercised their powers with discretion, particularly in their enforcement of regulations regarding ale sales and local festivals whose violators seldom incurred the status of criminals in local opinion.

Urban centers probably appeared much safer than rural areas to many early modern Europeans. Continental cities still sheltered behind their medieval walls and their gates were closed at night, locking out danger symbolically at least. Amsterdam was typical in this regard, not only nightly locking its gates, but also lowering iron barriers into the canals to prevent penetration of the city by amphibious criminals. Within their

---

[18] Quoted in Florike Egmond, *Underworlds: Organized Crime in the Netherlands, 1650–1800* (Oxford: Polity Press, 1993), p. 33.

walls most cities also regulated activities after dark closely, because the security provided by municipal street lighting dates only from 1667 (Paris) and 1669 (Amsterdam). Nuremberg closed taverns at sunset and two hours later sounded a curfew that permitted the arrest of suspicious persons found abroad. Such protective actions were almost universal, but in the establishment of regular urban policing, as in rural patrols, the French again led Europe for much of our period.

Travelers marveled at the policing of Paris in the late seventeenth and eighteenth centuries. In the capital in 1667 the French crown began upon the unique step of replacing traditional night watches with a professional uniformed force administered by the central government. The crown charged this force of the Lieutenant of Police, supported by the French Guards (a military unit we examined in Chapter 2), with all aspects of maintaining order in the capital, including trash collection and fire fighting. The Lieutenant of Police devoted some 3,000 officers to law enforcement and other tasks in a city of some 600,000 inhabitants by the late eighteenth century. This force included clerks and administrators, inspectors who were akin to modern detectives, *commissaires* in each of the city's forty-eight districts who investigated crimes and could order arrest and imprisonment, and uniformed mounted and foot patrolmen. Together these men constituted the largest and best-organized urban police force in western Europe. But even such a force barely approached the capacities of modern police agencies. The policemen were limited in number, illpaid, and lived in the very neighborhoods they patrolled, which meant they were heavily influenced by those they policed. Direct citizen action against offenders was frequent and the police often arrested only those the populace singled out to them. Similarly, they had to forgo apprehension of offenders who could depend on the silence of neighbors. Here, as in much of western Europe, the settled population of the city seems to have used the police for its own ends; the threat of a report to the force led many contesting parties to settle their differences in order to avoid legal entanglements. Officers seem to have served such disputants as mediators as well, and the full weight of this police authority seems to have fallen chiefly on the floating population of the poor, not on the settled population.

No other western European city in our period approached the level of policing in Paris, even with its limitations. Policing in London, the largest city in Europe by the late eighteenth century, functioned for much of the era largely with institutions created by the Statute of Winchester of 1285. That medieval statute required municipalities to create parish night watches of citizens to patrol the streets after dark as a supplement to the nonprofessional constable in every parish. Only in the 1730s did the municipalities of Greater London and the national government begin to create paid uniformed and nonuniformed forces to provide more comprehensive policing to the metropolis. In Amsterdam, a city of perhaps 200,000 by the late seventeenth century, the *schout*, an official who combined the functions of a public prosecutor and police chief, had a force of eighteen men. Only a few beadles represented the police authority of seventeenth-century Frankfurt, a city of about 20,000, where much rested on the citizenry. A decree of 1580 urged citizens personally to intervene to stop brawls and offered cash rewards to those who apprehended lawbreakers. Moreover, the authorities expected burghers to mount a "hue and cry" in response to the summons of a drummer.

Order in such cities rested perforce on the willingness of citizens to report offenses, serve in nightly patrols by elected citizens' watches, and ultimately employ their own strength. It is no wonder that a minor Dutch bestseller of 1674 was a work by a professional wrestler that must count as the first urban self-defense manual, complete with illustrations of prosperous burghers following the book's instructions on how to defend themselves against disreputable-looking assailants. The nature of early modern policing was thus such that those who finally endured state justice met their fate usually as a result of community cooperation with the authorities. Something of a community-based justice persisted amid the judicial revolution. Settled offenders, shielded by their neighbors and co-workers, were far less likely to experience state justice than marginals or outsiders. That justice was frequently brutal, because in much of Europe it depended on judicial torture to gather evidence, and everywhere it meted out corporal and capital punishment.

Judicial torture

Torture by state authorities to extort information from persons suspected of crimes or subversive activities has probably been practiced from earliest times. Our subject here is a particular manifestation of torture, unique to our period: judicial torture, that is, inflicting pain on defendants as part of formal trials to elicit evidence for a court conviction. This was torture that was an integral part of gathering evidence in a trial – indeed, courts kept written records of its applications – and was quite separate and distinct from the violence inflicted on the condemned in the form of corporal or capital punishment after sentencing.

Judicial torture developed in the late medieval period as a part of the Roman-canon legal procedure, the spread of which over much of western Europe was so central to the judicial revolution. Roman–canon procedure functioned quite differently from the English tradition with which most of us are familiar. It was inquisitorial in nature, which is to say that officials of the court took the lead in investigating and prosecuting crime. The English criminal law, by contrast, was an accusatorial system in procedure, that is, one in which crime victims or their kin initiated trials, and until the eighteenth century sustained court costs. Judgment in Roman-canon procedure, moreover, was in the hands of a panel of judges. These jurists, drawn from the small elite of law graduates, deliberated and ruled without a jury, quite unlike the judges who presided in English courts enforcing the conclusions of juries of local citizens. And, most importantly for our purposes, the Roman-canon procedure of the legal specialist required very specific proofs of guilt in order to convict. This was a system very different from the procedure of English courts in which all that is necessary for conviction is to persuade twelve jurymen of a defendant's guilt beyond reasonable doubt. Indeed, the law of proof in the Roman-canon tradition of jurisprudence was the root of torture in our period. Proof of guilt for conviction in capital crimes had to rest on either the testimony of two eyewitnesses to the offense, or the confession of the accused. Conviction was impossible without such proofs; the law precluded courts from weighing circumstantial evidence and ruling on the basis of such proof. Thus when judges lacked two eyewitnesses to an offense, but still possessed substantial proof of guilt, they required a confession to convict the defendant.

Such strict rules of proof were not part of England's common law tradition. Instead, juries weighed various kinds of evidence and could even convict on the basis of circumstantial evidence. Historians have therefore found the violence of judicial torture in England largely confined to the period from 1540 to 1640 when the Privy Council, and occasionally the monarch, ordered torture to gather evidence. While the victims of this torture included some common criminals, their ranks contained a large number of persons suspected of sedition and religious subversion during a period in which the crown's Protestant faith and foreign policy provoked considerable domestic challenge. It was the authorities' perceived need to protect domestic security that chiefly underlay the brief English recourse to torture.

On the European continent there is evidence in legal treatises of the use of judicial torture to gain evidence in Italy as early as the thirteenth century, and a decretal of Pope Innocent VI in 1252 confirmed the use of torture in canon law. By the sixteenth century, when a spate of continental law codes appeared to systematize the judicial revolution, all recognized the use of torture. The major law codes of the age – the *Constitutio Criminalis Carolina* (1532) of Germany, the Ordinance of Villers-Cotterêts (1539) of France, the *Nueva recopilación* (1567) of Spain, and the Criminal Ordinance of 1570 of the Spanish Netherlands – all provided detailed regulation of judicial torture. In some countries, such as France, torture could be applied at two junctures in a trial. "Preparatory torture" could be applied to the accused to elicit the confession necessary to convict, and in France, from the sixteenth century on, torture could only be applied once at this stage. "Preliminary torture" occurred after conviction and prior to execution with the goal of forcing the condemned to reveal the names of accomplices. Because the criminal had been condemned to death by this stage in the proceedings, there were no limits on the number of times preliminary torture could be applied.

Procedurally, there were a few general limits on torture. In France, for example, an appeals court had to ratify the decision of lower-court judges to proceed to preparatory torture. In most countries, too, preparatory torture had first to be threatened, a process known in Germany as torture *mit Güte*, that is, torture without pain. If the threat of torture failed to produce a confession, the real thing followed. But not every defendant suffered torture; most legal systems commonly exempted certain persons. As a general rule, anyone deemed unable to survive it was excluded from this brutality, so the feeble and aged, pregnant women, and children were safe from torture. In many areas aristocrats, state officials, clerics, physicians, and doctors of law also escaped torture. For those forced to endure torture there was, however, one way to avoid conviction. A defendant generally had to be released if he sustained the torture without confessing. This practice, echoing medieval trials by ordeal and clearly favoring the hardy and not necessarily the innocent defendant, persisted into the late seventeenth century. At that time, law codes such as the French Criminal Ordinance of 1670 began to provide for such defendants. When torture elicited no confession in capital cases, the courts in a growing number of continental countries might convict but assign a noncapital penalty on the basis of incomplete yet convincing evidence of guilt.

The modes of torture varied widely, but everywhere it had to be carried on in the presence of the judge and a scribe to record the questioning. The authorities intended every form of torture to inflict pain without causing death, and most maximized pain by afflicting the musculoskeletal system and the most innervated bodily tissue. One of the most widely used tortures was the strappado, in which the hands of the accused, tied behind the back, were fastened to a rope passing through a ceiling-mounted pulley. The torturer then pulled that rope, raising the accused off the floor and leaving him suspended. Common, too, were various vise-like devices, such as legbraces and thumbscrews, designed to crush limbs. Some courts employed the rack to stretch defendants, while some burned the soles of their feet. Other jurisdictions, like that of the Parlement of Paris, forced torture victims to ingest large quantities of water, or occasionally denied sleep to them.

Widespread use of judicial torture, however, did not characterize western European justice throughout the early modern period. Just as we will note a progressive reduction of the frequency of brutal punishments in our period, almost every continental western European state experienced a rapid late sixteenth- or seventeenth-century drop in the employment of torture. In France, where the Parlement of Paris ordered torture of 20 percent of appellants to its justice in 1533–42, only 5 percent suffered such pain in 1620. And the Parlement of Brittany, which ordered preparatory torture in 4.8 percent of its cases in 1600–50 used this torture in but 0.72 percent of its trials in 1650–1700; in the same periods that court's employment of preliminary torture decreased from application in 27.6 percent of all cases to 12.7 percent. In the various courts of Germany the same trend is evident. Tortures in Frankfurt, ordered in 59.3 percent of all cases in 1562–94, dropped to 15 percent of all cases in 1661–96. And in Bavaria the Court Council, which ordered torture in 44 percent of cases in 1650, required the infliction of such pain in only 16 percent of cases in 1690.

The decline of torture continued in the eighteenth century. In Rome the Sacra Consulta, the venue for serious crimes in the city, ordered twenty-six defendants to be tortured in 1737 but only four defendants in 1786. And one French regional court, the Sénéchaussée of Libourne, tortured but one of 1,529 defendants sampled over the period 1696 to 1789. Judicial torture, widespread on the continent at the outset of our period, was evidently disappearing by its close, and the question for historians has long been why this occurred. Historians noted early on the statutory abolition of judicial torture between 1740 and 1788 in almost all the major western European states. Traditionally, they explained this precipitate abandonment of torture as the result of the intense criticism of the practice by Enlightenment thinkers like Christian Thomasius, Cesare Bonesana, marchese di Beccaria, and Voltaire. But, as we have seen, the practical abandonment of torture predated its abolition in law by many years.

Eventually, though, in 1977, John Langbein convincingly explained that the end of torture predated the Enlightenment because it was rooted in legal and penal change, not in the publications of intellectuals.[19] According to Langbein, jurists increasingly found the old law of proof

---

[19] John Langbein, *Torture and the Law of Proof: Europe and England in the Ancien Régime* (Chicago: University of Chicago Press, 1977).

unsatisfactory because it did not necessarily produce reliable evidence and permitted hardy criminals to escape conviction. Their solution was to permit conviction and sentencing to noncapital penalties with less than the traditional proofs of guilt. At the same time, new forms of punishment, including incarceration, galley service and transportation, which we will discuss later in this chapter, emerged as noncapital penal options for judges who lacked full evidence to support the death penalty. The result was abandonment of torture and adoption of new modes of punishment that made our period one of transition not only in western European behavior but in penology as well.

Punishment

Lawbreakers unlucky enough to face conviction in early modern courts – through reluctant denunciations by their neighbors, the action of limited police services, or their own words extracted by torture – experienced punishments throughout much of the early modern period that added considerable violence to their society. At the outset of our period, few states possessed carceral institutions requisite for the prison sentences that are the usual fates of twenty-first-century lawbreakers. Although the fewer female offenders might experience some sort of incarceration, the authorities typically held male lawbreakers in jail only pending sentencing to penalties that required minimal state resources. For minor offenses such penalties might include fines or banishment, but more typically they consisted of corporal or capital punishment.

Corporal punishment was routine for nonaristocratic perpetrators of relatively minor offenses like petty larceny, minor sexual offenses, swindling, and blasphemy; it might also be the fate of offenders deemed by their judges to be worthy of mercy in capital offenses. Often judges combined corporal punishments with other penalties such as banishment, but a large number of corporal punishments were possible. The most severe of these, reserved for grave crimes, was physical mutilation, often applied to the body part associated with the crime, and so stigmatized the offender as to exclude him from respectable society. Some courts even ordered blinding of offenders, although by the sixteenth century the enforcement of this penalty seems to have been rare. More common was the amputation by ax of an offender's hand, or perhaps fingers, by the public executioner. Persons guilty of theft, fraud, perjury, and certain types of violence might forfeit their hands, and one seventeenth-century Nuremberg poacher lost his fingers so that he could not shoot again. Cutting off the ear was another option to which judges resorted in Germany, particularly for women involved in petty theft and sexual offenses. In many places blasphemy and perjury merited a hole bored through the offender's tongue or, in serious or repeated infractions, slitting or removing the tongue.

Flogging was another common corporal punishment, one that did not leave the kinds of obvious marks left by mutilations. A criminal could easily conceal with clothing a back scarred by a lash or sticks, but authorities always ordered flogging to be carried out with the greatest publicity. In France judges frequently ordered that offenders be flogged on market-day, with strokes to be applied at the four corners of the marketplace; in Germany, if banishment accompanied the sentence of flogging, the offender might be beaten as he was paraded through the streets and out through the city gate. Judges varied the extent of the flogging sentence according to the gravity of the offense, but usually this penalty drew minimal blood.

Another mutilation that might sometimes be concealed resulted from branding. Early modern judges, like our own today, punished repeat offenders more harshly than first offenders so, in an age without central criminal records, they often used the brand as a painful way both to punish and to record commission of an offense on the offender's person. Using a red-hot iron, the authorities signalled the offense on a lawbreaker's forehead or shoulder. French executioners used an iron with a fleur-de-lis device for this purpose, or, in some jurisdictions, a "v" (*voleur* is "thief" in French); in Frankfurt the branding device often employed by the authorities bore an eagle. Such a mark on the forehead stigmatized a person for life because it could not be concealed. Shoulder brands might be covered from public view by clothing, but judges often began legal proceedings with examinations of defendants' shoulders.

Other forms of punishment meted out by lower courts dealing with minor infractions debased the honor of offenders without recourse to mutilation. Those guilty of such crimes as minor thefts, fraud, and sexual offenses received shaming penalties either alone or in combination with such punishments as branding, flogging, or banishment. The most common shaming penalty was confinement in the pillory, a wood or stone structure located in a prominent place such as a marketsquare, in which the authorities displayed lawbreakers, often with symbols of their crimes. The pillory confined the head and arms of the standing offender, rendering the person defenseless. Spectators' responses to convicts thus displayed were often violent, depending on popular perceptions of the gravity of the individual's offense. The crowd might throw stones and refuse, or assault the offender in other ways; even maiming or the death of the condemned were possible. Few ordered to be confined in the pillory shared the fate of Daniel Defoe. Condemned in 1703 to three days of display in a pillory in his old neighborhood for seditious libel, Defoe found himself surrounded by a crowd throwing flowers. Various jurisdictions also used lesser shaming penalties that included parading offenders through town bearing symbols of their crimes. Violence by spectators was always possible during these punishments, too.

Those accused of more serious crimes risked capital punishment. Early modern law in principle imposed death for a long list of offenses. In eighteenth-century France, for example, death could be the penalty for offenses against the state such as treason, dueling, armed smuggling, counterfeiting, perjury, forgery of legal documents, and certain violations of the monarchy's press censorship. Violence against persons also called for the death penalty in the case of individuals found guilty of murder, attempted murder, infanticide, robbery, abduction, and rape. In addition, perpetrators of grave sexual offenses, including sodomy, incest, certain flagrant forms of adultery, bigamy accomplished with forgery, and sexual relations with a nun or between a male servant and his female employer, were liable to the death penalty. Persons guilty of certain property crimes, including breaking and entering, thefts by domestic servants, and stealing of property valued in excess of 3,000 *livres*, also faced possible execution, as did practicing French Protestant clerics from 1685 to 1787. The laws of other countries similarly imposed death for numerous offenses. The Swedish Criminal Code of 1734 mandated death in sixty-eight crimes ranging from treason and murder to adultery, bigamy, and arson. In some countries the number of capital crimes was growing in this period, especially for offenses against property. The British parliament, for example, added about 180 capital statutes to the laws of the land between 1660 and 1819, the majority of them for property crimes.

Most western European legal systems established a number of different modes of execution, with the precise form used in individual cases depending chiefly on the gravity of the offense. The status of the offender also determined the nature of the penalty; rarely were aristocrats or women, for example, subjected to hanging, a particularly degrading penalty in the view of early modern Europeans. The range of death penalties was evident in every major legal system. Especially brutal were punishments in which the executioner broke the limbs of the condemned man. In Germany this was the penalty of breaking with the wheel, in which the executioner struck the condemned man, prone and bound, repeatedly with a heavy wheel or other implement. In France, which adopted this penalty in 1535, the executioner bound the condemned man prone to a wooden structure in the shape of the cross of Saint Andrew and broke his limbs with a bar. Such a penalty chiefly befell males who had been convicted of aggravated murder, that is, an offense such as taking the life of a family member or killing in the course of a robbery.

Fire and water, traditional purifying agents, factored in capital punishments, too. Burning alive at the stake often awaited convicted arsonists, blasphemers, heretics, witches, counterfeiters, poisoners, and sodomites. In England until 1790 it was the penalty, too, for women guilty of petty treason, the label the law applied to a woman's murder of her husband. Drowning was a penalty generally applied to females guilty of moral and religious offenses like adultery, infanticide, and heresy. In Germany women convicted of infanticide, murder of their husbands, or other heinous crimes, might be buried alive, a mode of execution usually reserved for their sex, and equated by judges with breaking with the wheel for men. In such burials the executioner placed the bound woman in a shallow grave and buried her alive, shoveling dirt first on her feet and then continuing up her body. In the course of the burial, or immediately after, the executioner often drove a stake through the condemned's heart into the floor of the grave, perhaps to assuage popular fears of revenants.

A variety of capital punishments awaited other convicted criminals. Quartering was a penalty reserved for persons convicted of high treason and assassination. In Germany the executioner disemboweled the prone victim with a cut down the middle of the torso, and then sliced the body into quarters for public display at four different locales. In France dismemberment occurred when the executioner tied teams of horses to each of the four limbs of the condemned and drove them in different directions. Boiling in oil was a punishment sometimes used in France, Germany, and a few other countries for counterfeiters, but it was rare in our period, despite one recorded boiling in Germany in 1728. Most common criminals, including thieves and murderers, increasingly met with decapitation and hanging.

On the continent executioners typically administered decapitation with a large sword, an act that required considerable skill on the part of the executioner because the condemned was kneeling and unrestrained. In the British Isles decapitation proceeded slightly differently; most often, executioners employed the block, but in Halifax and in a few jurisdictions in Scotland executioners employed a primitive guillotine.

Hanging, however, was the most common form of capital punishment. It required that the executioner place the noose of a rope around the neck of the condemned and that the rope itself be affixed to a structure of two or three vertical posts, connected by horizontal parts. The condemned then mounted a ladder, and death came through strangulation when the executioner pushed the person from the ladder. This style of hanging did not employ the trapdoor and sudden drop of the condemned that became common in the nineteenth century. In the more modern procedure, death resulted from the breaking of the convict's neck. While certainly not instantaneous, death did come about much more rapidly than through strangulation, as it could in another form of strangulation coming into widespread use in Spain in the eighteenth century: the garrote was an iron collar that the executioner could tighten with a screw to kill.

Judges often compounded such capital penalties with additional aggravating circumstances that increased their pain or ignominy. In Germany and Florence, for example, condemned individuals might be paraded to the place of execution while the executioner tore their flesh with red-hot tongs. Mutilation could precede death in Spain, while in England executioners hanged convicted traitors briefly by the neck then, when they were still living, disemboweled them. Everywhere, too, posthumous display of the remains of the executed persons for purposes of deterrence denied them traditional burial. The executioner exhibited on the wheel the bodies of those who had been broken there and on the gallows the corpses of those who had died there. The heads of the decapitated hung from London Bridge as well as from the gates or battlements of continental cities.

Figure 7, the work of the Flemish artist Pieter Bruegel the Elder (*c.* 1525–69), is part of a series of engravings entitled *Virtues*. This particular engraving, *Justice*, portrays the varieties of violence employed in early modern legal processes. The Latin legend below the engraving reads: "The aim of the law is either through punishment to correct him who is punished, or to improve others by his example, or to protect society by overcoming evil." "Justice" stands at the center of the engraving, blindfolded to individual differences among those who seek her, and atop a block with shackles for holding prisoners. A number of figures surround her. In the left foreground is the artist's representation of a sixteenth-century trial, with a judge preparing to order death to defendants bearing crucifixes. On the right a judge, holding a thorny rod, presides over torture assisted by a scribe taking down the confession. The accused man is at once being stretched on a rack, burned with pitch dripping off the torch held above him, and forced to ingest large quantities of water. In the middle distance, on the right, an executioner prepares to decapitate a condemned man, while to the left, under the arches, another man is about to suffer amputation of his hand and a second man waits his turn. Further distant on the right, another man is being beaten with bundles of branches while, just to the left, the authorities inflict additional torture in a modified strappado. Finally, in the far distance, one condemned person is burned alive while four others swing from the sort of gallows we described earlier, and a number of decapitated corpses, having been

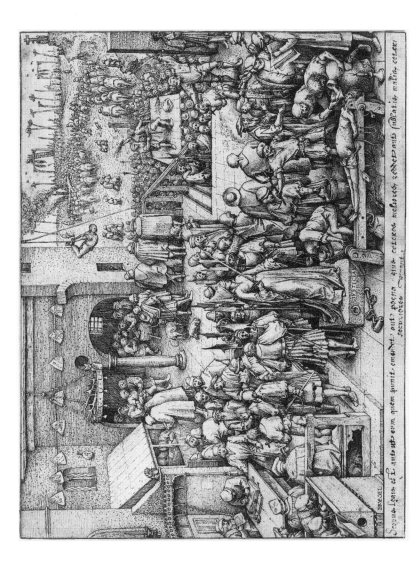

Figure 7. Pieter Bruegel the Elder, *Justice*. Pen and ink, 1559. Copyright Bibliothèque royale Albert Iᵉʳ (Cabinet des Estampes, S. II 133707), Brussels.

broken with the wheel, are displayed upon wheels fixed atop posts. All of this is an accurate portrayal of the state justice of our period, and the crucifix in the far upper right represents the approval of such practices by Christianity.

Bruegel's graphic portrayal of early modern justice is shocking to twenty-first-century viewers because it depicts a penology so different from our own. Early modern jurists, aware that the inadequacies of police services provided little deterrence to criminals from the fear of apprehension, seem to have sought to deter would-be lawbreakers with the brutality of the punishments they inflicted upon those malefactors who did fall into the hands of the law. It is this unfamiliar and brutal aspect of the age's penology that scholars have sought to understand better, and the work of the French philosopher Michel Foucault particularly shaped this quest.[20] Foucault saw such executions as public ceremonies intended not only to punish individual criminals but also to convey a message to those watching the events. That message was one aimed to deter would-be lawbreakers but additionally to demonstrate the power of the state. The mutilation of the body of the condemned expressed the arbitrary and sacred nature of the judicial power of the absolutist state.

The crowds that we see assembled to witness executions in Figure 7 convey the publicity of these highly ritualized acts of violence. Publicity was a large part of penology for much of our period and jurists of the age recognized that the crowd was present at executions, in part, to be taught a lesson, as Bruegel's inscription suggests. The publicity of such punishments compounded the severity of even relatively light corporal punishments through the shame incurred by the offender. Most punishments involved contact with the public executioner, a figure viewed as particularly dishonorable by early modern Europeans; such contact transferred that dishonor to the condemned. In addition, a person of honor was expected to defend himself. It follows from this that it was considered ignominious to be rendered defenseless, beaten, maimed or, worse, executed – especially as this latter punishment often ended with desecration of the body of the condemned.

Authorities therefore scheduled corporal and capital punishments to coincide with events like marketdays to assure big audiences for the infliction of punishments. Large crowds assembled to witness these events, especially in a major metropolis such as London, Paris, or Naples; eighteenth-century crowds at London executions sometimes approached 100,000. But even in smaller centers huge numbers gathered for executions. Some 20,000 regularly witnessed executions in Seville's Plaza de

[20] Foucault, *Discipline and Punish: The Birth of the Prison*, translated by Alan Sheridan (New York: Vintage Books, 1979).

San Francisco. A like number attended an execution in 1788 in the Thuringian backwater of Clingen. And the death of the French smuggler Mandrin drew some 6,000 witnesses to relatively isolated Valence in 1755.

Executions assumed certain patterns in small towns as well as in large urban centers. At first carried out at crime scenes, death penalties were soon relocated by the authorities to more easily policed permanent sites, like Tyburn Hill outside London, the Place de la Grève in Paris, and the Columns of Justice in Venice. Executions occurred at such sites with some frequency in major cities. London's chief criminal court, the Old Bailey, produced victims for the gallows at Tyburn eight times a year, for example. But outside the major cities executions seem to have been far less common events.

When executions did occur, they followed a ritual that was essentially similar throughout western Europe, constituting a kind of theater that mixed religious and political elements expressing, as Foucault suggested, a complex message for spectators to decode. Execution days proceeded according to a ritual familiar to early modern Europeans throughout our period because these events changed very little over time. Indeed, in Caen, France, that ritual remained unchanged from the fifteenth century to 1792.

The sacred played a major role in executions. In Christian theology execution, when accompanied by public acts of contrition even in the last moments of life, provided the opportunity for the spiritual reintegration of the sinner into the Christian community. Consequently, every western judicial system provided access prior to execution for the condemned to clergymen, or, in Italy and Spain, to members of religious confraternities specializing in aiding such criminals in their last hours. A penitential death would achieve the spiritual goal and, by the condemned's public acknowledgement of guilt, validate the taking of a life by a state justice that was not yet securely established.

The ritual of execution usually began with a procession from the place of confinement to the execution site. This phase of the execution put the condemned on wide public view, often with signs of penance and the crime itself. The condemned frequently wore the plain white garment of a penitent, with a placard proclaiming the offense for which the authorities had assigned execution. Often, too, this procession displayed religious symbolism; in parts of Spain, for example, the condemned rode an ass as Christ had done. Elsewhere, the condemned might be dragged to the scaffold, maimed along the way with red-hot tongs or other implements, or conveyed simply in a cart. But throughout Europe spiritual assistants and judicial officials accompanied the condemned on this journey, by their presence publicizing the execution's sanction by church and state. In Catholic countries the procession might often stop at religious shrines along the route and at the local church for the ritual that the French called *amende honorable*. In this rite the condemned, bearing a large votive candle or a torch, knelt and begged forgiveness of God, the king, and the law.

The procession then moved on to the scaffold where, typically, the sentence was read and the condemned was offered the right to utter a few last words. Ideally, these might be an edifying statement censuring the crimes that resulted in execution and urging the audience to avoid the primrose path that led to the executioner. Depending on the site of the execution, the condemned might then piously pardon the executioner, pray briefly with a spiritual advisor, or kiss a crucifix that he might proffer. In England and France, by the eighteenth century, peddlers might even be circulating through the crowd at this time hawking apocryphal accounts of the confession and last words of the condemned. Sometimes this scene might prove even more spiritually uplifting. Thus in 1762 a soldier named Corbelet chanted the "Miserere," "Veni Creator," and "Ave Maria" while the executioner of Caen broke his limbs on the wheel. Such a death, however, did not always occur, despite the best efforts of the clergy attending the condemned person. Occasionally uncooperative individuals ended their days shouting their innocence or defiance, but many executions did not fail crowd expectations of an edifying event.

The spiritual significance of the execution in the popular mind is evident in crowd behavior. Many spectators believed in the spiritual or curative power of certain elements of this spectacle, and they hastened to sop up the blood of executed criminals or to seize the limbs of those hanging by their necks. There was even a widespread belief in Denmark and Germany that drinking the blood of the executed cured epilepsy.

The wider significance of such ritualized state violence in early modern society is much debated by scholars, particularly the nature of the reaction of spectators and society at large to these ceremonies. Such debate goes right to the heart of central issues in cultural, political, and legal history. Historians have for a long time emphasized the powerful normative thrust of the early modern state and, more recently, the reformed Christianity of the sixteenth and seventeenth centuries that confessionalized modern society. Controversy abounds, however, over the way historians interpret the impact of these processes on various social groups. In the view of some, the agents of church and state, often operating through judicial institutions, crushed popular culture and regulated their subjects' behavior despite popular resistance. Courts, police, and most especially the executioner, became the agents of this process, criminalizing all resistance to it.

A substantial body of historical scholarship has appeared, inspired by the work of E. P. Thompson and others, centered on popular resistance to the normative thrust of the early modern state in such acts as its game laws, tariffs, and even its mode of execution. The scholars of this school of thought discerned intense resistance to new state power, and identified as "social protest crime" violations of the new laws. They found the perpetrators of such acts adhering to traditional norms of behavior that legitimized their actions.[21] Yet this view, resting as it does on a vision of a one-way flow of the normative power of state and church downward through society, seems no longer to accord with modern historical scholarship. As we have seen, police institutions were too weak simply to impose the behavior required by state law on unaccepting populations. Rather, at least some of the state's subjects must have been willing accessories to this process because the behavioral standards and the discipline process that the state imposed generally accorded with widely held notions of just behavior. We have also seen that the subjects of the early modern state were not ignorant of its laws; they used them, when they saw fit, to resolve their differences. Indeed, given the weakness of police resources in our period, a very large portion of defendants in state courts would have found their way to the bar of justice through action by their colleagues, neighbors, or kin. State law, it now seems, advanced because it often reflected popular standards of behavior and justice in early modern society. Both popular justice and state justice after all had the same goal: to preserve order.

If the fact that most condemned individuals began their path to the scaffold through action by members of their community indicates basic popular acceptance of this sort of justice, there is no better demonstration of this than the reaction of the crowd to executions. Historians have tended to view popular reactions to early modern execution with the perception of Enlightenment opponents of capital punishment. As a result, they traditionally viewed the capital punishment of our period as a penal system imposed on an unaccepting population that rebelled against it at the least opportunity. Such a characterization of early modern capital punishment is not entirely accurate.

In the early modern period death in general was more public than it is today, and its rituals were familiar to all, at least among social groups with sufficient education to comprehend fully the religious culture of the day.

---

[21] Douglas Hay *et al.*, *Albion's Fatal Tree: Crime and Society in Eighteenth-Century England* (New York: Pantheon Books, 1975); E. P. Thompson, *Whigs and Hunters: The Origins of the Black Act* (New York: Pantheon Books, 1975); and the works of George Rudé and Eric H. Hobsbawm, including *Captain Swing* (New York: Pantheon Books, 1968), particularly explore social-protest crime.

Aiding them in this was a large body of literature addressing the *ars moriendi*, the art of dying. Many early modern Europeans must have viewed execution in the light of such death practices. Recent historical examinations of execution, including the remarkable study of English popular reactions to capital punishment by V. A. C. Gatrell, now indeed suggest a basic popular acquiescence in this system of justice.[22] Such acceptance came not, as some suggest, from the violence of the age, which inured the populace to pain and suffering. Rather, the retributive aspect of this justice seems to have struck most early modern Europeans, at least for the most serious crimes, as a fundamental part of the divine order. Indeed, the rituals of the scaffold and even the pamphlet literature peddled at executions translated the state's taking of a life into visual forms and written words congruent with popularly accepted values. A particularly illuminating study of eighteenth-century justice in Württemberg by Karl Wegert reminds us that, while different social groups would have drawn different meanings from executions, even the most gruesome practices must have struck a familiar note for all in an audience imbued with early modern popular culture.[23]

Much of capital punishment practice, in Germany and elsewhere, drew on familiar primitive apotropaic rites, practices intended to purge evil, which merged with Christian symbolism in the early modern execution. Thus leaving the bodies of executed criminals hanging at the gallows was more than simply a deterrent; in a popular culture with an active belief in an underworld, this act blocked burial and prevented the diabolical sinner from regaining the earth and his chthonic home. Similarly, severing the criminal's head from the body harked back to early Germanic customs that emphasized that such a separation prevented the resumption of the sinner's evil career. Burning alive not only symbolically – and appropriately – penalized a crime like arson, it also utterly purged this world of the offender by completely consuming his body. And breaking with the wheel, an expression of the circle, a traditional magical symbol, perhaps resonated with the popular belief that the skeleton was the location of the soul and the root of life. Given such ideas, smashing the bones of an offender must have seemed natural to many.

Executions thus displayed much that was probably familiar and acceptable to their spectators. These spectators might have been noisy and uncouth according to the clerics and privileged lay people who left most written records of these events, but they did not normally oppose the

[22] V. A. C. Gatrell, *The Hanging Tree: Execution and the English People, 1770–1868* (Oxford: Oxford University Press, 1994).

[23] Karl Wegert, *Popular Culture, Crime, and Social Control in Eighteenth-Century Württemberg* (Stuttgart: Franz Steiner Verlag, 1994), pp. 99–110.

executions or resist the state authorities that presided over them. Even the chief such official, the executioner, a social outcast often dressed in distinctive garb and everywhere shunned by his neighbors, was not usually the object of particular violence by the crowd.

There is another possible root for this public acceptance of the rites of execution. Historians have found that early modern justice was highly selective, and that, in the popular mind, most individuals who mounted the scaffold richly deserved their fates. Judges almost everywhere reinforced this conclusion by using the tremendous discretionary power accorded them in most early modern law codes to invoke the death penalty chiefly for a category of heinous crimes that threatened the established political, religious, or social order. Called *cas énormes* in France, *kwade feiten* in the Low Countries, and *delictos atroces* in Spain, these offenses typically included witchcraft, heresy, parricide and infanticide, sodomy, incest, arson, and murder.

Judges also applied their discretion in selecting those executed for crimes. They most commonly ordered the deaths of intolerable repeat offenders or marginals like vagabonds. Seldom did they execute stable members of the community with good reputations who had simply run afoul of the law. When confronted with the need to repress disturbances by such people, like the riots and rebellions common in the seventeenth century, judges typically ordered executions of some of the most egregious offenders and allowed the majority to go free. They lacked the force necessary to preserve order had they instituted widespread repression.

When executions failed to express popular ideas of justice, however, crowd members did oppose them. The crowd expected justice to be fair, expeditious, and played out according to the "script" of the scaffold ritual we have examined. When these expectations were not met, crowd violence might ensue. Popular expectations of fairness required that the penalty more or less equal the crime. Perhaps the most widespread such protests in London occurred over the efforts of physicians to obtain corpses for medical instruction. Parliament, wishing to deter a perceived rise in violent crime, passed the Murder Act of 1752 allowing judges to order that the corpses of hanged criminals be turned over to the Company of Barber-Surgeons for dissection in medical research and education. Although such a use of corpses had occurred from time to time since the early sixteenth century, this large-scale expansion of the practice offended many. Dissections precluded Christian burial and, in the minds of many, by destruction of the body also prevented resurrection. It was therefore deemed an unacceptable amplification of punishment, and the Murder Act occasioned a number of riots by friends and relatives of the condemned.

The nature of a sentence and its mode of execution might also offend spectators' sense of justice. Unwarranted brutality, even in corporal punishment, could cause spectators to erupt in violence. In mid-eighteenth-century Paris a coachman accused of stealing an iron bar of little worth from his employer, a cab owner, was publicly flogged and branded. When the employer urged the executioner to lay his blows on harder the crowd rioted, breaking the cab owner's house windows and burning two of his cabs. A similar riot occurred in Amsterdam in 1732 at the flogging of a female servant for theft from her employers. Again, the crowd's wrath fell on the employers who had pressed charges in the first place. Conversely, a sentence popularly viewed as too light might also spark violence by spectators. Thus in 1612, when Nuremberg's judges sentenced the city messenger to a beating and banishment for moral offenses and treason, the crowd stoned the man to death.

Popular ideas of justice also held that there were circumstances that could free a condemned person. There was, for instance, a widely held popular notion that a condemned person could not be hanged twice. The nature of early modern hanging, as we have seen, meant death by strangulation, and occasionally executioners cut down from the gallows convicts who had only lost consciousness and not expired. In such circumstances, crowds often violently resisted attempts to rehang the condemned. Similarly, crowds might violently resist attempts to hang convicts again when the hangman's rope broke in the course of the execution. And many believed that a condemned man should be freed if a virgin offered to marry him. Such a bizarre eventuality occurred in Cologne in 1561. Tilman Isenhaupt, about to be hanged, received not one but two offers from young women, yet declined both. Nevertheless, the crowd demanded an end to the execution, hurled stones at the executioner, and cut Isenhaupt down from the gallows and freed him.

Spectators also demanded expeditious justice that would not unduly prolong the pain and suffering of the condemned. This sentiment meant that it was not unusual in the course of hangings for friends and relatives of the condemned to force their way to the gallows to pull on his legs in order to abbreviate the agony of his strangulation. What a crowd universally abhorred was a botched execution. For many in the crowd, execution represented the banishment of evil and the reestablishment of communal harmony after the crime. A bungled execution prevented this possibility and, for some people, raised the idea that the execution was unjust, the executioner's failings resulting from divine intervention. Bungled executions, unfortunately, were not unusual. Decapitation, as we have seen, required a skilled executioner. Nevertheless, the public expected that this official sever the head of the condemned in one blow, and violence could erupt when this did not occur. Hence spectators stoned to death the executioner of Florence on 29 March 1503 for taking several blows to sever a head. And in 1685 an English executioner barely escaped death at the hands of the crowd when he required five strokes of the ax to decapitate the duke of Monmouth.

Crowd violence might also flare up when the execution ritual went off course owing to the occasional refusal of the condemned to play the assigned role. Early modern authorities feared such eventualities because they raised popular doubts about the justice of the penalty and could lead to an assault on the executioner or local officials. Sometimes such a turn of events occurred at a cost to the condemned, however, as in the case of a Morisco in Seville in 1585. The condemned, sentenced to hanging for theft, used his last words to proclaim a tavern owner's debt to him. He then obdurately refused to grant the ritual forgiveness of the hangman, and when the latter placed the noose around his neck the condemned man called out to Mohammed. The crowd stoned him and burned his remains.

These examples notwithstanding, popular society, assembled as spectators for public executions, essentially accepted most public corporal and capital punishments. Indeed, the Amsterdam riot was the only such disturbance in that city recorded during our period. This apparent acceptance of penal brutality raises another question, of what accounts for the eventual disappearance in western Europe of the practices we have described. Drawing on Enlightenment criticism of this penology, historians have for long attributed its end in the late eighteenth or early nineteenth centuries to the *philosophes'* growing opposition to these practices. Such an explanation now seems untenable, as does that more recently advanced by Michel Foucault. Foucault alleged that the older penology based on punishing the body of the condemned disappeared in the early nineteenth century in favor of a better deterrent to rising crime: the penitentiary with its goal of reforming the mind and spirit of the criminal. Alleging that the new penology was one of a triumphant middle class aimed at confining all those who deviated from its norms, Foucault's ideas at first drew wide acceptance. The nineteenth century, after all, was the century in which the middle class gained political power, and Foucault's theory neatly explained the pattern of other institutional developments of the age, like the appearance of the asylum.

The present state of historical knowledge, however, at a very minimum negates the chronological framework advanced by both Foucault and historians who find the Enlightenment at the root of the new penology. We now know that the violence of western criminal law was diminishing everywhere from the sixteenth or seventeenth centuries onward, as the declining incidence of capital punishment decrees by western European courts demonstrates. In England the decrease in capital punishments dates from the 1630s. Executions carried out as a result of judgments by the Old Bailey sessions for London and Middlesex averaged about 140 per year in 1603–25 but fell to an average of 6.24 per year in 1701–25. While executions ordered by that court rose after 1750 to 33 per year as parliament extended capital punishment to a large number of property crimes and as the wars of the period also drove up the crime rate, they remained below sixteenth- and seventeenth-century levels. Provincial English court records also demonstrate a rapid seventeenth-century decline in death penalties. The court of Great Sessions at Chester issued 337 death sentences in 1580–1619, 274 in 1620–59, and 85 in 1660–1709.

In France sentences of the Parlement of Paris, an appeals court that dealt with very serious crimes, reveal the same trend. In 1535 34 percent of the court's penalties were death sentences, including two persons ordered to be boiled. By 1545 the proportion of death sentences had dropped somewhat, to 26 percent of the total, and by the 1780s capital punishments represented slightly less than 2 percent of the court's sentences.

Historians have noted the same trends in sentencing in the municipal jurisdictions of the Low Countries, Germany, and Italy. Thus executions in Brussels declined from 488 in 1506–1600 to 122 in 1600–1700, and but 40 in 1700–83. Amsterdam executions similarly diminished, from an average of slightly over six per year in 1524–52 to an annual average of about three in the second half of the sixteenth century. Despite a temporary increase from 1701 to 1750, executions continued their decline to an annual average of slightly more than one execution in 1751–1800. In Germany death sentences in Frankfurt fell from 91 in 1562–80 to 28 in 1621–40, and 8 in 1661–80. Court records of Florence exhibit trends parallel to those in northern Europe. Judges in that city executed 56 convicts in 1501–05, 33 in 1601–05, and 4 in 1701–05.

Despite occasional increases in executions, the decline in the numbers of death sentences carried out in western Europe in the course of the sixteenth and seventeenth centuries is clear. And virtually everywhere in western Europe, save England and Amsterdam, that decline seems to have continued steadily in the eighteenth century.

Historians have also noted that, in the declining number of cases in which authorities carried out death sentences, there was a growing tendency by judges either to reduce the brutality of the sentence, or to abandon entirely the most savage capital punishments. The Parlement of Paris, for example, ceased to boil counterfeiters after the mid-sixteenth century and that bizarre penalty disappeared in Germany, too. Quartering was disappearing, too; judges of the Parlement of Paris ordered it but twice in the last two centuries of the monarchy: for Ravaillac, the assassin of Henri IV in 1610, and for Damiens, the would-be assassin of Louis XV in 1757.

Where horrific penalties like the wheel and burning alive did persist, judges intervened to diminish the suffering of the condemned. In the course of the sixteenth century, for example, it became usual for judges of the Parlement of Paris to accompany a sentence to the stake or the wheel with a *retentum* providing for the executioner's quick strangulation of the condemned. In fact, in the cases of individuals condemned to the wheel, the historian of the Parlement of Paris in the sixteenth century has found a *retentum* with every sentence.[24] Strangulation of the condemned might occur after the first, second, or third blow by the executioner, or perhaps after a specified period of time under the executioner's rod. This was not a uniquely French practice; it became common in Prussia after 1779 and under the Habsburg monarchy after 1776. A similar desire to reduce suffering is evident in England. There women burned for petty treason were partially affixed to the stake with a noose attached to a rope passed through the top of the structure; a stout tug of the rope by the executioner, prior to igniting the fire, generally extinguished life and spared the condemned the agony of the flames.

By and large, it seems, by the eighteenth century hanging (or the garrote in Spain) and decapitation, inflicted with increasing rarity, were the typical western European modes of capital punishment. A close study of the punishments assigned in three successive round-ups of the *Bokkerijders*, a brutal eighteenth-century band of thieves operating in the Dutch Republic and northwestern Germany, demonstrates the same trend. In the sentences of the early 1740s only about half of the executions were by simple hanging; the others involved decapitation, garroting, and the wheel, often with aggravating circumstances. In the sentences of the 1750s and 1770s the brutal theatricality of punishment was largely absent, judges rarely added additional pain or ignominy to death sentences, and they assigned simple hanging in 97 percent of the executions.

By the eighteenth century, in short, the penal regime little resembled that of the sixteenth century. Its brutality was diminishing long before the late eighteenth or early nineteenth centuries, and several historians advance hypotheses to explain this development. The sixteenth and seventeenth centuries witnessed key innovations in penology that

---

[24] Alfred Soman, "La justice criminelle aux XVIᵉ–XVIIᵉ siècles: Le Parlement de Paris et les sièges subalternes" in Alfred Soman, *Sorcellerie et justice criminelle: Le Parlement de Paris (16ᵉ–18ᵉ siècles)* (Brookfield, VT: Ashgate Publishing/Variorum, 1992), pp. 30–33.

provided important sentencing alternatives for western European judges. One of these was penal servitude. Employing this at first mainly to remove growing numbers of vagrants from society, authorities soon included law-breakers among those assigned to hard labor. Spain, France, and other Mediterranean states maintained fleets of galleys that required large numbers of rowers, and judges increasingly spared lives to supply these fleets with their labor requirements. The decrease in capital sentences in the Parlement of Paris that we noted between 1535 and 1545 is in part explained by the fact that 19 percent of the court's sentences in the latter year involved galley service, while none did in 1535. Even when France and Spain abandoned galleys as warships in 1748, both countries contin-ued to use convict labor in naval arsenals, while Spain also employed it in the mines of Almadén and Cartagena and in the *presidios* of North Africa.

In the seventeenth century another alternative to physical punishment, transportation, emerged in England. Transportation entailed shipping offenders to overseas colonies in a condition of indentured servitude. A few other countries, including the Dutch Republic and Sweden, also experimented with this practice. And in eighteenth-century England naval or military service also emerged as alternatives to bodily punishment.

The most significant penal alternative, however, began to emerge in northwestern Europe in the mid-sixteenth century, initially as an answer to growing numbers of poor in a region unsuited to the use of galleys as warships. England took the lead in providing an institutional answer to poverty, founding its first carceral institution for vagrants in the old Bridewell Palace near London in 1555. The aim of this institution and others like it was to reform vagrants, through a regime of labor and pater-nalistic religious discipline, into hardworking and productive citizens. Amsterdam followed with the foundation of the Rasphuis and Spinhuis (1596), as did other cities, including Leyden (1598), Bremen (1608), Antwerp (1613), Stockholm (1621), Lyons (1622), and Brussels (1623). Called "houses of correction" in England because of their mission to rehabilitate vagrants, these institutions soon began to receive individuals guilty of crimes, too. Historians of criminal justice regard them as the first penitentiaries, and they appeared, in some areas, over a century before the period identified by Foucault as that of "the birth of the prison." Like galley service, the existence of this sentencing alternative had an immedi-ate impact on penal practice. In Brussels, for example, the number of eighteenth-century executions diminished as condemnations to the house of correction rose.

The increasing judicial recourse to these novel noncapital and non-corporal punishments, and judges' growing tendency to attenuate the brutality of the capital penalties they did order, provide evidence of more basic changes in western Europe. Many historians concur that the increasing stability of early modern states meant that their judicial systems did not have to engage as frequently in the rituals of public execution. Quite simply, they assert, as state authority became more firmly established the ritual demonstration of it became less necessary.

Other scholars add to this explanation. Pieter Spierenburg certainly concurs in finding a political basis for the evolution of early modern penology.[25] But most significantly, he also draws on the work of Norbert Elias to suggest the impact of the civilizing process on early modern penology. Growing sensibility among elite groups and increasing internalization of restraints on behavior led to the privatization of certain aspects of life in our period, including sex, bodily functions, suffering, and death itself. Changing attitudes among elites were also evident in the rejection of public execution by many. Thus the elites, the groups first affected by these changes, increasingly ceased to attend public executions, a reflection of their growing distaste for these bloody rituals, and judicial action came to reflect this sentiment. Spierenburg shows the number of executions declining in his study of Amsterdam; executions elsewhere also became more and more rare, and many jurisdictions entirely abandoned public capital punishments in the nineteenth century.

The English historian V. A. C. Gatrell offers the most recent explanation of the new penology in emphasizing the importance of both humane and functional causes for the ultimate decline of public execution in late eighteenth- and nineteenth-century England. Recognizing the growing security provided by the strengthened state, he has concluded: "hanging came to be repudiated for reasons greater than the fact that some people came to feel bad about it. We also take it for granted that many came to feel bad about it because they could afford to do so—as new controls bit deeper and made them safe."[26]

Our survey of justice indicates a number of significant trends in the history of violence. The growing power of the early modern state, so central to many of the historical theories that we explored in the Introduction, affected all that we have examined. State police agencies and courts, abetted by increasing popular support, began to erode infrajudicial and parajudicial processes of dispute resolution. By the end of our period the judicial revolution was almost assured, as the early modern

[25] Pieter Spierenburg, *The Spectacle of Suffering: Executions and the Evolution of Repression: From a Preindustrial Metropolis to the European Experience* (Cambridge: Cambridge University Press, 1984) and *The Prison Experience: Disciplinary Institutions and Their Inmates in Early Modern Europe* (New Brunswick, NJ: Rutgers University Press, 1991).

[26] V. A. C. Gatrell, *The Hanging Tree*, p. 24.

state advanced toward its goal of monopolizing both force and justice. Significantly, that justice sustained considerable modification in our period, as brutal corporal and capital punishments diminished in frequency and as a new penology emerged. We will find, however, that the interpersonal violence that those punishments aimed to control long remained part of the lives of the mass of early modern Europeans.

FURTHER READING

Astarita, Tommaso, *Village Justice: Community, Family, and Popular Culture in Early Modern Italy* (Baltimore: The Johns Hopkins University Press, 1999).

Beattie, J. M., *Crime and the Courts in England, 1660–1800* (Princeton: Princeton University Press, 1986).

Bennassar, Bartholomé, *The Spanish Character: Attitudes and Mentalities from the Sixteenth to the Nineteenth Century*, translated by Benjamin Keen (Berkeley: University of California Press, 1979).

Black-Michaud, Jacob, *Cohesive Force: Feud in the Mediterranean and the Middle East* (New York: St. Martin's Press, 1975).

Blickle, Peter, *Resistance, Representation, and Community* (Oxford: Oxford University Press, 1997).

Blok, Anton, "Rams and Billy-Goats: A Key to Mediterranean Codes of Honor," *Man* 16 (1981), pp. 427–44.

"The Symbolic Vocabulary of Public Executions" in June Starr and Jane F. Collier (eds.), *History and Power in the Study of Law: New Directions in Legal Anthropology* (Ithaca: Cornell University Press, 1989).

Cameron, Iain A., *Crime and Repression in the Auvergne and the Guyenne, 1720–1790* (Cambridge: Cambridge University Press, 1981).

Dülmen, Richard van, *Theatre of Horror: Crimes and Punishment in Early Modern Germany*, translated by Elisabeth Neu (Cambridge: Polity Press, 1990).

Dupont-Bouchat, Marie-Sylvie, "Criminal Law and Human Rights in Western Europe (14th-18th centuries): The Example of Torture and Punishment. Theory and Practice" in Wolfgang Schmale (ed.), *Human Rights and Cultural Diversity: Europe, Arabic-Islamic World, Africa, China* (Goldbach: Keip Publishing, 1993), pp. 183–97.

Evans, Richard J., *Rituals of Retribution: Capital Punishment in Germany, 1600–1987* (Oxford: Oxford University Press, 1996).

Foster, George M., "Peasant Society and the Image of the Limited Good," *American Anthropologist* 67 (1965), pp. 293–315.

Gatrell, V. A. C., *The Hanging Tree: Execution and the English People, 1770–1868* (Oxford: Oxford University Press, 1994).

Goffman, Erving, *The Presentation of Self in Everyday Life* (Garden City, NY: Doubleday, 1959).

Gowing, Laura, "Language, Power, and the Law: Women's Slander Litigation in Early Modern London" in Jenny Kermode and Garthine Walker (eds.), *Women, Crime and the Courts in Early Modern England* (Chapel Hill: University of North Carolina Press, 1994), pp. 26–47.

Greenshields, Malcolm, *An Economy of Violence in Early Modern France: Crime and*

Justice in the Haute Auvergne, 1587–1664 (University Park: Pennsylvania State University Press, 1994).

Herrup, Cynthia, *The Common Peace: Participation and the Common Law in Seventeenth-Century England* (Cambridge: Cambridge University Press, 1987).

Houlbrooke, Ralph A., *Church Courts and the People during the English Reformation, 1520–1570* (Oxford: Oxford University Press, 1979).

Ingram, Martin J., *Church Courts, Sex and Marriage in England, 1570–1640* (Cambridge: Cambridge University Press, 1987).

Kent, Joan R., *The English Village Constable: A Social and Administrative Study* (Oxford: Oxford University Press, 1986).

Landau, Norma, *The Justice of the Peace, 1679–1760* (Berkeley: University of California Press, 1984).

Langbein, John H., *Torture and the Law of Proof: Europe and England in the Ancien Régime* (Chicago: University of Chicago Press, 1976).

Lenman, Bruce and Parker, Geoffrey, "The State, the Community and the Criminal Law in Early Modern Europe" in V. A. C. Gatrell, Bruce Lenman, and Geoffrey Parker (eds.), *Crime and the Law: The Social History of Crime in Western Europe since 1500* (London: Europa Publications, 1980), pp. 11–48.

Linebaugh, Peter, "The Tyburn Riot against Surgeons" in Douglas Hay *et al.*, *Albion's Fatal Tree: Crime and Society in Eighteenth-Century England* (New York: Pantheon Books, 1975), pp. 65–117.

Muir, Edward, *Mad Blood Stirring: Vendetta and Factions in Friuli during the Renaissance* (Baltimore: The Johns Hopkins University Press, 1993).

Peristiany, J. G. (ed.), *Honour and Shame: The Values of Mediterranean Society* (Chicago: University of Chicago Press, 1966).

Peters, Edward, *Torture* (Oxford: Basil Blackwell, 1985).

Pike, Ruth, "Capital Punishment in Eighteenth-Century Spain," *Histoire sociale/Social History* 18 (1985), pp. 376–86.

Pitt-Rivers, Julian, *The Fate of Shechem: Or, the Politics of Sex: Essays in the Anthropology of the Mediterranean* (Cambridge: Cambridge University Press, 1977).

(ed.), *Mediterranean Countrymen: Essays in the Social Anthropology of the Mediterranean* (Paris: Mouton, 1963).

Reinhardt, Steven G., "Crime and Royal Justice in Ancien Régime France: Modes of Analysis," *Journal of Interdisciplinary History* 13 (1983), pp. 437–60.

Justice in the Sarladais, 1770–1790 (Baton Rouge: Louisiana State University Press, 1991).

Reynolds, Elaine, *Before the Bobbies: The Night Watch and Police Reform in Metropolitan London, 1720–1830* (Stanford: Stanford University Press, 1998).

Sharpe, James A., *Defamation and Sexual Slander in Early Modern England: The Church Courts at York*. York: Bothwick Papers, no. 58, n.d.

"'Last Dying Speeches': Religion, Ideology and Public Execution in Seventeenth-Century England," *Past and Present* 107 (1985), pp. 144–67.

Soman, Alfred, "Deviance and Criminal Justice in Western Europe, 1300–1800: An Essay in Structure," *Criminal Justice History* 1 (1980), pp. 3–28.

Spierenburg, Pieter, *The Spectacle of Suffering: Executions and the Evolution of Repression: From a Preindustrial Metropolis to the European Experience* (Cambridge: Cambridge University Press, 1984).

Tilly, Charles, *Coercion, Capital, and European States, A. D. 900–1990* (Cambridge, MA: Basil Blackwell, 1990).

Wegert, Karl, *Popular Culture, Crime, and Social Control in Eighteenth-Century Württemberg* (Stuttgart: Franz Steiner Verlag, 1994).

Williams, Alan, *The Police of Paris, 1718–1789* (Baton Rouge: Louisiana State University Press, 1979).

Wrightson, Keith, "Two Concepts of Order: Justices, Constables and Jurymen in Seventeenth-Century England" in John Brewer and John Styles (eds.), *An Ungovernable People: The English and their Law in the Seventeenth and Eighteenth Centuries* (New Brunswick, NJ: Rutgers University Press, 1980), pp. 21–46.

The random act of violence, in which an assailant injures or kills a person previously unknown to him or her, is always shocking. The very randomness of the act implicitly threatens everyone in the locale in which it occurs, and consequently the focus of the modern media on such incidents is often intense. Widespread fear is the frequent result of such media attention, and public opinion polls in the United States and elsewhere consistently report respondents' fears about such chance violent crime. Statistically, of course, such fears have relatively slight basis in reality. Robbery attempts gone awry, occasional acts of political terrorism, and opportunistic rapes are the main forms of such violence. Most modern violence, though, in fact pits assailants against those whom social scientists often style their "primary associates": the neighbors, friends and acquaintances, co-workers, and family members with whom they have ongoing relationships, and the greatest possibility for conflict.

The same criminological realities confronted early modern Europeans. The random act of violence always seized public attention, even in an age of few newspapers and limited literacy, but, as in our own day, the most common violence in early modern Europe, was actually violence between people with established relations with one another. This violence erupted as part of the discourse of human relations, and we must seek its roots in those relations and in the society of early modern Europe. We will find that society more violent than our own, one in which, as an insightful historian of the sixteenth and seventeenth centuries has written, that violence constituted: "the common thread of human relations and of the sociability characteristic of various groups in the population."[1] We will find much about early modern society revealed in judicial authorities' treatment of interpersonal violence. Theirs was a rather rigidly hierarchical society, one excessively concerned about matters of personal honor, and criminal law reflected this. The principle of equality of all before the law, which governs

---

[1] Robert Muchembled, *La violence au village: sociabilité et comportements populaires en Artois du XVe au XVIIe siècle* (Turnhout: Editions Brepols, 1989), p. 9.

our jurisprudence, was largely foreign to early modern Europeans, and the social status of both victim and defendant affected the treatment of the cases by jurists. Legists also designed criminal codes to uphold the existing social structure and concepts of right and wrong somewhat different from our own. In this chapter we will trace those differences in our examination of interpersonal violence in the form of homicide and assault, domestic violence, rape, and murder of the newborn child.

Homicide and assault

Historians' research in criminal justice records of the early modern period has turned up very little of the premeditated, carefully planned homicide that modern law classifies as murder and that is the stuff of traditional detective literature. Rather, this was an age in which many had recourse to sudden violent assaults that modern courts often classify as manslaughter because of their lack of prior malice or planning. These violent assaults, even those with fatal results, seem at first glance to have been sudden eruptions of brutality that appear strange to us and require some analysis to understand their causes and meanings. A fatal encounter in rural southwestern France may serve as a model.

This incident occurred as the sun was setting on the afternoon of 28 December 1739, and on a festive observance of the Feast of the Holy Innocents. The brothers Pierre and Jean Lavialle, both merchants, were drinking wine with friends in a cabaret, or tavern, in the small town of Gensac in the Dordogne River valley. The conviviality of the occasion quickly dissipated with the arrival of another merchant, Fouignet-Sauvel. The latter owed money to Pierre Lavialle who, in a room filled with local merchants, officials, and professional men, demanded payment. The verbal exchange grew increasingly heated, and Lavialle struck Fouignet-Sauvel with his walking stick. In response Fouignet-Sauvel drew a hunting knife with which he killed Pierre Lavialle and gravely wounded Jean Lavialle when he hastened to his brother's assistance. Fouignet-Sauvel then fled the area, returning only in 1741 when a royal pardon set aside the death sentence imposed on him in absentia by the local court.[2]

There is much here that is alien to us. While Fouignet-Sauvel, like modern assailants, struck down a primary associate – in this provincial crossroads community the principals in this case belonged to a relatively small circle of the local elite whose members maintained ongoing social, commercial, and perhaps even familial relations – the violence itself

---

[2] Archives départementales de la Gironde (France), Sénéchaussée de Libourne, Procédures civiles et criminelles, 5B633, and Registres des sentences, 5B83.

seems, by our standards, entirely disproportionate to the ostensible cause of the argument. We normally regulate debts in civil courts, and that course of action was an option in eighteenth-century France. The setting for this fatal encounter seems odd, too; the two men made no effort to conceal their confrontation, but rushed to violence in a crowded public house in front of a large number of witnesses. The men seem to have seen little wrong with a violent resolution of their dispute, and the site of their fight suggests that their contemporaries probably saw it as a legitimate and almost commonplace aspect of social discourse. The royal pardon reinforces the conclusion that such violence was deemed acceptable, at least in some circumstances.

We also probably find strange the status of the two actors in this violent drama. In the twenty-first century little reported violence is committed by members of social elites; most modern violence, instead, is perpetrated by those marginalized in our society by economic, cultural, or ethnic factors, or by ideologues seeking to advance their causes by terrorism.

This case thus raises many questions, none more fundamental than that of the frequency of such violence. This case was not unique; criminal records from all over early modern western Europe yield cases similar to this one in the seeming pettiness of their origins and the brutality of their outcomes. Quantifiable expression of that frequency is difficult, however. Any conclusions scholars make about the frequency of crime, whether in our own era or in the early modern period, must be based on offenses reported to the authorities, and even today, for a variety of reasons, not all crimes are reported. Thus an unknown amount of crime must always remain unknown, a "dark figure," at the extent of which scholars can only guess. This problem of unreported crime was much greater in the early modern period, when the disincentives to reporting crime to the authorities were numerous.

As we have seen, there were infrajudicial modes of dispute resolution that competed with judicial institutions; use of such practices kept much violence from official cognizance and thus official records. The cost of justice also inhibited the reporting of crime; throughout western Europe, well into the eighteenth century, most crime was prosecuted at the expense of victims, not the state. The isolation of much of early modern Europe's population in rural communities distant from cities that were the usual seats of the police and judicial authorities to which crime was reported also meant that many offenses never entered official records. And even where the authorities were near by, historians have identified a code of silence, bred of fundamental distrust of police and judicial officials, which affected crime reporting. Consequently, we must recognize the limitations of most statistical analyses of early modern crime.

Only the crime of homicide, which many scholars regard as an important indicator of a society's overall level of violence, seems to be a valid object of statistical analysis. This is a crime that is difficult to conceal, because it produces tangible evidence of its commission in the victim's body. Therefore there was a high reporting rate of homicide in our period, producing an abundant volume of records of legal actions that began, in most European states, with a procedure akin to modern coroners' inquiries. When such investigations suggested a suspect, moreover, prosecution resulted from the increasing willingness of many early modern governments to prosecute this gravest of offenses at state expense. Thus even in rural jurisdictions like the Sénéchaussée of Libourne in which the Gensac murder occurred, by the eighteenth century the French crown prosecuted almost all homicides at royal expense. Of course, many early modern killers escaped capture and trial – one study has found that only one in nine homicides in sixteenth-century Amsterdam came to trial – so historians must also search coroners' records and police reports of homicide as more accurate measures of real levels of violence than trial records.

Using all of these sources, however, historians have reconstructed homicide rates for a number of early modern locales in statistical terms commonly used in the twenty-first century, that is, the number of murders per 100,000 of the population. We must view these figures, however, as suggestive of the incidence of homicide rather than absolute rates. The population figures on which such rates must depend are imprecise for our period, and historians' research methods differ. Some, for example, use coroners' records, while others employ trial dossiers or indictments. And some include murder of newborn infants, a distinct form of violence that we will examine later in this chapter, with the taking of adult lives. But even with these qualifications, the early modern homicide rates advanced by historians highlight the significance of homicide and assault in the early modern period.

In the nations of western Europe most closely studied by historians twentieth-century national homicide rates have varied from a low of 0.5 murders per 100,000 (England and Wales and the Netherlands in 1929–31 for example) to almost 1.5 murders per 100,000 (England and Sweden in 1990) in the last years of the century, with the most marked increase since 1960. Recent United States homicide rates are much higher, varying from 10.2 per 100,000 in 1980 to 6.3 per 100,000 in 1998. But both North American and European homicide rates pale in comparison to many of those that historians have identified at the outset of our period and that are illustrated in table 1.

These sixteenth-century homicide rates are much higher than those of

Table 1. *Homicide rates 1480–1594 (sample)*

Locale	Period	Homicides per 100,000
Alost, Belgium	1480–1504	60
Arboga, Sweden	1493–1502	10
Arras, France	1526–1549	39
Cologne, Germany	1500–1599	10
Douai, France	1496–1519	16/17
Stockholm, Sweden	1545–1549	20
Stockholm, Sweden	1590–1594	36

Source: Xavier Rousseaux, "Ordre moral, justice et violence: l'homicide dans les sociétés européennes, XIIIe–XVIIIe siècle" in Benoît Garnot (ed.), *Ordre moral et délinquance de l'antiquité au XXe siècle* (Dijon: Editions universitaires de Dijon, 1994), p. 78.

late twentieth-century Europe, suggesting that fatal violence was much more common than it is today. But if the frequency of early modern violence is foreign to us, we will find much else about it that is far more familiar. That the causes of the Gensac case, for example, seem difficult to ascertain at first is in fact deceptive. Historians' analysis of such cases must rely on complaints lodged with police and judges, and these are not always completely candid about the origins of violence. As Natalie Z. Davis showed in her study of pardon requests, people confronted by the law attempt to put the best face on their actions, giving accounts that often little resemble the facts of a case.[3] Plaintiffs inevitably minimize their own roles in causing violence. As a result, in searching for the roots of early modern interpersonal violence we must look beyond the petty bickering that surprises us by escalating into violence. Another nonfatal tavern altercation from the same court district as that of Gensac suggests the fundamental issue underlying much of this interpersonal violence. In pressing assault charges for slaps he received when one of his neighbors took offense at his joke, Mathieu Robert wrote: "that which aggravates this action, which is as contemptible as it is reprehensible, is the publicity: it was in a cabaret that the blows were struck."[4] The primary concern, in this encounter as in many like it, was not so much the physical injury, but rather the emotional one. Robert found the public nature of the blows humiliating and he lodged charges. Similarly, the fatal violence in the Gensac case erupted because Lavialle accused Fouignet-Sauvel of

---

[3] Natalie Z. Davis, *Fiction in the Archives: Pardon Tales and Their Tellers in Sixteenth-Century France* (Stanford: Stanford University Press, 1987).

[4] Archives départementales de la Gironde (France), Sénéchaussée de Libourne, Procédures civiles et criminelles, 5B675.

negligence in meeting his obligations in front of neighbors and business associates, shaming him. These were affairs of honor, revolving around fundamental issues of reputation and, ultimately, status and local power.

While our examination of quasi-judicial dueling in Chapter 3 suggested the explosive nature of honor among aristocrats, the Gensac case brings the problem of honor down to the popular level. Upon analysis, the issues for the Lavialles and Fouignet-Sauvel reveal themselves as matters familiar to us in other terms. We are today still concerned about preserving what we call "face" and avoiding shame, and while we are better able to escape shame peacefully in the anonymity of modern urban life, it still produces violence. One North American psychiatrist who studies criminal behavior has written: "I have yet to see a serious act of violence that was not provoked by the experience of feeling shamed and humiliated, disrespected and ridiculed, and that did not represent the attempt to prevent or undo this 'loss of face'."[5]

Disagreements over money, cards, land, passage rights, sex, alcohol, or any of the multitude of other commodities of human interchange in this period, all, ultimately, involved honor or "face." And just as we saw the duels of early modern aristocrats in defense of honor governed by ritual, ritual was not absent from the more commonplace encounters that escalated petty disagreements toward violence. Again, the Gensac case may serve as an example. The confrontation began with a verbal interchange in which Lavialle demanded payment and questioned Fouignet-Sauvel's reliability in business. As we have seen in Chapter 3, professional reputation and family lineage were essential components of early modern concepts of honor. "Thief," "rogue," "bankrupt," or in Spain "Secret Moor" or "Son of a Jew," all were words calculated to offend male honor, just as "whore" affronted the moral probity central to female honor.

Nonverbal communication, in the form of gestures, could perform the same insulting function. A man showing his backside to another, or a woman lifting her skirt, was intentionally committing an offensive act. So, too, was the perpetrator of tricks like placing excrement in front of an enemy's door and drawing him out to step in it, or filling his hat with beer in a tavern. These acts all held the victim up to derision and demeaned his honor. Invasions of personal space also offended honor, whether it involved a herder leading his livestock across another's property, or two bourgeois encountering each other from different directions on a narrow path during a Sunday stroll and each refusing to yield passage to the other. All of these verbal and nonverbal messages usually expressed

---

[5] James Gilligan, *Violence: Our Deadly Epidemic and its Causes* (New York: G. P. Putnam's Sons, 1996), p. 110.

ongoing animosity between two people, and the fact that one of them had chosen to escalate the conflict by giving offense in public.

In the Gensac case a verbal interchange propelled the two businessmen toward violence. Doubtless one of the men added blasphemy to his insults, a widely recognized sign of his readiness to move beyond any pretense of civil behavior. Typically, unless friends or associates of the principals intervened at this point violence was likely to ensue. In this case Lavialle struck Fouignet-Sauvel with his stick. Such blows, whatever their origin, seldom fell haphazardly; instead, their targets on the victims' bodies further escalated the attack on honor. If the recipient of the first blows was a woman, they often landed on the lower torso, the flanks, or the loins. In this society, which linked female honor with personal morality, humiliation was especially great when blows fell in the region of the womb and vagina.

If the recipient of the blows was a male, however, the likelihood was very great that he received a blow to the head, as did Fouignet-Sauvel. This was certainly an obvious place to inflict serious injury, but perhaps more importantly the head assumed great symbolic significance in this society. The head was where an individual often displayed his pretensions; a gaudily plumed hat or an elaborate wig, for example, spoke eloquently about the wearer's self-image to all he encountered. And, for the most honorable members of society, the removal of the head in execution by decapitation spelled the complete loss of honor. Thus any action directed at the head was provocative, whether it was a blow, a slap, a tug at a beard, or even a stroke of the hand or walking stick knocking a hat or wig to the ground. Studies of court records in France, the Low Countries, and Rome show that blows to the head represented as much as 50 percent of all mortal wounds reported to the authorities.

As we have seen, this was a well-armed society and the initial violence, if simply that of a slap, punch, or kick, often escalated as each party resorted to weapons. Pointed weapons, especially swords and the knives most men carried to cut their food or perform their work were weapons of choice for much of our period. In seventeenth-century Castile 60 percent of reported murders were the result of knife or sword wounds, while in Amsterdam knifings accounted for 82.8 percent of all homicides in the 1710–26 period. Indeed, Amsterdam, like many other Dutch cities, was home to a lower-class culture of knife fighting, with its own special rules, for much of our period. The ritual was well known, and began when one man invited another to follow him outdoors in order that their impending fight might not embarrass their host. There, at the cry "Stand still!", both parties drew their weapons and spectators stepped back for a test of strength and skill that proceeded at least until the drawing of blood satisfied the participants. An informal etiquette governed such fights, and men often allowed opponents who had dropped or broken their weapons to secure others. Such courtesies notwithstanding, many of these confrontations were fatal.

Firearm usage in confrontations of this sort grew throughout our period. Gunfire, for example, resulted in but 2 percent of homicides in 1560–69 in Kent, England, an area in which, two centuries later, guns produced 22 percent of homicides. But much early modern violence was the result of an assailant wielding some more common weapon: a walking stick or peasant's staff; tools of a trade, like a butcher's cleaver, or a hammer; axes; and a mass of hastily chosen implements, including iron bars, billiard cues, whips, and furniture.[6] Even primitive weapons could be lethal in the early modern period, and turn a simple assault into a case of homicide, in part because of the rudimentary medical techniques of the age. Many victims survived for weeks after their attacks, only to succumb to infections.

The Gensac case raises one more issue for us, that of the social status of the principals. The individuals in this case were affluent businessmen, of a type not normally linked to violent crime in modern society. Their involvement in such violence is indication that a broad spectrum of society resorted to arms in this period. Indeed, in the sixteenth and seventeenth centuries social elites represented more than half of the accused in violent offenses in the Agenais region of France and fully half of those pardoned for homicide in the county of Artois in the Spanish Netherlands. Among others who engaged in the physical violence we have found so common in this period were even Catholic clerics, at least before the late seventeenth century when Tridentine reforms of clerical behavior began to take effect at the grassroots level in much of Europe. Until that time, priests in many areas, such as the Spanish Netherlands and Spain itself, routinely bore arms. Indeed, in Spain a third of the caseload of the Tribunal of Bref, a special sixteenth- and seventeenth-century ecclesiastical court charged with enforcing priestly discipline, consisted of clerics charged with bearing arms, and another 26 percent of its cases involved murder or attempted murder by priests bearing guns. Priestly violence featured other weapons, too, and even originated on the high altar. Such violence erupted at the cathedral of Elne in northern Spain at the Christmas Eve vigil of 1590. When Canon Hieronim Advart placed a small likeness of Christ on the tabernacle just before the service his colleague Miguel Tamarro told him to remove it. Advart refused and the two traded insults even as mass began; when Advart left the altar at the end of

[6] Ruff, *Crime, Justice and Public Order*, p. 79.

the service he lay in wait for Tamarro, seized his robes as he passed by, and wounded him with several knife blows.

The lowest orders of society also engaged in this quotidian violence, and the poverty of many serving only to magnify it. As we have noted, violations of property rights often became affairs of honor that could exacerbate existing differences. In 1708, for instance, a peasant named Gennai killed Giovanni Bianucci for taking turnips from his garden in Altopascio, Tuscany.

If this was a violence of all social groups, however, it was also a violence that only rarely crossed social barriers. Most assailants were of approximately the same social status as their victims. In the Sénéchaussée of Libourne, the district that produced the Gensac case, and the neighboring Sénéchaussée of Bazas, 43 percent of the principals in 603 reported cases of homicide, assault, and insult came from exactly the same social groups. Even when the assailant and his victim differed slightly in social terms, they generally were well acquainted as neighbors; about 89 percent came either from the same parish or from parishes within 3 miles (5 km) of each other. Research in the records of other jurisdictions produced comparable results.

Such violence among social equals and neighbors was, like violence in our own time, largely a male business. Police everywhere seem to have seen little threat in petty violence between women in marketplace disputes and the like, and one Paris police official wrote: "Disputes between women interest no one."[7] The result was widespread underreporting of much female violence. But even if we recognize that reports of much non-fatal female violence never reached the authorities, the record is clear. Most of early modern violence was the work of males. Research into pardons for crimes of violence suggests the highest rates of male criminality in the lands of the Spanish crown: 98.6 percent of murderers receiving Good Friday pardons in seventeenth-century Castile were men, while males received 99.6 percent of the pardons issued in Artois from the fifteenth to the seventeenth century. Elsewhere, other records suggest only marginally greater female participation in acts of violence. Research in the records of a number of jurisdictions in England, France, and the Dutch Republic yield evidence that only from about 1.5 to 11 percent of known killers in our period were women.

This male-dominated violence was, like much of twenty-first-century violence, largely produced by young unmarried men, long recognized by criminologists as the most violence-prone segment of any population. To

[7] Quoted in Arlette Farge, "Proximités pensables et inégalités flagrantes: Paris, XVIIIᵉ siècle" in Cécile Dauphin and Arlette Farge (eds.), De la violence des femmes (Paris: Albin Michel, 1997), p. 79.

cite one example, 78 percent of the individuals accused of physical violence in the Châtelet of Paris in samples from 1765, 1770, and 1775 were males under thirty-five.

This largely youthful male violence broke out in every locale of early modern socialization. The tavern or cabaret, the sort of establishment in which the Lavialle brothers fell, was the preeminent zone of early modern male sociability, and these places were numerous. Amsterdam in the seventeenth century, for example, had 518 alehouses, one for every 200 inhabitants of the city. In these establishments men consummated business deals and exchanged the news of the day; and in an age in which clean drinking water was not always readily available, they consumed large quantities of wine, beer, cider, or gin, depending on local customs. Such consumption contributed to violence. Alcohol's physical effects on its imbibers can be obvious, and include diminished reaction time and reduction of muscular coordination. But other effects of alcohol are more subtle. It reduces an individual's sensitivity to external stimuli, like cues to behavior; it also diminishes intellectual functions that govern self-control and inhibitions, and overconsumption of alcohol can produce euphoria. Such effects, combined with the possibility for conflict inherent in any large gathering, account for alcohol's role in provoking violence. One modern North American study found significant levels of alcohol in 56 percent of hospital emergency-room patients injured in fights. The link between alcohol and violence seems just as clear in the early modern period. In Artois in the fifteenth to the seventeenth century, for example, 55 percent of all violent acts for which pardons were issued occurred in taverns.

Figure 7 illustrates the conditions in an eighteenth-century Paris *guingette*, an establishment serving wine in the area outside the tax barrier that surrounded the city proper. These *guingettes* were very popular because their wines, free of the tax added to the price of spirits sold inside the city, were cheaper, and because they had space for dancing and even gardens that were generally uncommon in urban cabarets. Parisians made the trip out to such establishments at weekends particularly, but violence was common, both inside and on the trek back into the city. The artist makes this clear in his choice of the Ramponaux establishment for his picture. The name of this publican was the origin for the eighteenth-century French colloquialism for a hard blow: *ramponneau*.

The presence of alcohol in taverns facilitated violence, but violence was inherent in human relations and it occurred even where people gathered without the influence of spirits. In many early modern locales, such as Castile, this was often the street, the site of 46.8 percent of all Castilian homicides pardoned on Good Fridays in the seventeenth century. Streets

Figure 8. Anonymous, *Uproar at Ramponaux's*. Watercolored drawing, eighteenth century. Bibliothèque nationale de France (Cabinet des Estampes), Paris.

in most early modern cities were narrow and often crowded, and there-fore passers-by jostled and frequently offended each other. At night they were badly lit and afforded ready concealment for assailants in the dark. Other violent public spaces included cemeteries, where villagers in Artois routinely gathered after mass, and marketplaces like the Mercato Nuovo in Florence.

The workplace also frequently was the site of violence due to conflicts over wages and working conditions. The artisans' districts of most early modern cities were densely inhabited, and since much work was done outdoors the pettiest conflict generally had a ready audience whose pres-ence for an affair involving honor often assured its escalation to a violent outcome.

Just as violence flourished in those locales where early modern Europeans gathered, it was also most common at the times most condu-cive for them to assemble. Thus, just as in the twenty-first century, the warm-weather months were the months of greatest violence. Early modern Europeans were outside a great deal for agricultural work or other purposes and inevitably they came into conflict. Indeed, as the weather warmed, the incidence of violence increased. Interpersonal vio-lence also increased, just as it does today in all predominantly Christian countries, at the Christmas holidays, when people gathered in great numbers for indoor festivities often marked by consumption of alcoholic beverages. For early modern Europeans, however, the festive season extended from Christmas into January, as we will see in Chapter Five. The pre-Lenten celebration of Carnival began just after Christmas in many locales. In addition, January and early February were key times for marriage in Catholic populations, because the Church forbade matri-mony in the Advent and Lenten seasons that bracketed these months. Thus more gatherings and conflicts marked this period as well.

This pattern of warm-weather and holiday violence prevailed through-out Europe, as the records of pardons for violent crimes in Castile dem-onstrate. In seventeenth-century Castile, on average, the quarter of the calendar year represented by May, June, and July produced some 28 percent of all pardoned violent crimes for which the date was known. Holiday violence in December and January, together representing 16.7 percent of the calendar year, accounted for about 23 percent of the Castilian pardons of homicides and assaults.

Early modern interpersonal violence also followed a pattern of daily incidence quite similar to that of the twenty-first century, when violence mounts at times of greatest leisure, chiefly during weekends and holidays. Everywhere in the early modern period Saturdays, Sundays, and the numerous days of religious observance, marketdays, and local festivals

were days of above-average incidence of assault and homicide. In Artois
in the fifteenth to the seventeenth century pardons reveal that fully 42
percent of assaults and murders occurred on Sundays and days of religious festivals. Weekend violence often extended into the working week,
too. In eighteenth-century Paris the records of district police officials
(*commissaires*) show that more than half of all reported violence happened
on Sunday or Monday; "Holy Monday" was long a continuation of
weekend revelry for Parisian artisans.

Crime rates, of course, vary not just seasonally and daily, but even by
the time of day. In twenty-first-century societies nonworking hours, after
dark for much of the year, are peak periods of human conflict because
opportunities for social interaction increase at the end of the workday.
While early modern officials were often less precise than their modern
counterparts in recording the times of crimes, historians can determine
the general time of day for many offenses. The dangers of night, in an age
of considerable superstition, were deeply felt, and in the Spanish
Netherlands a popular saying was that "The night is no friend." Records
of violent acts prove the validity of this old saying. In Castile 51 percent of
cases of interpersonal violence pardoned on Good Fridays in the seventeenth century occurred at night; an additional 16 percent occurred in the
evening, often in cabarets. Daylight hours accounted for 34 percent of
acts of violence. Study of pardons in Artois shows that nocturnal violence
was common in northern Europe, as well: the evenings produced 55
percent of assaults and murders and the night an additional 22 percent;
the daytime accounted for only 23 percent of these offenses.

Early modern Europeans regarded violence, whether of the daylight or
of the evening hours, as a routine part of the discourse of daily life for
much of our period. The authorities often tolerated it, unless, of course,
an assailant was particularly brutal in maiming or killing the victim. Such
behavior might provoke either citizens or local officials to action, but in
the normal course of events the fate of Fouignet-Sauvel was not atypical.
The merchant fled the Gensac area and returned only when he had
secured a royal pardon. In France pardons like that he received often
required that the assailant pay compensatory damages to the victim's
family to settle the matter. Flight like that of Fouignet-Sauvel was
common elsewhere, too, including the seventeenth-century Dutch
Republic, where the law did not even penalize relations who hid family
members charged with assault or homicide.

The evolution of the criminal law in much of western Europe increasingly reflected such attitudes. In England manslaughter evolved as the
charge for the most common type of violence, that epitomized by the
Gensac case. In Francophone areas homicides like that in Gensac came

to be called *homicide simple*, as opposed to killing with premeditation, *homicide qualifié*. Homicide without malice aforethought was thus becoming quite distinct in law from murder, the taking of life with deliberate purpose. In many jurisdictions murder usually remained the initial charge in most homicides but, depending on the circumstances of the case, courts often reduced charges to manslaughter or even accidental homicide.

Even as the law increasingly reflected society's recognition of the commonplace nature of violence, criminal assault, manslaughter, and murder indictments were diminishing considerably in many jurisdictions by the end of our period. Again, rates of reported homicide prove the most reliable indicator of the trend, and two remarkably complete series of rates are illustrative. The longest data series comes from England, where a large number of local court studies permit calculation of approximate national homicide rates from the medieval period to the present century. That research shows a dramatic decline in violence, from an annual average of about 20 reported murders per 100,000 of population in 1200 to about 15 in the late medieval period, approximately 7 in 1600, between 4 and 5 in 1700, about 2 in 1800, and roughly 1 in 1900.

Data drawn from official inspections of bodies of murder victims in Amsterdam demonstrate a similar decrease in homicides. In the Dutch metropolis the average annual homicide rate declined from 47 per 100,000 of population in the mid-fifteenth century to about 28 in 1524–65, 1.66 in 1752–67, and 1 in 1800–16. As in England, the Amsterdam decline was not consistent and steady; there were temporary periods of increases in homicides in both places. But in both the English and the Dutch early modern data there is a marked overall decline in the number of reported homicides by 1800 to a rate approximating that of the twenty-first century. Less complete data sets from Belgium, France, Germany, Spain, and Sweden suggest similar, long-term trends in homicide, albeit at differing times and rates.

While this decline in violence occurred widely in our period, it affected different social groups at different times. So, even as aggregate rates diminished, violent subcultures persisted. In seventeenth- and early eighteenth-century Dutch cities, for example, the knife-fighting culture continued to flourish among the urban lower classes, especially in and around drinking establishments. Western Europe in our period therefore remained a somewhat more violent place than it is today.

Historians have detected changes in some aspects of justice that may explain some part of this precipitate drop in homicide rates by the eighteenth century. By that time, many English jurisdictions, for example, were no longer sending forward indictments in cases in which the killer was unknown, a fact that has an impact on rates derived by those historians who rely on indictment records. But such procedural alterations can account only in part for the decreasing rate of homicide, and we certainly cannot ascribe the fall to a crackdown by the authorities that deterred violence. As we have seen, policing began to improve only at the very end of our period, and judges started to assign harsher penalties for violence only very late in the early modern era. Most scholars believe, instead, that real changes in human behavior were underway. Violence seems to have become increasingly unacceptable to larger segments of the European population, evidence of the civilizing process described by Norbert Elias that we will find affecting other forms of violence, including that within the household.

Domestic violence

In 1608 an English woman named Margaret Bonefant visited her neighbor, Anne Young, concerned about the latter's safety at the hands of an abusive husband. She found her friend in a frightful state, "as though she were more lyke to die of that beating then to recover and lyve."[8]

The fate of Anne Young illustrates the results of an early modern domestic violence that is in many ways similar to that of our own society. Like this sort of brutality in our century, early modern domestic violence typically consisted of abuse by the male head of the household directed at his wife. Early modern, as well as modern, criminal court records do yield evidence of violence by women, but such cases are relatively rare; in many early modern jurisdictions three out of four victims of domestic violence were women assaulted by men. Early modern children, like their modern counterparts, were victims of abusive fathers, but with scant rights in early modern law, they left few records of their experiences – in contrast to the school, hospital and social services records of today. Those who perished at the hands of a parent, though, as many did, at least left a large body of court records; in some early modern English jurisdictions as many as half of all homicides within the family were of children older than the newborns whose deaths we will analyze later in this chapter. The early modern household, however, did contain one group of victims not generally found in modern cases of domestic violence. These households frequently had servants and apprentices, and heads of households also victimized these individuals.

Early modern domestic violence was similar to modern domestic violence in another way, too: it flourished behind a wall of silence maintained

[8] Quoted in Laura Gowing, *Domestic Dangers: Women, Words, and Sex in Early Modern London* (Oxford: Oxford University Press, 1996), p. 209.

by all affected by this behavior. The psychological effects of abuse some-times render victims incapable of seeking assistance outside the home. Other household members frequently hesitate to report domestic vio-lence for fear of the shame that will accrue to the family if the violence in its midst becomes known in the larger community. Neighbors and friends are often reluctant to intervene in the domestic problems of others, too.

Despite the broad similarities between early modern and modern domestic violence, however, there was a key difference between the two; domestic violence seems to have been far more common in the early period, and it merited little legal sanction. We will find the causes of this widespread and often unchallenged violence in the social and legal struc-tures of early modern western Europe.

In principle the full weight of religious tradition, civil law, and custom endowed the husband and father with almost total power in the early modern household. Biblical authority especially shaped religious thought on the governance of the household. Saint Paul, in his letter to the Ephesians, wrote: "Wives, submit yourselves unto your own husbands, as unto the Lord . . . Children, obey your parents in the Lord: for this is right . . . Servants, be obedient to them that are your masters according to the flesh, with fear and trembling." And while by the sixteenth century some religious thinkers, Protestant and Catholic alike, were beginning to counsel restraint in the application of force to maintain the dominance of the male head of the household, all agreed that the authority of the husband and father required occasional reinforcement with corporal punishment. But the sixteenth-century Catholic moralist and theologian Jean Benedicti, while affirming male dominance in the household, raised an increasingly troubling issue. If the wife did disobey her husband, Benedicti asserted, he was justified in administering punishment to her that did "not overstep the bounds of modesty and reason; for even though she is inferior, nevertheless she is not the slave or the chambermaid but the companion and flesh of her husband."[9]

Many Protestant theologians echoed their Catholic counterparts, but among Calvinists there was a clear break with the traditional assertion that the male head of household had the right to assert his dominance by force. John Calvin recognized that violence could be counterproductive with children, writing: "Severity and petty strictness rouse children to obstinacy."[10] Moreover, in Calvin's Geneva spouse beating became a

[9] Quoted in Jean-Louis Flandrin, *Families in Former Times: Kinship, Household and Sexuality,* translated by Richard Southern (Cambridge: Cambridge University Press, 1979), pp. 126–29.

[10] Quoted in Beatrice Gottlieb, *The Family in the Western World from the Black Death to the Industrial Age* (Oxford: Oxford University Press, 1993), p. 170.

crime. Nonetheless, while such religious condemnation of domestic violence became more frequent in the last years of our period, it was not universal, even among pacifist groups. Thus a late seventeenth-century
religious-instruction book produced by English Quakers, a pacifist group
that denied the Catholic doctrine of original sin and believed all children
were born innocent, quoted the book of Proverbs on childrearing: "Thou
shalt beat him with the Rod, and shalt deliver his soul from Hell."

Western customary and statutory law reinforced religion in regard to
the disciplinary force of the male head of household. Ancient Roman law
had actually given the husband the right to kill his wife for certain
offenses, especially adultery, and in France until 1907 a husband discovering his wife engaged in adultery could legally kill her. But almost everywhere else, by the early modern period husbands could not legally kill
their wives. They retained, however, tremendous legal authority over their
wives. In continental countries the principle of the all-powerful husband
and father (*patria potestas*) became entrenched in civil codes after the
recovery of Roman law in the late medieval period. In English common
law the principle of coverture obtained, under which the wife had no legal
standing apart from the husband. This was a relationship summed up by
the eighteenth-century jurist William Blackstone as: "The husband and
wife are one, and the husband is that one."[11]

In both England and continental countries these principles created
certain legal responsibilities of husbands for their wives' actions. Legal
liability for their wives' behavior justified husbands' rights to discipline
their spouses with physical punishment. Similar legal principles sustained
the right of the male head of household to chastise his children, servants,
and apprentices. He ultimately bore responsibility in law for their behavior, too. The exact degree of discipline was the question. Gratian, the
twelfth-century legal scholar whose *Decretum* was so essential to the adap-
tation of Roman law to the needs of late medieval western Europe, offered
something of an answer on this score: "A man may chastise his wife and
beat her for her own correction; for she is of his household and therefore
the lord may chastise his own . . . so likewise the husband is bound to
chastise his wife in moderation."[12]

Thanks to Gratian, perhaps, "moderate correction" was the rule, but
the precise severity of that chastisement was still ambiguous. In parts of
England it seems to have meant beating with a rod or stick no larger in
diameter than the householder's thumb, the origin of the expression
"rule of thumb." In the customs of parts of France "moderate correction"

[11] Quoted in *ibid.*, p. 91.
[12] Quoted in G. G. Coulton (ed.), *Life in the Middle Ages*, 4 vols. (Cambridge: Cambridge
University Press, 1928–30), 3, p. 234.

permitted beating until blood flowed. All of these parameters, however, were rather imprecise and suggest the obvious: there was tremendous potential for "moderate correction" to escalate into a fatality. When death did occur, however, both early modern statutory law and judicial practice were ready to overlook male excesses. A Swedish law of 1734 provided that if a child died as a result of a parental beating the charge was not murder but manslaughter by misadventure, a fining offense. And English juries and continental judges regularly gave a verdict of accidental death and waived penalties in cases of domestic violence.

For much of the early modern period there was little questioning of this legal situation. As we have seen, popular opinion viewed women as passionate and naturally unruly, and in many people's minds unruly wives were prone to follow the insatiable sexual desires that the thought of the age ascribed to females. Hence discipline seemed necessary to many men of this time. Limited criticism of the principle of moderate correction began to emerge only in the seventeenth century, and not until two centuries later did most western European states begin to extend their criminal codes and case law to include domestic violence. Until that time, victims of domestic violence found scant legal relief from officials of the state. Only homicide and the most egregious nonlethal domestic violence ever reached state courts, and judges were extremely reluctant to intervene. Accordingly, when the father of Françoise Ouairy removed her from the home of an abusive husband in early seventeenth-century France, the court ordered her father to desist his interference and to return the young woman to her husband. A Nuremberg wife of the same period, who complained to a local court of a husband's brutality, was imprisoned briefly as an example to wives who questioned their husbands' authority.

This judicial reluctance to intervene in marital matters extended to the approach of courts to abuse of servants and apprentices. Masters assaulted these unfortunates with various implements, but judges generally acquitted those whose force could be considered "moderate" in any way. If justices could not acquit, they tried to admonish or arbitrate, and ruled against masters only in the most extreme cases, like that of Bartholomew Clifford, an English pewterer's apprentice burned on the face by an angry master wielding a hot iron. Generally, courts acted only in cases like this of excessive violence; the jury in Clifford's case set him free of any obligations to his master.

In some countries an administrative procedure also existed that provided relief in cases of domestic abuse. In France the *lettre de cachet*, a royal confinement order, permitted victims to secure the state's incarceration of a violent or dangerous family member. Research has shown that, of the estimated 100,000 to 200,000 of these orders issued in the king's name in the 200 years from 1589 to 1789, the vast majority came at the request of people seeking incarceration of rebellious children, adulterous wives, alcoholic relatives, and abusive husbands. In the cities of the Austrian Netherlands and the Dutch Republic in the eighteenth century a similar procedure existed whereby family members could request an alderman to order the confinement of a relative in a house of correction.

Where such confinement was unavailable, or courts were unwilling to act in the face of domestic violence, the state offered little other relief to victims. Civil divorce for battered wives was virtually impossible before the French Revolution. As a result, many turned to ecclesiastical authorities for adjudication of domestic violence. Ecclesiastical divorce, however, was seldom an option for battered wives. In the few Protestant areas in which it was legal, such as the Dutch Republic, violence and incompatibility were usually not acceptable reasons for divorce. In Catholic countries the Church's position on divorce, which still obtained in much of Protestant Europe, was clear: a valid marriage was dissoluble only upon the death of one spouse. Canon law in Catholic states and statutes in some Protestant areas like England, however, allowed for annulment and judicial separation from bed and board. Annulment was possible if a plaintiff could show that the marriage had occurred despite such ecclesiastical "impediments" as: both partners being underage at marriage; permanent impotence or frigidity in either partner; the existence of a prior marriage contract at the time of matrimony; or the relationship of the couple within forbidden degrees of kinship. Annulment permitted the remarriage of both partners but deprived the woman of her share in her former husband's estate, and rendered illegitimate any children of the dissolved union.

If a wife could prove none of the impediments permitting annulment, separation at the orders of a church tribunal was another possible release from a violent spouse. Catholic and Protestant authorities could typically grant separation if either spouse could prove certain forms of adultery or extreme cruelty, although wives filed the bulk of these requests. The handling of separation requests revealed the courts' double standard for male and female behavior. In France, for example, male adultery constituted grounds for separation only if a husband introduced the other woman into his household; any act of sexual infidelity, however, constituted female adultery. But separation did not dissolve the marital bond so that the partners could remarry; all it provided was the right of the partners to reside separately. A state civil court then, typically, undertook division of the property of the couple. A study of separations in the diocese of Cambrai, France, between 1710 and 1791 reveals that Catholic authorities granted separations with surprising frequency – but chiefly in those cases deemed so brutal that the woman's life seemed endangered.

Clergymen and ecclesiastical institutions also struggled with the problem of restoring peace to marriages without the extreme step of separation. Pastors tried to reconcile marital difficulties, but when problems exceeded the local cleric's mediation skills the ecclesiastical institutions sought to identify and chastise as culprit one partner or another. Yet everywhere they were reluctant to impose discipline on the husband and father, and did so only when the local pastor and respected witnesses confirmed wives' charges of domestic violence. In eighteenth-century Neckarhausen, Germany, Anna Hentzler discovered this when she complained to the local consistory about her husband's violence. Directed by her husband Jacob to lead the horse while he plowed, she refused, claiming to be ill. In response Jacob beat her with a rope. The consistory answered Anna's complaint with a finding that she had provoked her husband, after briefly considering jailing her for a night as an object lesson.

If church and state provided little relief in cases of domestic violence, neither did the intervention of family, friends, and neighbors always offer relief from male violence against wives, children, and servants. This was not because those outside violence-prone households were unaware of domestic brutality; people lived cheek by jowl in most early modern communities and knew of the goings-on in their locales. Instead, they seem to have taken low levels of domestic violence for granted or, like their twenty-first-century counterparts, preferred not to get involved. Such attitudes even marked the behavior of social elites. In seventeenth-century France when Marguerite de la Vergne sought the aid of her brother-in-law in drafting a separation petition from her abusive spouse, he told her to be patient with her husband, "since she had married him."[13] And in Spain, in the same period, the aristocratic Doña Teresa de Parejà of Lucene wrote to an abused relative: "Cousin, bear these beatings patiently since it is the Lord Our God who has given you the cross."[14]

If ready intervention by friends and family in domestic violence was not forthcoming, it is clear that there were certain thresholds of violence that, if exceeded, did produce action. In Scotland publicity seems to have been key; when the wife's screams attracted attention, or if she ran from the

[13] Quoted in Julie Hardwick, *The Practice of Patriarchy: Gender and Politics of Household and Authority in Early Modern France* (University Park: Pennsylvania State University Press, 1998), p. 86.

[14] Quoted in James Casey, "Household Disputes and the Law in Early Modern Andalusia" in John Bossy (ed.), *Disputes and Settlements: Law and Human Relations in the West* (Cambridge: Cambridge University Press, 1983), p. 196.

home, some sort of community act of intervention generally occurred. In Languedoc in southern France the use of a weapon against the wife, or infliction of severe bodily injury, seems to have rallied assistance to battered wives. Especially illustrative is the case from eighteenth-century England of Elizabeth Spinkes in which publicity and extreme violence provoked intervention. Her notoriously abusive husband locked her in an upstairs room, she broke her foot in a fall during an attempted escape, and when her husband rushed at her in the street where she lay, neighboring women blocked him. He reached his wife only when he threatened to have the women's husbands arrested under the traditional principle that held them accountable for their wives' behavior. Nevertheless, other neighboring women summoned a constable who rescued Spinkes from her husband; this abused wife subsequently sued successfully for separation and won £28 per year from her husband.

In similar circumstances, the community occasionally responded in cases of child abuse. When the escalating violence of a drunken father against his two young sons in Geneva in 1765 culminated in the father throwing the boys to their deaths from an upper-story window, authorities had to restrain a mob of neighbors prepared to lynch the parent.

The Genevan intervention, however, came too late. The reluctance of the law, the Church, and even friends, family, and neighbors to mount early intervention to aid victims of domestic violence, in combination with the power of the male head of household under law and custom, suggests that domestic violence must have been frequent in the early modern period. Precisely how frequent is the subject of a debate among historians that revolves around the development of the affective family.

The scholars who pioneered modern family history – Philippe Ariès, Edward Shorter, Lawrence Stone, and others – saw the early modern family as especially devoid of affection.[15] They placed the appearance of the affective western family only in the late seventeenth and eighteenth centuries. The family, for such scholars, was characterized by considerable violence, and Shorter commented: "As a practical matter, wife-beating was universal."[16] Stone also portrayed early modern aristocratic parents as cruel to their offspring. Other historians, however, advance a different vision of the early modern family. Alan Macfarlane, Linda Pollock, and others restore affection and sympathy to the early modern

---

[15] Philippe Ariès, *Centuries of Childhood: A Social History of Family Life*, translated by Robert Baldick (New York: Vintage Books, 1962); Edward Shorter, *The Making of the Modern Family* (New York: Basic Books, 1975); and Lawrence Stone, *The Family, Sex and Marriage in England, 1500–1800* (New York: Harper and Row, 1977).

[16] Edward Shorter, *A History of Women's Bodies* (Harmondsworth: Penguin Books, 1984), p. 5.

family; for these historians brutality was not the norm.[17] Neither view, of course, can be quantitatively proven; the wall of silence around the family was even higher half a millennium ago than it is today, and so much violence went unreported as to invalidate statistical analyses of its nonlethal forms. Nevertheless, certain quantitative indicators suggest a greater frequency of domestic violence in the early modern period than in our own time.

Criminal court records of capital offenses – largely homicide – can suggest the relative frequency of the most brutal form of domestic violence; it is difficult, as we have noted, to conceal homicide. In eighteenth-century samples from French appeals courts, like the Parlements of Paris and Toulouse and the Conseil Supérieur de Nîmes, capital crimes within the family constituted a large part of the tribunals' work: 23 percent of all capital offenses in the Paris jurisdiction; 26 percent in urban areas of the Toulouse court and 47.5 percent in its rural regions; and 45.5 percent of all capital cases in the Nîmes court. Within cases of domestic violence, abuse of a spouse constituted between a third and two-fifths of all serious domestic offenses, followed in frequency by violence against parents, children, other family members, and servants.

Other court records confirm the validity of the French experience. Court records of homicides in Essex in the period 1560–1709, for example, carry the same message. Fatal violence directed at family members consistently constituted about a quarter of the homicides judged in the county over a century and a half. In this Essex sample a third of the victims were spouses (with wives outnumbering husbands two to one) and half were children.

The Essex data showing a high rate of fatal violence against children can only suggest another aspect of domestic violence that must have been extensively underreported. Apprentices and servants seem to have figured in official records only when they were victims of the most extraordinary physical violence or of homicide. Both had few legal rights in early modern Europe and lacked the material means to carry charges to law. With this in mind, samples of cases involving adolescent servants and apprentices' charges against masters in quarter sessions in Northumberland, County Durham, and Newcastle upon Tyne from 1600 to 1800 are suggestive. Ten percent of all cases in this period concerned charges by these employees against masters. Understandably, most of the cases involved wage

---

[17] Alan Macfarlane, *The Family Life of Ralph Josselin, a Seventeenth-Century Clergyman: An Essay in Historical Anthropology* (Cambridge: Cambridge University Press, 1970) and *Marriage and Love in England, 1300–1840* (Oxford: Basil Blackwell, 1986); also Linda A. Pollock, *Forgotten Children: Parent-Child Relations from 1500 to 1900* (Cambridge: Cambridge University Press, 1983).

disputes, but a fifth of all servants' cases and a quarter of all apprentices' cases alleged physical violence by their employers.

Church court records, too, bear eloquent witness to the apparent frequency of domestic violence against wives. In the dioceses of Córdoba and Granada in Spain 47.5 percent of all the applications for separation of couples in the centuries from 1500 to 1800 allege physical violence by the husband against the wife, while another 25.9 percent charge the male head of household with insults and general cruelty. Other issues that might end domestic life, including neglect, dissipation of the wife's dowry, adultery, and venereal disease constituted slightly more than a quarter of the charges. Violence and incivility were the preeminent causes of separation requests, and women who had experienced such intense violence that they had fled to the shelter of the homes of their birth families filed two-thirds of separation requests.

Analyses of police, court, and ecclesiastical records reinforce the impression of a high rate of domestic violence. Records of requests for confinement under *lettres de cachet* in France and aldermanic orders in the Low Countries reveal large numbers of requests for incarceration of violent husbands. And the difficult process of securing incarceration suggests that the requests probably represent just a small part of the total domestic violence in this society. Requests had to be sustained by a record of growing violence and of the husband's mounting bad habits, like alcoholism, an unwillingness to work, or dissipation of family resources. Submitting a request was not a step taken lightly. Confinement deprived the family of its major wage earner, no matter how unreliable, and in seven of ten applications for confinement in Antwerp, Bruges, Brussels, and Ghent, the family unit included children. Consequently, women seem to have endured abuse for some while; the average length of an eighteenth-century marriage at the time of the request for confinement was twelve years in Paris and twelve and a half years in Antwerp. Domestic violence had probably marred many of those years.

Domestic violence, therefore, seems to have been quite common. It was not, however, constant in its frequency throughout our period. Most historians detect a subtle change in early modern Europeans' response to domestic violence at about the mid-eighteenth century. It was becoming increasingly unacceptable to many, the result of the evolving behavioral norms identified by Norbert Elias, and a rising number of cases in official and ecclesiastical records suggest not necessarily a real growth of domestic violence but simply a greater willingness of victims to prosecute it. Such evolution affected the social elite first, of course, but by the late eighteenth century the new norms of behavior had spread to their dependants. Cissie Fairchilds, for example, found servants reporting physical chastisement by their masters to police authorities for the first time by the mid-eighteenth century.[18]

Other evidence also points to evolving behavioral norms in regard to domestic violence that began with social elites in the sixteenth century and progressively affected groups of descending standing on the social ladder. By the mid-nineteenth century a new threshold of acceptable behavior increasingly prevailed even in the tenements of working-class London, where neighbors began to report wife beating to the police with frequency for the first time. Domestic violence had become unacceptable to the industrial-age poor of the metropolis.

Rape

Our inclusion of rape, the act of sexual intercourse between a man and a woman coerced by violence or its threat, in a chapter essentially devoted to acts of physical violence reflects the attitude of modern western Europe toward this crime. Through its laws and the criminal classifications established by such agencies as the United States Federal Bureau of Investigation, our society treats rape as a form of assault, an act of violence. But it is also a sexual offense, and it is this aspect of rape that both complicates its study and offers its students significant insights into the attitudes of the society that produces it.

The great problem in studying rape is its chronic underreporting. Modern criminologists concur that this crime, like domestic violence, is vastly underreported, and some of these scholars estimate that perhaps only one rape in twenty comes to the official attention of the authorities through a crime report. Modern women fail to report rapes for a variety of reasons, many of which, as we will see, would have been familiar to their early modern ancestors. Certainly many rape victims hesitate to report the crime because of a sense of shame at their victimization in this most personal of crimes. But the legal procedures for establishing the commission of this crime and securing conviction of those who perpetrate it are also deterrents. Criminal justice officials traditionally have been suspicious of the charge, assuming that the victim's dress or deportment somehow provoked the attack, and thus have sometimes forced the victim to establish her innocence in the attack she sustained. The laboratory and medical procedures necessary to establish the veracity of the victims' allegations, and the loss of personal privacy involved, have also deterred many women from lodging rape charges.

In the early modern period, an era considerably more violent than our

---

[18] Cissie Fairchilds, *Domestic Enemies: Servants and Their Masters in Old Regime France* (Baltimore: The Johns Hopkins University Press, 1984), p. 122–33.

own, the number of reported rapes was extraordinarily low by modern standards, even in major population centers. Tribunals in Amsterdam tried only two rapes in the seventeenth century and six in the eighteenth; Frankfurt judges heard but two such cases in the years from 1562 to 1695; Genevan magistrates judged forty accused rapists in the period from 1650 to 1815; and the Parlement of Paris, the French appeals court with the largest jurisdiction in the kingdom, ruled in but forty-nine rape cases in the period from 1540 to 1692, less than three per decade. Such a low incidence of reported rape strongly suggests widespread underreporting of the offense. But there are also tangible indicators of a much greater frequency of the crime, although we shall never be able to quantify its extent precisely. Notebooks kept by English justices of the peace, recording local events of which they had knowledge but which never came to trial to become part of the judicial record, reveal a much higher rate of rape than statistics based on court documents might imply. But even trial records themselves can suggest the extent of unreported sexual assault. To cite one example, legal proceedings revealed a serial rapist in the 1580s in the region of Hénin-Liétard in the Spanish Netherlands. The arrest and prosecution of François Sauwel for rape in 1589, perhaps accompanied by a *monitoire* read from the pulpits of Catholic churches and requiring listeners to report evidence relative to a crime on pain of excommunication, produced a number of denunciations of the accused for previously unreported rapes dating back nine years.

Through such records historians have been able to reconstruct the character of rape in this period. Early modern rapists victimized females who were most vulnerable to assault because of their physical isolation, economic dependency, or age. Women regularly worked outside of the home, as agricultural laborers or as domestic servants. In some areas, like northeastern England, women often did heavy agricultural work, like reaping and tending fields of turnips or potatoes, which frequently left them alone and thus vulnerable. Court records suggest the problems posed by such work. Those of the Northeast Assizes in England, for example, show that 43 percent of reported rapists assaulted victims walking to their agricultural labors across remote fields or moors. A further 22 percent of rapists found their victims working alone in remote fields, and one such assailant near the coastal town of Whitby taunted his victim: "No one but the ships will hear your screams."[19]

If the physical isolation of agricultural labor rendered women vulnerable to rape, their economic and social dependence also put many women

[19] Quoted in Anna Clark, *Women's Silence, Men's Violence: Sexual Assault in England, 1770–1845* (London: Pandora, 1987), p. 25.

at risk of sexual assault. Women in domestic service were frequent rape victims. Their residence in their masters' homes, often in crowded conditions, put them in close contact with male servants, young men of the family, and the master himself. Much sexual violence, therefore, began in the household or its vicinity. In Geneva, in the 1650 to 1815 period, 60 percent of rape victims were domestic servants, while fully 67 percent of the rape victims heard by the Old Bailey in late eighteenth-century London were in such employment. Much of this sexual assault in the household doubtlessly resulted from simple intimidation of dependent women by their employers or other male household members. But physical violence was not unusual; Thérèse Cavaillon, an eighteen-year-old servant in the household of the receiver of the *gabelle* in Berre, France, was the victim of a rape at knifepoint by her master's son in the mid-eighteenth century. And even when victim and assailant were not from the same household, records of reported rapes suggest that assailants had some prior acquaintanceship with their victims within an urban neighborhood or a country district, and that they employed that knowledge to pick the most vulnerable women.

Rapists victimized another sort of vulnerable female, too: young girls. Even though most early modern statutory and customary law recognized an extraordinarily young age of consent by modern standards, in some places twelve years of age, assailants seldom respected such legal conventions. A third of the forty-nine rapes documented in Florence in 1495–1515 involved girls aged between six and twelve years and 30 percent of accused rapists tried in Geneva in 1650–1815 had assaulted females aged ten or younger.

Another aspect of early modern life also contributed to the frequency of sexual violence. The youth groups that we will find in Chapter 5 so common in early modern Europe engaged in sexual assault. Those of eastern and southeastern France, Spain, and Italy, often composed of journeymen and artisans' sons, practiced a violent rite of passage: they demonstrated the virility that was such an important component of male honor in gang rapes. These rapes were brutal, indeed, as ten or fifteen young men might break into a woman's home to rape her there or to drag her into the street for the assault.

Gang rapes were not infrequent in the first years of our period. Indeed, one historian estimates that in Dijon, France, fully half of the young men of that city probably participated in such a rape at least once in their lives. And Dijon records show that 80 percent of the 125 reported sexual assaults in that city in the years 1436–86 were gang rapes. But only a fraction of these rapes incurred legal repercussions; even 300 years later, in Paris, the authorities seldom pursued the perpetrators of gang rapes.

They were the work of young men who often had important connections in the powerful guilds, and the very violence of the youths' actions must certainly have deterred witnesses from intervening in their assaults, or victims from reporting them after the fact. Consequently, most gang rapists did not bother even to disguise their faces when they committed such violence.

Also helping to assure the virtual legal immunity of gang rapists was the social status of their victims. Abandoned wives, women suspected of being mistresses to priests, servants kept as concubines, and even the daughters of poor day laborers were their victims. In short, these were women already on the margins of a society that equated respectability with social status. Few such women would have had the means to undertake costly legal action, and even if they had, much of public and judicial opinion would have regarded them, not their assailants, as guilty.

Early modern society regulated many rapes through infrajudicial measures that kept such matters out of the courts. At a most basic level, the father or other male guardian of a victim might seek to recoup part of his family's honor by an act of vengeance against the assailant. Alternatively, the attacker might avoid criminal charges by a payment to the woman and her male guardian. And, most bizarrely by our standards, a rape might also be concluded by marriage. Indeed, the matrimonial conclusion of rape drew on traditional canon law, which stipulated that rapists be forced to marry their victims or to provide them with a dowry sufficient to permit marriage to another. This sort of settlement was even possible after a trial. Thus Christophe Fleuvrey, aged fifteen or sixteen, raped a thirteen-year-old girl while he was drunk in May 1596. This resident of the Spanish Netherlands received a pardon of his conviction on the condition that he marry the girl or provide her with a dowry.

As important as these considerations were in limiting the number of reported early modern rapes, the greatest deterrents were issues very familiar to modern criminologists and law-enforcement personnel: the shame felt by the victim and the nature of the legal procedures applied in rape cases. The tragedy of rape is its effect on the victim in both physical and emotional pain. Forced penetration is agonizing in itself, as are the effects of physical violence. But the victim's greater pain is often emotional. And in early modern Europe, a society that defined female honor in terms of chastity and moral probity, rape was a heavy burden of shame for a woman to bear. It was one, indeed, that often precluded marriage, and understandably rape victims were loath to take charges to court and thus to call attention to themselves.

It was not only unwanted attention, however, that deterred potential plaintiffs from going to the authorities. The attitude conveyed in the words of the English jurist Sir Matthew Hale (1609–76) pervaded European jurisprudence regarding rape: "it must be remembered . . . that it is an accusation easy to be made and hard to be proved, and harder to be defended by the party accused, tho never so innocent."[20] Thus, in this age of primitive forensic medicine, judges were skeptical about the charge of rape, and conviction was not even certain in cases of rape discovered *in flagrante delicto*. Judges demanded evidence of resistance, reports of cries for help, and prompt reporting of the offense (in England, normally within five days of the crime), and even then they were not always convinced of the crime. Indeed, one eighteenth-century French jurist confidently wrote: "Whatever the superior strength of the man over the woman, nature has furnished the latter with innumerable resources for avoiding the triumph of her adversary."[21]

Courts also frequently inquired into the backgrounds of rape victims, and the statutes of much of early modern Europe forbade women of loose morals even to lodge rape charges. The authorities simply assumed that such victims would have encouraged their assailants. Judges regularly admitted testimony intended to impugn plaintiffs' reputations, and any hint of immorality led to the acquittal of the defendant. Indeed, it was virtually impossible for girls employed in taverns, women with friends among the soldiery, or females who strayed too far from home to get a fair hearing on rape charges. A Swedish case from 1702 may illustrate not only judicial suspicions of rape victims but also the real legal risks sometimes entailed in bringing a charge of sexual assault.

Anna was the wife of a soldier serving abroad in the Great Northern War. In her husband's absence she was living in Bråbo with another woman on an isolated farm, where a drunken soldier raped her. Anna offered little resistance, as the attack seems to have triggered an epileptic seizure. The soldier fled after the assault, and Anna's housemate returned to find her badly bruised from the attack. The housemate counseled Anna to do nothing, at least until she had determined if she was pregnant, because of the stigma attached to rape. Nevertheless, Anna told a neighbor, who notified the soldier's commanding officer of the attack. A military inquest failed to convict the man, and by the time the local court took up the case the soldier had been shipped to the battlefront and killed in Poland. The local court ignored Anna's injuries and prompt reporting of the assault, and found her guilty of voluntary adultery under an ordinance of 1698. Fortunately, a superior court overturned this conviction,

---

[20] Quoted in G. Geis, "Lord Hale, Witches, and Rape," *British Journal of Law and Society* 5 (1978), p. 26.

[21] J. F. Fournel, *Traité de l'adultère*, quoted in Georges Vigarello, *Histoire du viol (XVIᵉ–XXᵉ siècle)* (Paris: Editions du Seuil, 1998), p. 53.

but in the light of such a judicial approach we might reasonably doubt that the higher court would have reversed the verdict easily if its decision would have affected a living defendant.

Pregnancy resulting from rape impacted negatively on a victim's case, too, owing to the era's faulty medical knowledge. Early modern Europeans believed that a female's eggs were released only if the woman had an orgasm, and for male jurists of the period orgasm signified the woman's enjoyment of the sexual act. One seventeenth-century English legal scholar wrote: "Rape is the forcible ravishment of a woman, but if she conceive it is not rape, for she cannot conceive unless she consent."[22]

In the face of such social and procedural realities, many adult women refrained from pressing rape charges. This may account for the large percentage of rape cases involving children that we have noted. Rape of children outraged most early modern Europeans, so prosecution of such cases was much more likely and judges were inclined to find in favor of the plaintiff. Many adult rape victims seem to have preferred to claim attempted rape, rather than rape itself. The lesser charge avoided close inquiry into a woman's morals and the circumstances of the assault, and, most importantly, required no admission on the woman's part that she had had sexual intercourse. Often, too, the less serious charge could be tried in a local court that was cheaper and more accessible than the higher courts that had to hear the graver charge. And conviction on the lesser charge was far easier. In the late eighteenth-century Old Bailey juries found guilt in only 17 percent of rape cases, but Quarter Sessions in the London area in the same period convicted in 47 percent of attempted rape cases.

If a rape victim, regardless of these considerations, took her case of sexual assault to court as a charge of rape and secured conviction of her assailant, the treatment of convicted rapists reveals much about early modern society. In the Dutch Republic, England, France, and Germany, the law regarding rape was completing a slow evolution in the first century of our period. The medieval statutory law here focused chiefly on the abduction of young women by suitors rejected by the parents of the prospective brides. The abductors sought to force marriage upon the parents, who, like the law, assumed that sexual intercourse occurred when young women were seized from their homes. In the law of the period abduction represented theft of the father's property, his daughter, and the law aimed to protect fathers against such loss, as well as from the threat to the rest of their property posed by an unworthy marriage to a ne'er-do-well suitor.

[22] Nicholas Brady, *The Lawes Resolution of Women's Rights or the Lawes Provision for Women*, quoted in Nasife Bashar, "Rape in England between 1550 and 1700" in *The Sexual Dynamics of History: Men's Power, Women's Resistance* (London: Pluto Press, 1983), p. 36.

In the course of the sixteenth century the criminal law in most countries came to distinguish between rape and abduction, but elements of the older jurisprudence persisted in practice and sometimes even in statutes. Thus the *Constitutio Criminalis Carolina* of 1532, the law code of the Holy Roman Empire, retained an element of an older approach to rape based on definition of the crime as a property offense. The code specified death as the maximum penalty for the crime of rape – the same penalty, its author noted, as for robbery. Nevertheless, in Germany, as elsewhere, rape had become by the sixteenth century an offense separate and distinct in law from abduction, and it was a crime severely punished in principle. An English statute of 1576, a Florentine law of 1558, and French laws of the same period all echoed the *Carolina*'s provision of capital punishment as the maximum penalty for rape, just as death remained the penalty for abduction in many countries. But it seems quite clear that most jurists still regarded the latter offense, one against property and parental authority, as considerably graver than rape.

To be sure, courts weighed the circumstances of individual rape cases, considering such factors as the amount of force employed by the assailant; any breaking and entering of private property involved in the crime's commission; the age and marital and social status of the victim; and the social status of the accused. But, in practice, early modern tribunals decreed death rarely, applying it mainly in cases that shocked the public – those of rapists who assaulted children, killed their victims, or infected them with venereal disease. Penalties for those who raped adult women with no aggravating circumstances were often extraordinarily light, and perhaps reflected jurists' perpetuation of the old tradition that held that rape was theft. Thus, just as penalties in property crimes increased with the value of the property loss, the penalties in rape cases increased with the social status of the victim. Indeed, this was a practice recognized by the most prominent legal scholars of the age. Daniel Jousse, the foremost French commentator on criminal law in the eighteenth century, wrote: "Rape can be committed against all sorts of women . . . It is punishable with more or less rigor according to their rank." Then he cited examples: "There are cases in which one can condemn to breaking on the wheel for this crime, as when vile persons seize a girl of good character on the road and rape her," but "A master who abuses his servant ought to be condemned to pay damages and interest to her to serve as a dowry."[23] In sixteenth-century Germany fines, banishment, and the pillory were the usual penalties for rape of most women. In Geneva in the 1650 to 1815 period only 10 percent of convicted rapists, all assailants of children,

---

[23] Quoted in Vigarello, *Histoire du viol*, pp. 24–26.

received the death penalty, while the rest were given sentences of banishment, imprisonment, or fines. And in Renaissance Italy courts in cities such as Florence and Venice imposed fines structured according to the status of the victim extensively.

In a society that resorted easily to violence, rapists were undeterred by either ready prosecution or harsh penalties, and rape was undoubtedly widespread in early modern western Europe. Undesired pregnancies, the result of some rapes, contributed to the violence of this age when they ended in the killing of infants.

Newborn-child murder

The birth of a child, so often the source of unbounded joy to parents in a stable and materially secure household, can be a personal disaster in other circumstances. In the early modern period, largely bereft of today's social-welfare agencies, the birth of a child to married parents in dire economic straits could raise the prospect of material ruin. And unwed mothers, in this age that placed so much value on female chastity, found themselves stigmatized by their situation, without the means to care for their children because they were unemployable except in the most menial occupations or as prostitutes. We will see that to avoid such consequences of the birth of a child, many early modern Europeans were prepared to consider extreme measures.

The work of almost two generations of modern demographic historians has shown that unwanted pregnancies were numerous in early modern Europe, because preventing conception was seldom a possibility in the first place. For much of our period contraceptive measures were little understood, and for most of the population were limited to *coitus interruptus*. As a result, early modern western Europe experienced a fertility rate three or four times that of the early twenty-first century, and many women had to deal with the consequences of pregnancies they were unable to prevent.

Especially difficult was the problem of conceptions outside of marriage, and modern historical scholarship suggests that their rate was quite high almost everywhere. Some women, especially domestic servants, as we have seen, were coerced into sexual relations with their employers, or other males of the household. Many more women had consensual sex with young men who had made promises of marriage to them. Contributing to the number of extramarital conceptions was a widespread misunderstanding about when the conjugal relations of married life might begin. Many people believed – incorrectly – that such relations might begin at the time of betrothal, instead of after the actual marriage.

In the majority of cases of premarital conceptions, simple arrangements seem to have resolved the situation of most women. Employers sometimes regularized their servants' situations by finding a marital partner for the women or by providing them with a dowry to facilitate marriage. Many men hastened to marry the young women they had impregnated, conduct attested to by the intervals of only a few months between the entries on parish registers of their marriages and the births of their first children. Researchers in judicial records have also found that the law sometimes propelled such hasty marriages, either through charges of rape or, in some parts of Europe, the charges of the father of a minor daughter that his "property" rights had been violated by the young man's "trespass and damage." Only when a man refused to marry the woman carrying his child did that woman confront the limited range of options open to those in such circumstances in our period.

Early modern ecclesiastical and temporal authorities universally condemned abortion, today a controversial but legal procedure (before a specified number of weeks) in much of modern western Europe, and midwives in England had to swear an oath not to use their skills to terminate pregnancies. Nevertheless, many early modern women knew of primitive abortive techniques, and information circulated among them about strange concoctions reputed to be abortifacients. Most historians agree, however, that successful abortions seem to have been relatively rare. Indeed, there were many deterrents to such termination of pregnancies. Abortion generally required a pregnant woman to share the secret of her condition with another, either a woman skilled in birthing and abortive techniques or someone to supply the knowledge and ingredients for preparing an alleged abortifacient. Moreover, whatever method a woman chose to try to end her pregnancy, there were risks: sepsis induced by primitive procedures or outright poisoning by potions said to induce miscarriage. The risks of these measures, in combination with their often substantial costs, probably deterred most women from attempting to terminate their pregnancies.

Carrying the pregnancy to term and offering the infant for adoption was not a viable option for early modern women as it is for their modern counterparts, either. Culturally, early modern Europeans put a great deal of value on blood lineage for the inheritance of property, and few of them, therefore, wished to adopt. Nevertheless, many poor women abandoned their newborns on the steps of churches, or in other public places where they would be found readily, in the hope that they might be cared for by others. Indeed, by the mid-seventeenth century, especially under the impulse of the work of Saint Vincent de Paul, foundling hospitals were appearing in major cities and were receiving increasing numbers of infants, even though their charges experienced very high mortality rates. Average annual admissions to the Paris foundling hospital rose from 305 in the 1640–49 period to 1,675 in 1710–19. But notwithstanding such growing numbers of admissions, relatively few unmarried women availed themselves of these institutions. Unwed mothers risked detection and their honor in delivering children to them.

In the absence of other options, most women with unwanted pregnancies carried them to term, and the most desperate sometimes resorted to murder of their newborns. Such killing has been widely practiced throughout history as a way of dealing with unwanted children. We have chosen to call this act (termed "neonaticide" in law) "newborn-child murder" in lieu of "infanticide," another term widely applied to this crime; the latter term is imprecise because it has been used to refer to the murder of children of any age, even as old as nine years.

For married women newborn-child murder could be relatively easy. No one questioned their condition; the high rate of early modern fertility made frequent confinements common for early modern married women. And the poor nutrition of the age, the lack of modern prenatal care, and the primitive state of medicine led to a rate of infant mortality so high that as many as half of early modern infants perished before the age of ten. So an infant might be strangled to death at birth, and the curiosity of neighbors about the newborn's fate could be satisfied easily with the explanation that the baby had been stillborn. Parents might also intentionally smother an infant during the first days or weeks of life and plausibly explain to those who inquired about their dead child that the infant had suffocated under a blanket as a result of the common early modern practice of placing newborns in bed between their parents. And intentional neglect, like denial of food, could be concealed by claiming some sort of sickness that had killed the child. Few would have questioned yet another infant mortality within a family in any case, and the forensic medicine of the age was unequal to providing reliable determinations of fact in such cases.

The circumstances of pregnant unmarried women were far more difficult. Neighbors closely monitored the activities of young unmarried women, always noting with whom they kept company, and were quick to observe any physical changes, even when artfully concealed under the billowing skirts of the age. A woman pregnant out of wedlock must constantly have feared detection of her condition by nosy friends and neighbors. One whose family had both sympathy for her situation and the resources to aid her, of course, could put her beyond such prying. She might be shipped off to an urban "lying-in" institution operating in a shadowy existence, or go to visit country relatives to deliver her child, who might then be given up to a foundling hospital or to the care of servants or poor relations. If, however, the woman was poor and had no such support, she was in desperate straits. If she was a servant, as many of these women seem to have been, detection of her condition usually meant dismissal, in part because pregnancy put the master in some legal danger. In parts of Germany, for example, the law required a master to inquire into suspected pregnancies among his employees, and he could be fined if one of them murdered her newborn infant. Certainly, too, few householders wanted a woman pregnant with an illegitimate child under their roofs, given community mores. And since no one else wanted a "fallen" woman with an illegitimate child in his or her employ, reemployment elsewhere was very difficult. Nor was marriage a ready option, except in areas of extreme labor shortage. Indeed, community attitudes could be positively hostile to women who had violated the standards of chaste behavior associated with female honor. Hostility especially originated in locals' fear of area poor-relief funds being expended on supporting illegitimate children, and in the laws in many parts of Europe that forbade sheltering unwed mothers.

A case originating in Württemburg in 1730 provides an extreme example of the lot of many unwed mothers. Anna Schneider, aged twenty-three, was marginalized in her community because of her poverty and lack of any family support. Her mother had died when Anne was a child and her father was an impoverished day laborer. She was usually employed as a tavern maid and had apparently delivered an illegitimate child six or seven years earlier. But in 1730 she found herself pregnant again, ill, and consequently without work. She begged for a time, but when contractions began she sought aid at a local farm. There her waters broke in front of several witnesses, who promptly loaded her on a litter, carried her to the middle of an isolated field, and abandoned her. She was found the next day, ill and frightened, with her dead infant near by. Taken into criminal custody, she deposed that she had strangled the newborn, and local authorities tried and executed her for the baby's murder.

Anna Schneider's experience casts in sharp relief the desperate situation of poor and unwed mothers in the early modern period. To avoid such degradation and hostility, many women sought to conceal their conditions, deliver their infants alone, kill the babies and hide their remains, then resume their daily routines as quickly as possible. Laws forbidding the killing of newborns date back to the fourth century A. D. in western Europe, but prosecution under such statutes seems to have been rare before the sixteenth century. In that century a number of developments seem to have hardened official and popular attitudes toward the crime and to have produced everywhere in Europe widespread prosecution of newborn-child killers that endured into the eighteenth century.

This was the age of the Protestant and Catholic Reformations and was marked by heightened sensibilities regarding all forms of immorality that were quickly made manifest in statutory form. Killing of the newborn was the murder of God-given children and the crime joined all sorts of behavior that increasingly came under the regulation of the state. Sixteenth-century statutes also controlled more closely drinking, gaming, Sabbath violations, blasphemy, and dress.

This was also an age of sweeping economic change, epitomized by the enclosure movement in England, and sixteenth-century population growth that burdened many societies with increasing numbers of poor. The result was a heightened fear not only of the criminogenic potential of beggars and "masterless" men and women, but also of the possible burden of their support on local charitable resources. Bastardy thus also came under increasing scrutiny by officials who sought either to prevent the problem in the first place or to force fathers to support their offspring.

Finally, our period was also one of increasing state power. As the agencies of the state sought to solidify households for tax purposes and to codify inheritance laws, nothing was more disruptive of these efforts than illegitimate children who could pose a claim on property. The promulgation and enforcement of new statutes aimed at newborn-child murder indicated state recognition of the fact that simple concerns about preserving property from the claims of illegitimate offspring also contributed to the killing of infants.

Taken together, these developments produced a remarkably uniform pan-European criminal law response to newborn-child murder in the sixteenth and seventeenth centuries. Almost everywhere new statutes appeared addressing in very similar terms both this crime and some of the issues raised by illegitimacy. These laws usually required that women pregnant out of wedlock register their condition with civil authorities. This requirement forced the women to name the fathers of their babies in an attempt to solve the problem of child support while alerting the local authorities to the possibility of a later newborn-child murder. But most importantly, these statutes modified the criminal law dealing with newborn-child murder so as to address the problems of conviction for this crime under traditional law. Because the crime was generally one without witnesses, and often had to be prosecuted with only circumstantial evidence, these statutes declared that the law would assume the guilt of an unwed mother whose child died if she had concealed her pregnancy by not registering her condition, telling friends and family of it, or having assistance at the birth. The first law of this sort, establishing a presumption of guilt that essentially forced the woman to prove her innocence, seems to have been that adopted in Bamberg, Germany, in 1507. The essential aspects of this law reappeared in the German *Constitutio Criminalis Carolina* of 1532 and in statutes promulgated in Denmark, the Dutch Republic, England, France, most of the German states, Lithuania, Russia, Scotland, and Sweden in the sixteenth and seventeenth centuries.

Such statutes at first let loose an avalanche of prosecutions for newborn-child murder, and some historians of criminal justice write of a "craze" of prosecutions of this offense in some of the same terms in which they write of the witchcraft "craze" of the sixteenth and seventeenth centuries. Certainly, with the new statutes facilitating prosecution of a crime regarded as murder in western law for more than a millennium, prosecutions grew rapidly in number. With promulgation of the French statute of 1556, prosecutions of newborn child murders rose in the Parlement of Burgundy from 0.5 percent of all cases in 1583–92 to 4.4 percent in 1646–49, 5.9 percent in 1668–71, and 8.1 percent in 1687–1700. In Württemburg enactment of that state's statute of 1658 inflated the number of cases of newborn-child murder from 14 in the entire sixteenth century and 58 cases in the period from 1600 to 1659 to 127 cases in 1660–1700. Such an increase in prosecution occurred almost everywhere, and in western Europe in the sixteenth and seventeenth centuries courts executed more women for newborn-child murder than for any other offense save witchcraft. Indeed, some tribunals executed more women for killing newborn infants than for witchcraft. The Parlement of Paris executed 625 women for this offense in 1565–1690 but only 57 women for witchcraft. And Genevan judges executed 25 of 31 accused newborn-child murderers, but only 19 of 122 accused witches in 1595–1712.

From the records of these trials, historians have learnt a great deal about the killers of newborn infants. They were overwhelmingly women, the mothers of the infants acting alone or occasionally with the assistance of a family member. They were also young, generally between the ages of twenty and thirty, and unmarried. The defendants tried by the Parlement of Paris for newborn-child murder between 1569 and 1608 are typical: 63 percent of these women were unmarried, 18 percent were young widows, and 13 percent were married women with absentee husbands. In addition, the women who committed this crime seem to have been the poorest in society. Servants predominated among the accused almost everywhere, and three-quarters of the alleged newborn-child killers tried in the Sussex Assizes in the 1660–1800 period were farm or household servants. Many of these women had been in service for a long time, had always had good character references, and sought through their crime to preserve the semblance of that respectability. Many of the women charged with the crime also seem to have been without relatives to provide them with material or emotional support. Their economic and social positions in early modern society are also evident in their frequent illiteracy and their ignorance of their bodily functions; many claimed not to have even realized they were pregnant until they delivered.

Despite our employment of quantitative data to describe samples of women who killed their children, newborn-child murder, like rape and domestic violence, is a crime that must remain imprecisely known to historians because it, too, seems to have been underreported. Keith Wrightson concluded from his reconstruction of the population and society of Terling in Essex, England, that perhaps as many as two and a half times as many newborn-child murders occurred there as were reported.[24] Material evidence bears up the validity of the conclusion that this offense was underreported. Many urban victims of newborn-child murder ended up in city drains, and work in Rennes, France, reconstructing such conduits after a fire in 1721, revealed the skeletal remains of eighty infants.

The penalty for newborn-child murder was uniformly death under sixteenth- and seventeenth-century statutes: early modern Europeans viewed this offense as a particularly heinous crime. In the Spanish Netherlands until the mid-seventeenth century, for example, conviction for witchcraft accompanied that for newborn-child murder; the "unnatural" character of the crime prompted judges to assume that only women in league with the devil could have committed it. Thus, punishments here assumed some of the gruesome forms reserved chiefly for witches. In Liège judges ordered the drowning of convicted killers of infants; elsewhere in the Spanish Netherlands courts ordered the impaling, strangling, or beheading of such persons. Punishments displayed similar brutality in other parts of Europe, even without the added charge of witchcraft. Burning or impaling might be employed under the *Carolina*. Even by the eighteenth century only England, France, and Geneva were moving away from such brutal forms of capital punishment for newborn-child murder.

However, historians do discern an evolution in Europeans' view of newborn-child murder beginning as early as the first decades of the seventeenth century. One consideration propelling changes in judicial attitudes toward this crime was a growing awareness of the inadequacies of forensic medicine. Conviction rested on proof that the infant victim had been born alive, only to be murdered by the mother. Judges therefore

[24] Keith Wrightson, "Infanticide in Earlier Seventeenth-Century England," *Local Population Studies* 15 (1975), p. 19.

called on midwives and physicians to identify evidence that a victim had been delivered at the full term of a pregnancy and had not been stillborn. They based their conclusions on such dubious evidence as the position of the infant's hands; if the fists were clenched, early modern medical professionals averred, the baby had been stillborn. They also examined tiny corpses for evidence of violent acts that might have terminated life, but they proved generally incapable of distinguishing between the effects of intentional violence and the results of birthing accidents that commonly occurred when women attempted to deliver without assistance. And physicians performed a primitive test on the lungs of victims to determine if they had ever drawn breath. The lungs were put in a vessel of water; if they floated, physicians assumed that the lungs had received air, that the victim, therefore, had been born alive, and that the probability of murder was quite high. But medical authorities as early as Galen in the second century A. D. had observed aspects of fetal lung development that contra-indicated such conclusions, and even as the test came into general use in the late seventeenth century many doubted its validity. European tribunals thus increasingly demanded proof of the commission of a crime, refusing simply to assume guilt. As early as 1619, judges of the Parlement of Paris eschewed the death penalty in these cases unless there was evidence of criminal violence on the corpse. Such standards of proof inevitably reduced the numbers of convictions.

Women, moreover, began to advance defenses increasingly acceptable to judges and juries. One that was particularly effective, in England at least, was evidence that a pregnant woman, even while concealing her condition, had made preparations anticipating a live birth. Such evidence as the preparation of a layette convinced juries of a defendant's lack of intent to kill her newborn. Other women mounted successful defenses based on their claim that the infant's death resulted from their temporary insanity induced by the pain of childbirth. And many women advanced plausible arguments that their newborns perished as a result of delivery accidents due to their lack of experience in the birthing process.

Judges' and juries' growing acceptance of such defenses was the result of both their mounting doubts about the validity of medical evidence and the evolution of early modern attitudes toward punishment in general and this crime in particular. We have already noted an increasing revulsion among some western Europeans at the brutality of their criminal law as early as the late seventeenth century. For some, state violence appeared an inappropriate response to criminal violence, and in the eighteenth century the Enlightenment progressively eroded the religious and moral attitudes that had criminalized extramarital sex and that partially underlay prosecution of child killings. A religious approach to the latter crime increasingly gave way to one founded on analysis of the motive, intent, character, and psychology of the mother.

Most importantly, however, application of the law reflected such attitudinal changes, even while newborn-child murder has remained a crime. Judicial consideration of the emotional state of the accused seems evident in many individual cases, like that of Marie Hanotte of Sprimont in the Spanish Netherlands, who won acquittal in 1702. This young domestic servant testified that her employer dismissed her and expelled her from his household as she began her labor, that she delivered a stillborn child and baptized the infant with her spittle, and that she then buried the tiny corpse eventually discovered by the authorities. Historians have found changed attitudes widely evident in court records. The English experience is especially well documented. In Surrey, from 1722 to 1802, all accused killers of newborns were either discharged by grand juries or found not guilty by trial juries. And growing judicial leniency toward this crime seems to have been common elsewhere, too. Württemburg courts, which executed fifteen women in the three decades prior to 1748, killed but three in the four decades from 1748 to 1787.

While courts adopted an approach to newborn-child murder that still informs western legal practice, other developments in the late eighteenth and early nineteenth centuries combined to diminish the incidence of this crime. The decriminalization of extramarital sexual relations, and the emerging attitude on the part of state authorities, especially evident in Germany, that able-bodied citizens, bastards or not, increased the national prosperity progressively diminished the stigma attached to pregnancy out of wedlock. At the same time, the dissemination of techniques of contraception limited the numbers of unwanted children, while the opening of foundling homes and other institutions provided some refuge for those who were born. Thus the frequency of newborn-child murder seems to have begun to fall considerably as our period drew to a close, making this crime one that was characteristic of the early modern era rather than its successor.

The prevalence of violence in various aspects of interpersonal relations that we have explored suggests that early modern Europe was indeed a violent place, one that makes our modern society appear relatively safe by comparison. The household, the inn, the workplace, and the street all produced interpersonal violence half a millennium ago. In Chapter 5 we will find that ritualized group violence, too, was a feature of the early modern period.

FURTHER READING

Alloza, Angel J, "Crime and Social Change in Eighteenth-Century Madrid," *International Association for the History of Crime and Criminal Justice Bulletin* no. 19 (1994), pp. 7–19.

Bashar, Nasife, "Rape in England between 1500 and 1700" in *The Sexual Dynamics of History: Men's Power, Women's Resistance* (London: Pluto Press, 1983), pp. 28–42.

Beattie, J. M., *Crime and the Courts in England, 1660–1800* (Princeton: Princeton University Press, 1985).

Brownmiller, Susan, *Against Our Will: Men, Women, and Rape* (New York: Simon and Schuster, 1975).

Cameron, Ian, *Crime and Repression in the Auvergne and the Guyenne, 1720–1790* (Cambridge: Cambridge University Press, 1981).

Casey, James, "Household Disputes in Early Modern Andalusia" in John Bossy (ed.), *Disputes and Settlements: Law and Human Relations in the West* (Cambridge: Cambridge University Press, 1983), pp. 189–217.

Castan, Nicole, *Les criminels de Languedoc: Les exigencies d'ordre et les voies du ressentiment dans une société pré-révolutionnaire (1750–1790)* (Toulouse: Association des publications de l'Université de Toulouse-Le Mirail, 1980).

Castan, Yves, *Honnêteté et relations sociales en Languedoc, 1715–1780* (Paris: Plon, 1974).

Clark, Anna, "Humanity in Justice: Wifebeating and the Law in the Eighteenth and Nineteenth Centuries" in Carol Smart (ed.), *Regulating Womanhood: Historical Essays on Marriage, Motherhood and Sexuality* (London: Routledge, 1992), pp. 187–205.

Cockburn, J. S., "Patterns of Violence in English Society: Homicide in Kent, 1560–1985," *Past and Present* 130 (1991), pp. 70–106.

Cohen, Elizabeth S., "Honor and Gender in the Streets of Early Modern Rome," *Journal of Interdisciplinary History* 12 (1972), pp. 597–625.

Cohen, Thomas V., "The Lay Liturgy of Affront in Sixteenth-Century Italy," *Journal of Social History* 25 (1992), pp. 857–77.

Dobash, Russell P. and Dobash, R. Emerson, "Community Response to Violence against Wives: Charivari, Abstract Justice and Patriarchy," *Social Problems* 28 (1981), pp. 563–81.

Dolan, Frances, *Dangerous Familiars: Representations of Domestic Crime in England, 1550–1700* (Ithaca: Cornell University Press, 1994).

Emsley, Clive and Knafla, Louis A. (eds.), *Crime History and Histories of Crime: Studies in the Historiography of Crime and Criminal Justice in Modern History* (Westport, CT: Greenwood Press, 1996).

Fairchilds, Cissie, *Domestic Enemies: Servants and their Masters in Old Regime France* (Baltimore: The Johns Hopkins University Press, 1984).

Farge, Arlette, *Fragile Lives: Violence, Power and Solidarity in Eighteenth-Century Paris*, translated by Carol Shelton (Cambridge, MA: Harvard University Press, 1993).

Farr, James R., *Authority and Sexuality in Early Modern Burgundy (1550–1730)* (Oxford: Oxford University Press, 1995).

Ferraro, Joanne M., "The Power to Decide: Battered Wives in Early Modern Florence," *Renaissance Quarterly* 48 (1985), pp. 492–512.

Fletcher, Anthony, *Gender, Sex and Subordination in England, 1500–1700* (New Haven: Yale University Press, 1995).

Forbes, Thomas R., "Deadly Parents: Child Homicide in Eighteenth- and Nineteenth-Century England," *Journal of the History of Medicine and Allied Sciences* 41 (1986), pp. 175–99.

Franke, Herman, "Violent Crime in the Netherlands: A Historical-Sociological Analysis," *Crime, Law and Social Change* 21 (1994), pp. 73–100.

Garrioch, David, "Verbal Insults in Eighteenth-Century Paris" in Peter Burke and Roy Porter (eds.), *The Social History of Language* (Cambridge: Cambridge University Press, 1987), pp. 104–19.

Gaskell, Malcolm, *Crime and Mentalities in Early Modern England* (Cambridge: Cambridge University Press, 2000).

Greenshields, Malcolm, *An Economy of Violence in Early Modern France: Crime and Justice in the Haute Auvergne, 1587–1664* (University Park: Pennsylvania State University Press, 1994).

Heijden, Manon van der, "Women as Victims of Sexual and Domestic Violence in Seventeenth-Century Holland: Criminal Cases of Rape, Incest, and Maltreatment in Rotterdam and Delft," *Journal of Social History* 33 (2000), pp. 623–44.

Hoffer, Peter C. and Hull, N. E. H., *Murdering Mothers: Infanticide in England and New England, 1558–1803* (New York: New York University Press, 1981).

Jackson, Mark, *New-Born Child Murder: Women, Illegitimacy and the Courts in Eighteenth-Century England* (Manchester: Manchester University Press, 1996).

Jansson, Arne, *From Swords to Sorrow: Homicide and Suicide in Early Modern Stockholm* (Stockholm: Almqvist and Wiksell, 1998).

Johansen, Jens Chr. V., "Falster and Elsinore, 1680–1705: A Comparative Study of Rural and Urban Crime," *Social History* 15 (1990), pp. 97–109.

Johnson, Eric A. and Monkkonen, Eric H. (eds.), *The Civilization of Crime: Violence in Town and Country since the Middle Ages* (Urbana: University of Illinois Press, 1996).

Kloek, Els, "Criminality and Gender in Leiden's *Confessieboeken*, 1678–1794," *Criminal Justice History* 11 (1990), pp. 1–29.

Leboutte, René, "Offense Against Family Order: Infanticide in Belgium from the Fifteenth through the Early Twentieth Centuries," *Journal of the History of Sexuality* 2 (1991), pp. 159–85.

Lis, Catharina and Soly, Hugo, *Disordered Lives: Eighteenth-Century Families and their Unruly Relatives*, translated by Alexander Brown (Cambridge: Polity Press, 1996).

Malcolmson, R. W., "Infanticide in the Eighteenth Century" in J. S. Cockburn (ed.), *Crime in England, 1550–1800* (Princeton: Princeton University Press, 1977), pp. 187–209.

Osterberg, Eva, "Violence among Peasants: Comparative Perspectives on Sixteenth- and Seventeenth-Century Sweden" in Göran Rystad (ed.), *Europe and Scandinavia: Aspects of the Process of Integration in the Seventeenth Century* (Lund: Scandinavian University Books, 1983), pp. 257–75.

and Lindström, Dag, *Crime and Social Control in Early Modern Swedish Towns* (Upsala: Acta Universitatis Upsaliensis; distributed by Almqvist and Wiksell International, 1988).

Perry, Mary Elizabeth, *Crime and Society in Early Modern Seville* (Hanover, NH: University Press of New England, 1980).

Gender and Disorder in Early Modern Seville (Princeton: Princeton University Press, 1990).

Phillips, Roderick, *Putting Asunder: A History of Divorce in Western Society* (Cambridge: Cambridge University Press, 1988).

Porter, Roy, "Rape – Does it Have a History?" in Sylvana Tomaselli and Roy Porter (eds.), *Rape* (Oxford: Basil Blackwell, 1986), pp. 216–36.

Roper, Lyndal, *The Holy Household: Women and Morals in Reformation Augsburg* (Oxford: Oxford University Press, 1989).

"Will and Honour: Sex, Words and Power in Criminal Trials," *Radical History Review* 43 (1989), pp. 45–71.

Rousseaux, Xavier, "Crime, Justice, and Society in Medieval and Early Modern Times: Thirty Years of Crime and Criminal Justice History: A Tribute to Herman Diederiks," *Crime, histoire et sociétés/Crime, History and Societies* 1 (1997), pp. 87–118.

"Criminality and Criminal Justice History in Europe, 1250–1850: A Select Bibliography," *Criminal Justice History* 14 (1993), pp. 159–81.

Rublack, Ulinka, *The Crimes of Women in Early Modern Germany* (Oxford: Oxford University Press, 1999).

Ruff, Julius R., *Crime, Justice and Public Order in Eighteenth-Century France: The Sénéchaussées of Libourne and Bazas, 1696–1789* (London: Croom Helm, 1984).

Ruggiero, Guido, *The Boundaries of Eros: Sex Crime and Sexuality in Renaissance Venice* (Oxford: Oxford University Press, 1985).

Violence in Early Renaissance Venice (New Brunswick, NJ: Rutgers University Press, 1980).

Sharpe, James A., *Crime in Early Modern England, 1550–1750*, 2nd ed. (London: Longman Publishing, 1999).

Defamation and Sexual Slander in Early Modern England: The Church Courts at York. York: Bothwick Papers, no. 58, n.d.

"Domestic Homicide in Early Modern England," *The History Journal* 24 (1981), pp. 89–108.

Soman, Alfred, "Anatomy of an Infanticide Trial: The Case of Jeanne Bartonnet (1742)" in Michael Wolfe (ed.), *Changing Identities in Early Modern France* (Durham: Duke University Press, 1997), pp. 248–72.

Spierenburg, Pieter, "Faces of Violence: Homicide Trends and Cultural Meanings: Amsterdam, 1431–1816," *Journal of Social History* 27 (1994), pp. 701–16.

"How Violent Were Women? Court Cases in Amsterdam. 1650–1810," *Crime, histoire et sociétés/Crime, History and Societies* 1 (1997), pp. 9–28.

"Knife Fighting and Popular Codes of Honor in Early Modern Amsterdam" in Pieter Spierenburg (ed.), *Men and Violence: Gender, Honor, and Rituals in Modern Europe and America* (Columbus: Ohio State University Press, 1998), pp. 103–27.

Strocchia, Sharon T., "Gender and the Rites of Honour in Italian Cities" in Judith C. Brown and Robert C. Davis (eds.), *Gender and Society in Renaissance Italy* (London: Longman Publishers, 1998), pp. 39–60.

Symonds, Deborah A., *Weep Not for Me: Women, Ballads, and Infanticide in Early Modern Scotland* (University Park: The Pennsylvania State University Press, 1997).

Trexler, Richard C., "Infanticide in Florence: New Sources and Results" in Richard C. Trexler (ed.), *Dependence in Context in Renaissance Florence* (Binghamton, NY: Medieval and Renaissance Texts and Studies, 1994), pp. 203–24.

Vigarello, Georges, *Histoire du viol, XVIe–XXe siècles* (Paris: Editions du Seuil, 1998).

Wrightson, Keith, "Infanticide in Earlier Seventeenth-Century England," *Local Population Studies* 15 (1975), pp. 10–22.

"Infanticide in European History," *Criminal Justice History* 3 (1982), pp. 1–20.

5   Ritual group violence

"Actions speak louder than words" is an old saying with which we are all familiar. It conveys a truism of interpersonal relations, but it also expresses much more; it reminds us that our behavior is a form of nonverbal communication that often reveals much about us as individuals and about the cultural forces that shape us. Collective behavior can reveal much about the society that produces it, too. Recognizing this, historians and cultural anthropologists in recent years have concerned themselves increasingly with what we will call ritual group behavior.

Ritual behavior consists of all those acts that are repeated, as almost instinctual conduct, and that thus reflect the learnt behavior of a society. Rituals are highly symbolic and express religious belief, political ideology, societal norms, and other aspects of the life of a given culture. In the present chapter we will examine the rituals of early modern society especially associated with violence, and we will search for the rituals of violence in the behavior of early modern youth groups and the festive life of the period. We will find that, while ritual violence inflicted physical injury on its victims, it often did so in pursuit of goals beyond the simple imposition of pain. Ritual violence enforced behavioral standards by harming or degrading those who transgressed them, and at times it tested society's limits of tolerance, too.

Youth groups

Contrary to the image of the adolescent lovers in Shakespeare's *Romeo and Juliet*, most early modern Europeans seldom married at a young age. Rather, they seem to have married in their middle to late twenties: demographic samples from sixteenth- and seventeenth-century England, for example, have placed the average age of first marriage for males in some regions at as late as twenty-eight years. Marriage, after all, meant establishing a new household, and that required the accumulation of at least a small amount of wealth, or the realization of an inheritance. When economic conditions worsened and amassing such resources became harder,

average age at first marriage rose; this seems to have occurred, for
example, in much of eighteenth-century France. Thus for many males
"youth," the period between puberty and marriage, could be as long as a
decade and a half. Young men therefore forged their identities in this
period less as heads of young households than as members of the youth
groups of their towns and villages, or their neighborhoods in cities. These
groups, found more or less formally organized in much of western Europe
in our period, had a number of names, depending on local custom, and
were often headed by elected leaders called "abbots" in order to mock
ecclesiastical hierarchy. We will employ the name applied to them in
southern France, "youth abbeys."[1]

The abbeys derived their identity from certain functions they performed within their communities, many of which added to the violent
tenor of life. Frequently led by the sons of the local social elite, these
groups' prime function was to monitor local morals and marriages. Young
men were vitally interested in any events that might affect the local availability of marriageable young women, and they were prepared to exact a
rough justice upon matches of which they disapproved. They had symbolic jurisdiction of village youth and placed May bushes or other
symbols before the homes of young women who had achieved matrimonial age to indicate their availability and character. They also presumed to
object to some marriages that these women might undertake. They
frowned, for example, on marriage to an outsider because such an act
diminished the local pool of marriageable women. They especially disapproved of marriages between spouses of unequal ages, particularly of
older widowers to young women who might have wed a male of their own
local age cohort. Their opposition could be symbolic, like placing barriers
before the couple at the church, lowering them peacefully only upon a
small payment from the groom or the bride's father. Or it could take the
more boisterous form of a noisy charivari.

The charivari, known as the *mattinata* in many parts of Italy, the *zabra-
mari* in Piedmont, the *vito* in Andalusia, and "rough music" in England,
was a performance of coarse music accompanied by the beating of pots
and pans (the Dutch name, *ketelmusik*, indicates this essential aspect of
the charivari). Young men sometimes added to this cacophony by pulling
the fur of cats, and abusing these creatures in other ways, too, to produce
loud squalling. Indeed, in much of Germany the charivari was known as
Katzenmusik ("cat music") and in Burgundy as *faire le chat* ("to do the
cat"). The youths performed the charivari under a couple's window on

---

[1] Natalie Z. Davis, "The Reasons of Misrule" in *Society and Culture in Early Modern France:
Eight Essays* (Stanford: Stanford University Press, 1975), pp. 97–123.

the wedding night, and perhaps on subsequent nights as well. Often the event was threatening, too, as the youths frequently carried guns and discharged the weapons both into the air and at the bridal couple's residence. By their exercise of such force, the young men asserted their jurisdiction over such matters and reminded their victims of their vulnerability. Nevertheless, the victims were expected to respond with good humor. A gift to the youths of money or refreshments from the couple or their families generally ended the noise, but it was not uncommon for a humiliated bridegroom angrily to open fire on his harassers.

Youth abbeys might also stage similar rites to rebuke a husband who deviated from stereotypical male behavior by accepting domination by his wife. The youths paraded an impersonator of the husband, his effigy, or sometimes the man himself, through town, mounted backwards on an ass, a horse, or a pole (called a "stang" in England), symbolizing his irregular behavior. Frequently they attached to his head the horns traditionally associated with the cuckold, that is, the husband of an unfaithful wife. They accompanied the procession with rough music and sometimes beat the man or effigy with sticks or, in England, with a skimmington, a tool used by women to skim cream. This act was known in France as the *assouade* and in England as "riding the skimmington" or a "stang-ride." The symbolism of all this highlighted the perceived abnormality of the browbeaten husband in a male-dominated society by reversing natural relationships. Sometimes, too, in England, domineering wives might be ducked by youths in a local pond. Everywhere the young men often carried guns or other weapons that forced the cooperation of their victims in their own humiliation.

Violations of community morals could produce such popular explosions of youthful activity as well. Youths seem seldom to have penalized premarital sex between their peers, but other violations of communal norms elicited action, especially on festive occasions when there were ready audiences. In a tradition common in the Languedoc region of France and in Italy, youths forced adulterous men and women, as well as prostitutes sometimes, to race nude or seminude through the streets while being whipped along the way. In early modern Brescia youths ironically forced prostitutes to run on the Feast of the Virgin, and in seventeenth-century London apprentices attacked bawdy houses.

Youths reproved other violations of traditional mores, too. Thus in 1618 a crowd in Burton upon Trent, England, beating drums and pans and ringing cowbells, pulled William and Margaret Cripple from bed and dragged them through the streets to the town stocks, where they received the abuse commonly meted out to criminals confined there. The couple, the crowd claimed, were not husband and wife but brother and sister.

Formal investigation of the couple's relationship became impossible, however, because the pair hastily left town for good after such treatment. Like many crowds at early modern charivaris, this one numbered in its ranks local elites, including the constable.

Although the charivari disappeared first in the anonymity of growing cities, where fewer people could know their neighbors' activities well enough to monitor them, it continued in rural areas, like southwestern France, well into the twentieth century. The charivari was not just a quaint folk custom; it was a kind of rude justice, in which the youths imposed their morality on their victims. Force was implicit in this process, because few were willing victims of such humiliation, and thus violence was a frequent concomitant of the charivari.

A second function of youth abbeys was to inculcate in their members traditional masculine character traits. Central to these was the ideal of courage, which had to be proven by public displays of fighting prowess and risk taking. Youths frequently coursed from town to town, seeking fights with the young men of rival towns. Crippling injuries, and even death, were sometimes the outcomes of these battles. Much of this occurred after dark on festive occasions, but in times of danger youthful strength and exuberance could be useful. Youth abbeys sometimes served as a sort of militia or auxiliary police, as in Nivelles in the Spanish Netherlands, and elsewhere.

Finally, youth abbeys often organized local festivities. The abbeys sponsored much that went into Carnival and other festivals, including contests with the youth of neighboring towns. In some parts of France they staged the *fête des Brandons* at the outset of Lent by carrying burning brands of straw through town, dancing and jumping to assure local fertility. And they rang bells on All Souls' Day. They financed these and other activities by soliciting money and gifts from community members. Although many householders, doubtless remembering their own youths, may have given liberally to the solicitors, it is clear that intimidation was an element of all of this. Property damage and assault might befall those who did not give money commensurate with their perceived wealth.

Carnivals and festivals

Festive events, framed by the religious and agricultural calendars of the age and often staged by youth abbeys, punctuated the lives of early modern men and women. One historian has observed that they probably lived their everyday lives with vivid memories of the most recent festival even while they looked forward to the next such event. These occasions were numerous. Indeed, in seventeenth-century Bordeaux days of religious observance recognized by the local synod, ranging from high holy days to modest local ceremonies marked by simple processions, numbered about 100, and frequent missions and pilgrimages also brought people together.

Usually far more than pious expressions of faith, these festivities were inherently dangerous in the eyes of both religious and civil authorities. Religiously, they were not entirely Christian, even in our period, and they embraced many aspects of pre-Christian culture that drew the opposition of the Tridentine Catholic Church and the Protestant reformers alike. For civil authorities concerned with public order, these festivities provided a cover for violence. Most also featured a symbolism seen as dangerous by elite administrators. This was a symbolism of social inversion, drawing on the biblical stricture "that the first should be last and the last should be first." We can recognize these dangers in the festivities associated with the liturgical calendar of early modern Catholic Europe.

The liturgical calendar opened with Advent, a season of prayer and penance that was not entirely devoid of joyful anticipation of Christmas. Christmas itself was a time of feasting and drinking that opened twelve days of celebration, one of the high points of which was 28 December. The Christian observance of the Massacre of the Innocents by King Herod, this day became the popular Feast of the Boy Bishop in early modern England and the Feast of the Fools in France, Germany, and Spain. Organized by young clerics and marked by bacchanalian celebrations, this festival culminated in the selection of a Bishop of the Fools from among the youthful clergy who mocked Church sacraments and clerical functions. The day's observance was also an occasion for pre-Christian rites to assure the fertility of the fields and marriages in the new year.

Carnival began just after Christmas, as early as the feast of Saint Stephen (26 December) in Venice, and reached a climax on Mardi Gras, or Shrove Tuesday, just before the beginning of Lent on Ash Wednesday. The word "carnival" probably derives from the Old Italian *carnelevare*, "the taking away of flesh," but we can read several meanings into this phrase. Lent, the forty days prior to Easter, was a period of penance, prayer, and fasting. Carnival therefore represented a last period of feasting and celebration before the spiritual rigors of Lent. Meat was plentiful at Carnival time, because early modern peasants slaughtered much of their livestock in the first months of the new year as fodder from the autumn harvest ran out. This sudden surfeit of meat sustained other festivities, too, especially marriage celebrations in these months between Advent and Lent (seasons in which Catholics, as we have seen, could not marry). Thus eating meat was an integral part of Carnival, and butchers played a prominent role symbolically in it. Their guild organized the Schembartlauf carnival in Nuremberg, and in Koenigsberg's carnival in 1583 butchers marched in the festive procession with a 440-pound sausage.

"Flesh," of course, can also refer to the sexual intercourse forbidden to Catholics during Lent in this period. Carnival was therefore a time of sexual license before a spell of enforced abstinence. Symbolically, the masks of Carnival revelers often featured long phallic-like noses and, more tangibly, French demographers have found that both legitimate and illegitimate conceptions rose at Carnival time. All of this doubtless drew on timeless aspects of the agricultural calendar and primitive pre-Christian fertility rites, for the early spring was also the time of planting.

Carnival was most widely observed in southern Europe, perhaps because the weather there is more conducive to outdoor festivities in the months of late winter and early spring than is that of northern countries. But northern Europeans celebrated spring and summer festivities with many of the elements of southern Carnivals. Indeed, Carnival was the prototypical festival, observed with all manner of events and themes that recur at other times of the year. There were parades with floats, masked balls, music making, the kindling of bonfires, poetry recitals, games, and, of course, feasting and drinking.

The danger in Carnival and its attendant disorders was great, for as Mikhail Bakhtin has observed: "Carnival is not a spectacle seen by the people; they live in it, and everyone participates because its very idea embraces all the people . . . During Carnival time life is subject only to its laws, the laws of its own freedom."[2] Carnival was a time of license, and elements of the carnivalesque infused all festivals. Bodily barriers fell to sexual license. Spatial barriers fell, too, as festive life transgressed the bounds of the public sphere, intruding freely on to private property, as the crowd invaded the home of the English couple, the Cripples. Most ominously, perhaps, social hierarchies also tumbled; a fool was often crowned "king" of the festivities, as the last, symbolically at least, did become first.

Revelers transgressed other norms of behavior, too. Festivities frequently mocked the sacred, and the language of the celebrants employed oaths, curses, and obscenities seldom heard in polite speech. Magnifying the inherent threat of violence emerging from the festivities was the custom in some parts of Europe, like southwestern France, of celebrants marching armed with their guilds or confraternities. Violence often resulted; in late sixteenth-century Venice one English visitor reported seventeen deaths on Shrove Tuesday alone. Almost universally, too,

[2] Mikhail Bakhtin, *Rabelais and his World*, translated by Helene Iswolsky (Cambridge, MA: MIT Press, 1968), p. 26.

Carnival concluded with symbolic and highly suggestive acts of violence in which an effigy representing Carnival sustained some sort of execution. Thus, in the Abruzzi, in Normandy, and in the Ardennes, Saintonge, and Aunis regions of France, revelers often burned an image of Carnival. In Lerida, Catalonia, and in upper Brittany inhabitants buried images. Often images received mock trials, too, before symbolic stonings and beheadings in Provence, Swabia, and Franche Comté. Elsewhere such images might be thrown into rivers for symbolic drownings.

The ritual death of Carnival, of course, prepared early modern Europeans for the abstinence of Lent, the devotions of Easter, and the prayers of the spring Rogation Days (the feast of Saint Mark on 25 April and the three days prior to Ascension Thursday) followed by those of Ascension Day. But spring and summer brought other expressions of the carnivalesque on more festive occasions. May Day, religiously the celebration of the festivals of Saints Peter and James, meant the erection of May poles in many locations, dancing, drinking, and sexual license as young people traversed the woods "gathering the may" – activities with pre-Christian origins frowned on by all Christian clergy. Because Rogation Days sometimes overlapped May observances such ribald behavior as male crossdressing marred this period occasionally. Whitsunday or Pentecost (the seventh Sunday after Easter) brought more such disorder that revelers often observed over an extended period. Similar behavior occurred on the feast of Saint John the Baptist, or midsummer (24 June). Celebrated in much of northern Europe as a virtual fertility rite in which youths sought purification by bathing in rivers, and potency by jumping over bonfires in the period of summer solstice, this day's antics bore little resemblance to religious observance. Indeed, in Chaumont, France, revelers dressed as devils and threw fireworks at festive crowds.

Late summer and early fall brought additional festivities associated with the harvest and fertility. In Bologna, for example, Saint Bartholomew's Day (25 August) provoked feasting, drinking, and ritual slaughtering of pigs. The same behavior marked observances of key autumn events. All Saints' and All Souls' Days (1 and 2 November), today observed by many Catholics with devout cemetery visits and prayers for the dead, were very worldly celebrations for early modern Europeans, affirmations of life with dancing, drinking, and athletic contests.

Other events filled out this ritual calendar. The visit of a bishop, an itinerant preacher, or passing pilgrims, drew large crowds and often created a festive atmosphere following religious ceremonies. Any parish of any size commemorated the dedication of its church with an often wild parish festival called the wake in England, the *ducasse* in France, and the *kermis* in the Low Countries. Fairs frequently coincided with religious observances and provided additional opportunities for celebration, disorder, and, as we will see, violence. Indeed, in the Angoumois region of France in the eighteenth century there were some 450 local and regional fairs. Carnivalesque motifs invaded more secular observances as well, such as royal entries, victory celebrations, and even wedding festivities.

The Protestant Reformation modified this festive calendar a little in England, parts of France and Germany, and Scandinavia. It also presaged a general assault on the festive events by both Catholic and Protestant leaders to which we will return. In many places, like Nuremberg, the authorities forbade Carnival entirely as the reformed faith grew in adherents. Nevertheless, the spirit of Carnival endured, as the festive calendar of Protestant England demonstrates.

There, despite Puritan attacks in the seventeenth century, Advent was still followed by the festivities of the twelve days of Christmas, the period between 25 December and 6 January. Work resumed afterward, but not for long, because Plow Monday, the first Monday after 6 January, when agricultural work was supposed to begin again, was a traditional day of feasting, drinking, and other celebrations. Shrove Tuesday remained as another winter holiday, characterized, as we will see, by cockfights, football, and other events. Easter, too, endured as a festive occasion, and May Day followed, with the May pole that the Puritans never successfully banned, and its sexual license. In some locales, like Middleton, the night was known as "Mischief-Neet" and it was considered acceptable behavior to topple the fences and gates of one's enemies. Whitsunday followed with more license, sometimes two weeks of it, as in Woodstock. In the autumn the Puritans successfully replaced Halloween (All Saints' Eve) and its ghosts and goblins with Guy Fawkes Night (5 November), a celebration of the discovery of the Gunpowder Plot of 1605 to blow up James I and parliament. In our period Guy Fawkes observances were very anti-Catholic in tone, and were celebrated with bonfires and fireworks. But much of the old remained. Not only did crowds burn effigies of Fawkes and the Pope, they also consigned to the flames ones of prominent and unpopular local figures. And tricks inflicted by revelers resembling Halloween goblins awaited those who refused to contribute to the festivities. Local parish wakes continued unabated, too. In the 1720s Northamptonshire's 290 parishes observed 198 wakes. Wakes usually began on the Sunday after the anniversary of the church's dedication and extended for much of the following week with feasting, drinking, and various jocund events.

All of these carnivalesque festivities featured events that at first glance we might classify as entertainments or even sports. Certainly crowds gathered to view these events, but to describe them in such terms is anachronistic, as two pioneers in the social history of sport, Norbert Elias and Eric Dunning, have suggested.[3] Today remnants of these events have become so commercialized and divorced from the festive calendar as to permit us legitimately to call them sports or entertainments. But in the early modern period the events attending the festive calendar were really part of the carnivalesque ritual of the age. The events we will examine certainly added to the violent nature of the carnivalesque, but they performed certain cultural functions, too, that we seldom ascribe to modern entertainments and games that do not require mass participation.

Violent team games were part of early modern festive life. They were a ritual affirmation of community, for "in hierarchical social structures *communitas* is symbolically affirmed by periodic rituals not infrequently calendrical or tied in with the agricultural cycle."[4] But the cost of these violent games was great, as we will see, and we must also understand them as affirmations of communal, neighborhood, or factional solidarity and honor. They in fact represent the "deep play" analyzed by anthropologist Clifford Geertz, activities that are so dangerous or costly that they are pursued not for themselves but as expressions of the self-vision of the societies that perform them.[5]

Just as their modern descendants enjoy playing or simply watching a ballgame like soccer, rugby, cricket, baseball, or American football, early modern Europeans attended similar matches as part of the festive calendar of their age. Many of these games were of considerable antiquity – the first record of English football seems to date from 1175. But "football" is a term used by many historians of sport to designate a game that in the early modern period little resembled modern European soccer or American football. The game was played on foot, but, depending on local custom, the ball was not necessarily propelled by the feet. Most significantly, there existed few of today's rules, many of which aim at limiting physical harm to players. So while these games were organized around local teams, they also provided opportunities for revenge and physical assault under the guise of a sporting event on a festive occasion. Many degenerated into riots between teams from neighboring towns or competing factions from the same locales.

In England, in fact, many ballgames involved almost as much fighting as ball playing, and the first efforts by monarchs to ban such games date

[3] Norbert Elias and Eric Dunning, *Quest for Excitement: Sport and Leisure in the Civilizing Process* (Oxford and New York: Basil Blackwell, 1986), p. 180.

[4] Victor Turner, *Drama, Fields, and Metaphors: Symbolic Action in Human Society* (Ithaca: Cornell University Press, 1974), p. 53.

[5] Clifford Geertz, "Deep Play: Notes on a Balinese Cockfight" in his *The Interpretation of Culture: Selected Essays* (New York: Basic Books, 1973), pp. 412–53.

from 1314. Indeed, in forbidding football at court in the early seventeenth century James I commented: "From this court I debarre all rough and violent exercises, as the foot-ball, meeter for lameing than making able the users thereof."[6] And a sixteenth-century witness to a ballgame in Chester recorded: "Much harme was done, some in the great thronges fallinge into a trance, some having their bodies brused and cracked; some their arms, heades or legges broken, and some otherwise maimed or in peril of their lives."[7]

Local custom governed English ballgames, and some players kicked, threw, or carried the ball, while others propelled it with sticks as in field hockey. The ball varied, too, from one locale to another; in some areas it was an inflated animal bladder encased in leather while in others it was a smaller, harder sphere. Play differed, too, some places permitting only wrestling and kicking on the field, while others also allowed boxing. Playing fields varied widely in size, as well.

Everywhere, however, games were generally associated with important days of the religious festival calendar, including Shrove Tuesday, Good Friday, and Christmas Day. Just as universally, games were expressions of local rivalries that involved hundreds of people. This was the case in the rivalry between Saint Peter's and All Saints' parishes in Derby that drew hundreds of players and a large regional audience throughout our 1500–1800 period. The games typically occupied two days, with men playing on Shrove Tuesday and boys on Ash Wednesday. The game started as the ball was thrown into the air in the marketplace, and the objective was for a team to get the ball to its goal. The goals were located at opposite ends of the town, about a mile (1·6 km) beyond the municipal limits in each case. In this game players carried the ball, and it was sometimes called "hugball," but there were few other rules. The game sometimes lasted six hours, with the Saint Peter's team often trying to get the ball into the Derwent River for a waterborne approach to the goal. Sometimes teams attempted a direct crosscountry assault on the goal, too. But if the defense of the opposing team was tenacious, all sorts of stratagems might be employed. On several occasions players emptied the woodshavings that filled the ball, concealing it under their clothing for stealthy approaches to the goal. And on one occasion a player carried the ball through a sewer under the town. Such play caused numerous injuries, property damage, and occasional deaths. It also produced enthusiastic fans: supporters had to be dispersed by troops when the authorities

[6] Quoted in Joseph Strutt, *The Sports and Pastimes of the People of England* (originally published in 1801; reprinted, Bath: Firecrest Publishers, 1969), p. 94.
[7] Quoted in Christina Hole, *English Sports and Pastimes* (London: B. T. Batsford, 1949), p. 52.

banned the game in 1847. Rowdy football fans, it seems, are not a uniquely modern phenomenon.

In some locales strange and violent rites were added to games. In the Shrove Tuesday games at Leicester the teams played a kind of field hockey in the castle grounds. The match ended at about one o'clock in the afternoon when the "Whipping Toms" appeared, dressed in blue smocks and bearing whips that they used to drive players and spectators from the castle confines. Serious injury from falls could occur here because it was customary for the Whipping Toms to strike people below the knees. And while immunity from whipping by a Tom could be bought with a one-penny fee, many people brought sticks with which to defend themselves. The mêlée ended at about five in the afternoon when all involved retired to local pubs where the consumption of alcohol only encouraged further violent behavior.

Matches could serve as convenient covers for collateral violence, too. Playing-field injuries embittered local rivalries still more, of course, and football games were convenient venues for violent acts of revenge. Thus Scots players at a game in 1601 at Lockton-in-the-Merse, Berwick, employed firearms during the game. Matches could provide useful cover for other activities, as well; on the Isle of Ely, for example, where there was considerable popular resistance to landowners' enclosure and drainage plans, players in a ballgame of June 1638 contrived to destroy drainage ditches in addition to their more customary property damage.

The French played an equally rough version of all of this, *la soule*. As in England, the game was played crosscountry, often between the newly married men and single men of one town, or between youths of rival towns. In France, too, the game was largely without rules. The players propelled the ball with hands, feet, or sticks and their number was unlimited; in Normandy games of between 700 and 800 players drew audiences of from 5,000 to 6,000 onlookers in our period. In France, as in England, the game was closely linked with the festive calendar, played especially on village feast days and Mardi Gras. And the French were just as brutal as their English counterparts. They settled old scores on the playing field, and football fatalities were not unknown. The antiquity of the game is suggested by certain customs and superstitions associated with it. In Normandy, for example, the ball was provided and thrown out by the most recent bride, and players believed that the winning team would have a bountiful apple crop, which hints at the possible origins of the games in a pre-Christian fertility rite.

Rather better regulated by the sixteenth century were the Italian football games, the *calcio* of Florence, the *pallone* of Sienna, and the games of other Italian cities in the January to March Carnival season. Nevertheless, the origins of these sports in ballgames like those of England and France seem clear; sources from prior to the sixteenth century refer not to the playing of a football game but to a *battaglia*, that is, a battle. The battle aspect of the game endured despite playing rules. Florentine players enjoyed the *calcio* on the Piazza de Santa Croce on a fenced playing field. The object of this game, engaging teams of twenty-seven players each, was to kick, strike, or throw the ball down the field to the goal line without propelling the ball above the head of an average man. To do so incurred a *fallo* (foul) and two *falli* resulted in one goal, or *caccia*, for the opposing team. Both offense and defense in such games pursued their respective roles with methods resembling assault and battery (and that evoke images of an early version of American football's "wedge offense"). The authorities vainly attempted to contain such violence with new rules; one seventeenth-century English visitor to Florence noted approvingly that a local ordinance decreed the death penalty for players who continued their sporting violence off the playing field.

If human combat was a collateral result of ballgames, combat itself, between either individuals or groups, was also part of early modern European festivals. Individual combat assumed many forms, but wrestling was very popular. Indeed, the Brighton Green Fair in Northamptonshire, England, reportedly drew 10,000 to its annual wrestling tournaments in the 1730s. Boxing was popular, too, at local fairs and religious festivals all over Europe and, in an age prior to Marquess of Queensbury Rules, could be quite brutal. Indeed, an English champion boxer drew up the first modern boxing rules in 1743 after his blows killed an opponent.

Combat events' popularity led to their early commercialization and an increasing independence of the festive calendar. Most great cities, and many smaller ones, provided a continuous schedule of combat events, in addition to those that a country spectator could attend at festivals and fairs. In addition to wrestling and boxing, promoters during our period offered matches with cudgels, quarterstaffs, or swords to a public that apparently wanted to see blood. One advertisement of 1753 for an English singlestick match, in which players' left hands were tied down and they defended and attacked with sticks in their right hands, noted that the goal was to "break a head." The advertisement also claimed: "No head to be deemed broken unless the Blood runs an Inch."[8]

Ritualized mass battles, group combats staged for religious festivals and such secular celebrations as royal visits, also figured on the early modern festive calendar. The practice of such combat was widespread

---

[8] Quoted in Robert W. Malcolmson, *Popular Recreations in English Society, 1700–1850* (Cambridge: Cambridge University Press, 1973), p. 43.

and flourished in neighborhood or regional rivalries between young men. In Bocairante in Valencia, Spain, a February festival is still staged, more peaceful in the present century than in an earlier era, and featuring a mock battle between citizens costumed as "Christians" and "Moors." The citizens of seventeenth-century Lille witnessed youthful street battles in the Carnival season that local authorities proved incapable of controlling. And in the French Périgord region festivals customarily concluded with stick fights between local youths and their counterparts visiting from neighboring towns. Such violence, with occasional fatal results, persisted in the area into the 1830s.

Ritualized combat seems to have flourished most widely in Italy. In Florence, Pavia, Pisa, and many other Tuscan and Umbrian cities, ritual battles between residents of rival urban neighborhoods took place on festive occasions such as Saint Anthony's Day, and especially at Carnival. Many of these battles were on bridges joining rival neighborhoods on opposite sides of a river, and in Florence the fighting on the main bridge over the Arno was called the *Giocca del Ponte* ("Bridge Game"). Combatants waged these battles with clubs and shields, or sometimes barehanded, and the passions they aroused produced injuries as well as violence that spread beyond the bridge into general rioting. Some of these battles featured stone throwing, too, but in Orvieto, Perugia, and Sienna, such combat, in the *Battaglia de' Sassi* ("Battle of the Stones"), seems to have been the activity of choice. The season for such sport could extend from All Saints' Day to Lent – even, in Perugia, until May. Combatants, dressed in their factional colors for a full day's battle, could number as many as 2,000 in Perugia, and many of them sustained injuries.

The most closely studied of the ritualized Italian group combats are the *Guerre dei Pugni*, the "Wars of the Fists" in Venice, typically fought on the bridges over the city's canals. These were battles between residents of rival districts within the city, chiefly the fishermen resident in one part of Venice and state naval arsenal workers dwelling in another. These battles, first mentioned in official sources in 1369, seem initially to have been fought with sticks, but by the sixteenth century they had assumed their classic form of a fist fight to gain control of the bridge. The fights always drew large numbers of spectators, who viewed them from the windows and rooftops of neighboring buildings, or from gondolas that blocked canals. And the crowds grew in the seventeenth century as the Venetian Carnival increasingly became commercialized and an early tourist attraction.

This sport was quite dangerous. Despite precautions such as the placement of haybales at each end of the contested bridge to break combatants' fall from the structure, injuries occurred. The fisticuffs hurt many, others fell into the canals, and, with tempers high, the mere appearance of a knife at the scene was sufficient cause for street warfare in which spectators joined by throwing rocks and rooftiles.

Venetians staged these battles on numerous festive occasions throughout the year: Saint Stephen's Day (feast of the patron saint of Venice), Carnival, Candlemas, Saint Giustina's Day (anniversary of the Battle of Lepanto), All Saints' Day, and Christmas. Numerous civic observances also featured these battles, including the visit of Henri III of France in 1574. The French monarch's reaction to one of these fights aptly described this event: "too small to be a real war and too cruel to be a game."[9]

Even so, the violence sustained by humans seems to have been less common than that universally inflicted on animals by early modern Europeans on their festive occasions. Certain animals appear repeatedly in this violence, especially bulls and cocks. Both creatures traditionally represented the male sexuality that figured in both pre-Christian and Christian festivities, and their sacrifices seem to have symbolized the purging of lust. The owners of both bulls and cocks often found their sacrifice easy; herds and hen yards, after all, require only one male of a species for breeding purposes. And many of the bloody spectacles involving cattle and pigs typically occurred in the early spring when, as we have seen, diminishing stocks of fodder mandated slaughter of livestock.

The simplest festive event involving bulls was bull baiting, so accepted in early modern England that even Elizabeth I held bull baitings for visiting dignitaries. In the countryside these entertainments occurred on Whitsunday, Guy Fawkes Night, wakes, and election days, when a local gentleman or a butcher might provide a bull. Indeed, in some localities ordinances required the baiting of bulls before slaughter. In this spectacle the bull was tied to a stake in the ground, or to a ring embedded in the pavement, by a rope of perhaps 15 ft (4·5 m) in length, thus confining the bull's movements to an area some 30 ft (9 m) in diameter. Securely tethered, the bull was then attacked by dogs as a crowd watched it toss its attackers about before succumbing to their numbers.

Equally bloody were two English variations on this entertainment form, bear baiting and badger baiting. Bear baiting was growing less and less common in our period because by the sixteenth century the beasts had to be imported into England. As a result they were not cheap and their owners, part of a nascent commercial entertainment industry, seldom allowed bears to be killed. Nevertheless, as they stood on their hind legs fending off attacking dogs, or rolled on those who had secured a

---

[9] Quoted in Robert C. Davis, *The War of the Fists: Popular Culture and Public Violence in Late Renaissance Venice* (Oxford: Oxford University Press, 1994), p. 47.

hold on them, the bears' agonies attracted many paying spectators. Far more usual, though, was baiting of the smaller but ferocious native badger. The object here was for the dogs to draw the badger out of a hole or box to which it was attached, and to attack and kill the creature.

Bulls figured very widely in other entertainments apart from baiting. The annual running of the bulls in Pamplona, Spain, on the feast of San Fermin, is the modern survival of an ancient festive ritual that was far more widespread than bull baiting. Indeed, we find bull running in early modern England, France, and Italy, as well as in Spain.

The objective in early modern England was to catch the bull. This task was made more difficult than usual at Tutbury in Staffordshire, where the organizers of the event held annually on the day after the feast of the Assumption (16 August) cropped the bull's ears, cut off its tail, slathered the beast with soap, and blew pepper up its nose. The annual running of the bull at Stamford, Lincolnshire, on the town's 13 November wake was especially famous and persisted until 1840. Local organizers released the bull at eleven in the morning to the peeling of church bells. Spectators cheered from the upper windows of houses whose ground floors were securely shuttered as the bull ran down streets whose exits had been barricaded. In those streets young men, called "bullards," teased and taunted the animal. This sort of persecution occupied much of the day until the young men drove the bull to the town's bridge, where the bullards attempted to "brig" it, that is, to toss the animal over the bridge parapet into the Welland River. After the bull had fallen into the river, it would struggle to escape on to dry land, whereupon it would be attacked by dogs and led back to town for slaughter.

Bull running seems to have grown popular in southern France in the fifteenth century. On festive occasions bulls ran through towns, maddened by spectators' shouting, dogs' barking, the sound of musket shots, and the blows of young men with banderillas, until they charged into a barricaded marketsquare for harassment by young men before butchering. Such bull running was costly to participants and spectators alike. Many fell victim to the bull, but the event also permitted much wine consumption and armed young men used it as an opportunity to settle personal scores. Despite such dangers, in the sixteenth and seventeenth centuries these events drew large audiences in Bordeaux at Carnival, Bazas and Saint-Sever at midsummer, the feast of Saint Madeleine (22 July) at Mont-de-Marsan, and the feast of Saint Vincent (1 September) at Dax, and at other celebrations of local festivals or victories.

The bull was part of festive observances in Italy, too. Records in Rome reveal Carnival games with animals as early as the twelfth century. Of equal antiquity was the annual bull running on the last Sunday before

Lent that, by the sixteenth century, culminated in a fight in Saint Peter's Square between bulls and mounted, armed, and costumed young men representing the districts of Rome. Bull runs and fights occurred elsewhere, too, including in Sienna and Venice.

It was in Spain, however, that taurine entertainments were most varied and extensive. Bull baiting and bull running still occur in that country, and there are distinct local practices like the *toro de fuego* in which the bull is run at night with incendiary devices on its horns. But bull fighting, historically the culmination of the running of bulls to an enclosed public square, was the most common event in the early modern period, and remains so today.

The best-known manifestation of modern Spanish bull fighting is the highly stylized *corrida de toros*, in which the matador on foot faces the bull. This form of bull fighting emerged only in the eighteenth century. For much of our period mounted aristocrats, *rejoneadores*, who displayed knightly equestrian skills while lancing the bull, waged combat with the animal. Only if he failed to kill the bull with his lance did the horseman dismount and attempt to kill the beast with a sword. But this was not done in the style of the modern matador; the dismounted horseman had the aid of assistants on foot who cut the bull's legs with various weapons to immobilize it for the final sword thrust. The first record of such a bull fight dates from 1080, when one occurred as part of the entertainment at an aristocratic marriage. Indeed, aristocratic and royal weddings were prime occasions for such entertainments, as were religious festivals, royal visits, and the opening of the cortes. When such taurine events took place, they were held in front of large audiences in important public spaces like that of San Francisco in Seville.

A combination of developments led to the decline of this traditional form of bull fighting in favor of the modern *corrida de toros*. The nobility was increasingly abandoning the sport by the late seventeenth century, reflecting an evolution of European aristocratic taste to which we will return. And the exit from the sport of its traditional participants was hastened by the accession of Philip V (r. 1700–46) to the throne. The new Bourbon monarch not only disliked bull fighting, he also favored a new riding style requiring a light, fast horse quite unsuited for traditional bull fighting, which demanded a heavy jousting mount. The sport therefore came increasingly to be dominated by dismounted commoners as the aristocracy abandoned it, and it assumed more and more its modern form of mass entertainment.

By the 1730s individual matadors, initially often drawn from among slaughterhouse employees, were gaining fame. Purpose-built *plazas de toros* appeared as early as 1617 in Madrid, but the great building boom in such structures began in the next century. Bull fighting, increasingly independent of the festive calendar, became commercialized entertainment early on, and the first advertising posters appeared as early as 1761. Moreover, rules increasingly governed the actions of matadors and spectators alike. The event's traditional origins in bull running, in which all might participate, were obscured as royal orders, beginning in 1659, required spectators to go directly to their seats and remain in the stands rather than join in the fray as in the old days. The result is a modern spectator event in which in the 1980s some 25,000 bulls annually died in a sporting season extending from spring into fall.

Various smaller animals suffered in violent public rituals, too, especially fowl. On festive occasions Dutch peasants engaged in "goose pulls," and a seventeenth-century ordinance in the town of Rijnland suggests that geese were not the only victims. Seeking to maintain municipal order, not protect animals, the city fathers decreed: "No one, no matter who he is, will be allowed to ride, to stick, to pull, to hit, or otherwise cut open any swans, geese, roosters, rabbits, eels, herring or other animals without exception, on foot, on horseback, on water, or on land."[10]

The Dutch were not alone in their violence toward fowl. All Saints' Day observances in the Champagne region of early modern France combined drinking and dancing with a competition in which men hurled forked sticks at a live goose hanging from a tree, with the thrower who knocked down the bird winning it. In the Birmingham area in England the usual wake games included one in which men on horseback tried to grab by the neck a live goose suspended from a rope stretched across a street. In a Rome variant of this game, played especially during Carnival and on Saint Bartholomew's Day, contestants in boats grabbed at the necks of geese suspended over the Tiber. And, in Toledo, Spain, on the feast of Santiago (25 July) mounted men at full gallop attempted to tear the heads off geese affixed to the ground.

The rooster, as we have noted a traditional symbol of lust, factored most prominently in violent events involving fowl, however, for destruction of these birds represented defeat of carnal urges. In England, for much of our period, an entertainment for boys and adolescents on Shrove Tuesday, wakes, and at fairs was cock throwing. In this game a cock tied to a stake became the target of those who paid a modest sum to throw cudgels or sticks at the bird from a distance of about 20 yards (18 m). If a thrower knocked the bird out and could grab it before it rose, he won the cock. One Frenchman traveling in England noted that it was dangerous

---

[10] Quoted in A. T. Van Deursen, *Plain Lives in a Golden Age, Popular Culture, Religion and Society in Seventeenth-Century Holland*, translated by Maarten Ultee (Cambridge: Cambridge University Press, 1991), pp. 109–10.

for humans even to approach the sites of these events because so much was being thrown. But the French also staged these sorts of events in the *abattis*. In this game at local festivals the participant who killed the creature became the festival "king" for the year.

As boys grew into men, however, they often attended another violent event involving the rooster: the cock fight. Around the globe, the appeal of such events has been virtually universal. All social groups in England attended cock fights in the sixteenth and seventeenth centuries, for example, and the event became increasingly commercialized in our period, as many larger inns had cockpits that resembled small amphitheaters. Promoters staged cock fights at fairs and festivals, too. But whatever their venue, the fights drew large crowds attracted by competitions that often reflected local or regional rivalries and the potential for gain through wagering. The sport itself was brutal entertainment. Cocks were specially bred for fighting, and their owners prepared them for the ring by clipping their wings, wattles, and combs, and affixing metal spurs to their feet. Thus readied, cocks most usually entered the rings in pairs, matched by weight, for combat to the death.

Like the rooster, the cat was a frequent victim of festive violence. We have already seen its mistreatment in charivaris, and the cat seems to have figured importantly in the imagination of early modern Europeans. It held obvious links to witchcraft for them, and in France and other countries it was also a sexual metaphor. Consequently, the cat figured in Carnival and festive rites in our period, and symbolic purging of the evil that the cat represented was widespread. In Paris, well into the eighteenth century, the Saint John's Eve bonfire featured a sack full of live cats suspended over the flames. As the fire consumed the sack, the cats perished in its flames. Similar cat burnings occurred elsewhere in France, but such festive cruelty to cats was not uniquely French. At Ypres, Flanders, other festive abuses of cats are similarly shocking to modern sensibilities. In the second week of Lent, on the day known locally as *Kattenwoensdag* ("Cat Wednesday"), residents annually enacted a ceremony in which they threw several live cats from the belfry of the town hall. Dating back to perhaps the tenth century, the custom endured until 1814. Another festive event in Ypres involved jousters aiming blows at cats suspended above the street in clay pots. When the cats fell to the street, children pursued the animals with the goal of killing them. Elsewhere, less ritualized, episodic violence also afflicted cats on festive occasions. A seventeenth-century London crowd, for example, once observed Guy Fawkes Night by stuffing live cats into an effigy of the Pope and igniting it.

Festivals and violence

Youth groups' abuses of their fellow citizens, periods of license throughout the year often accompanied by the symbolism of a world turned
upside down, and ritualized violence on humans and animals all pose
interpretive problems for students of the European past. Some historians
and cultural anthropologists have long argued that these rites provided a
safety valve of sorts for early modern society. The events of the festive calendar, they say, provided periods of masked equality that were a kind of
liberation from the constraints of a hierarchical age. They argue, too, that
such rites gave society cohesion and even reinforced its basic structure.
Max Gluckman, for example, contended that a society's occasional lifting
of traditional constraints serves to emphasize and thus reinforce them.[11]
The Russian scholar Mikhail Bakhtin, on the other hand, centered his
analysis of Carnival on the event's cultural elements. The world was
indeed turned upside down in the fascination of revelers with a grotesque
orgy of food, sex, and ritual violence.

Such analyses certainly capture much of the essence of the festive life of
our period. But they do not capture it all. Armed men roamed the streets,
beer and wine flowed, and normally lawabiding citizens discovered anonymity, and diminished responsibility for their acts, behind masks. The
ritualized violence occurring under such conditions could be dangerous
in itself, but the festivities gave rise to much ancillary violence, as well.
What started as mocking satire and ritual violence could escalate easily
into direct hostility, mass violence, riot, or rebellion. Riots and rebellions
frequently erupted when festive occasions coincided with problems, like
the introduction of new taxes. A Flemish Jesuit, writing in 1615, estimated that 1,300 people perished annually at parish festivals in his province.

For much our period, Carnival itself presented a constant threat to
public order. We have already noted in Chapter 3 how Carnival in Udine
in 1511 gave rise to both vendetta violence and a widespread peasant
revolt. Carnival in Bern in 1513 produced a peasant revolt, while
Carnival ended in rioting in Dijon in 1630 and in a massacre in Romans,
in Dauphiné, in 1580. Shrove Tuesday, the culmination of pre-Lenten
festivities, was always the most dangerous day of Carnival. In
seventeenth-century London Shrove Tuesday ended in rioting twenty-
four times during the first two Stuart reigns (1603–49).

May Day was dangerous, too. Its observance in London in 1517

---

[11] Max Gluckman, "Rituals of Rebellion in South-East Africa" in his *Order and Rebellion in
Tribal Africa* (New York: Free Press, 1963).

erupted into a riot against foreigners. Other religious festivals also produced real threats to public order, and sometimes even outright revolt arose on festive occasions. Thus Naples exploded in revolt in 1647 when the feast of Santa Maria della Grazia (7 July) coincided with a new tax on fruit. A ritual battle, like those common in Italy, degenerated into a general riot in which the crowd attacked the tax office, grain storehouses, and the palace of the Spanish governor. General revolt spread as a fisherman, Masaniello, emerged as a popular leader. The Pilgrimage of Grace of 1536, a revolt against the religious reforms of Henry VIII of England, similarly grew from a religious observance. And Kett's Rebellion, one of the greatest threats to the early modern English state, had its roots in the assembly of people in Wymondham, Norfolk, for the feast of the Translation of Saint Thomas à Becket on 7 July 1549.

Such violence, however, was slowly – though perhaps imperceptibly to contemporaries – diminishing in the last two centuries of the early modern era. Culturally, historians such as Peter Burke long ago identified the increasing separation of social elites from "popular culture."[12] Such a separation of the social elites from mass culture, a result of the forces that shaped the civilizing process, had widespread consequences. Socially, these were the people who had organized, led, and often financed youth groups. Elite patronage often made popular entertainments possible, too: gentlemen bred fighting cocks, contributed bulls to bull runs and baitings, and donated prizes to football, boxing, and other competitions. The withdrawal of such patronage certainly weakened all of these phenomena. Moreover, all the worse for the old ways, as such figures came under the influence of the civilizing process they often became instruments of an organized attack on popular culture. That attack came from two directions.

Religious reformers, Catholic and Protestant alike, objected to many of the elements we have observed in early modern festivities. Reformers knew their classical literature and recognized much that was pre-Christian in Carnival and other festivities. They also objected to much of early modern festive life on moral grounds. Carnival was a period of complete license, and post-Tridentine Catholic leaders, as well as their Protestant counterparts, found all that it stood for contrary to the ethic of order, decency, self-control, and hard work they embraced. Catholic reformers often tried to modify these practices, attempting to control confraternities better, for example. And, in the decree *Universa* in 1627, Pope Urban VIII began to restrict the number of religious festivals.

Protestant reformers tried frequently to ban many popular celebrations completely, often provoked by merrymakers. Thus in 1539, when

---

[12] Peter Burke, *Popular Culture in Early Modern Europe* (New York: Harper and Row, 1978).

Nuremberg city fathers found Carnival revelers parodying the local Lutheran reformer Andreas Osiander on a float designated the "Ship of Fools," they banned the festivities thereafter. In England the religious assault on popular festivities dated from the 1570s and grew with Puritanism; even Christmas festivities came under attack. Everywhere Protestant reformers' zeal to attack the old festive calendar only increased as they perceived in it holdovers of Catholicism. Calvinists in the Dutch Republic often banned observance of the feast of Saint John the Baptist, Mardi Gras, Epiphany, and New Year.

By the late seventeenth century, in much of urban western Europe at least, popular celebrations were in transition owing to the work of religious reformers. At first, events organized by society's weaker elements, like the Feast of the Fools of the young clergy, fell to the reformers' onslaught. But then, as we have seen, Carnival itself came under attack. What remained, increasingly, were mere representations of the carnivalesque. Theatrical performances, for example, represented Carnival to audiences who no longer participated actively in the event.

The centralizing early modern state quickly allied itself with religious reformers in most countries, with the initial exception of England. There the crown's opposition to the Puritans meant that the King's Declaration on Sports of 1618 (expanded in 1633 to become known as "The Book of Sports") condoned festivities of which the Puritans disapproved but "which shall not tend to the breach of our aforesaid laws and canons of our church."[13] Usually, however, the state found the disorder of youth groups and popular festivities increasingly a problem that required containment. Municipal rules and royal laws regulated Sabbath behavior; and wedding feasts, Carnival observances, games, and charivaris also came under the normative control of the state. Regulations as early as the sixteenth century in the Spanish Netherlands, for example, set the size and duration of wedding celebrations and attempted to confine parish religious festivals to one nationally uniform day per year to prevent merrymakers from journeying from festival to festival disturbing whole regions.

In Venice the last ritual fist fight on a bridge occurred on 29 September 1705, as the city's aristocratic rulers found such violence less and less acceptable. In 1705 a riot following the bridge battle had impeded efforts to fight a fire at the church of San Girolamo. Venetian authorities, who had winked at such goings on in the past, acted now in large part because the fights had in the seventeenth century become increasingly plebeian affairs abandoned by Venetian elites who had come to view attendance at the

---

[13] Quoted in Malcolmson, *Popular Recreations*, p. 11.

fights as *déclassé*. So there was not much protest that mattered when the authorities banned the fist fights.

The attack on ritual violence advanced elsewhere, too. By the 1760s provincial authorities in southwestern France sought to eliminate disorder by banning bull running. In relatively well-policed Paris no record of a traditional charivari can be found after the 1750s, when police began arresting those beating on pans. Such events had been similarly outlawed in England by the early eighteenth century.

The authorities everywhere also sought to control the spaces that hosted disorder. The streets, squares, and open spaces around city walls – traditional points of congregation for youth groups and revelers – were better patrolled, first by night watchmen, then by regular policemen. Sustaining the law's spirit were new attitudes among social elites increasingly affected by a civilizing process in which we can discern much that was antithetical to traditional festive life and ritual violence. The civilizing process stood for self-control and courtly manners. It also gave increasing currency to such principles as the right of all living creatures to decent treatment. Montaigne expressed this sentiment in the late sixteenth century thus: "If I see a chicken's neck pulled off or a pig sticked, I cannot choose but grieve; and I cannot well endure a silly dew bedabbled hare to groan when she is seized by the hounds."[14] Men of Montaigne's circle made and enforced the laws and, if at first they were concerned more with general problems of civil order, they increasingly saw to the welfare of humans and animals.

Blood sports were the first object of attack. In England cock throwing resulted in arrests as early as 1752 in London, Reading, Bristol, and Northampton, and it began to die out. Cock fighting proved more resilient in the face of laws and organizations concerned with animal welfare. And while bull running and fights persisted in Spain, English and French authorities ended that violence with difficulty in the first half of the nineteenth century. The Royal Society for the Prevention of Cruelty to Animals, for example, conducted a concerted legal attack on bull running at Stamford, only to be greeted by defiance and signs reading, "Bull for Ever." The bull ran last in 1839 despite the attempted intervention of twenty metropolitan policemen, ninety local constables, and forty-three dragoons. The local decision to terminate the practice in the end was based on the cost of such efforts at control, however, not the fate of the animal. Attempts to end brutality against humans encountered similar resistance: in 1852 cancellation of the annual *soule* game in Saint-Pierre-d'Entrement, France, required five brigades of the Gendarmerie.

[14] Quoted in Keith Thomas, *Man and the Natural World: Changing Attitudes in England, 1500–1800* (London: Allen Lane, 1983), p. 173.

If some popular festivities and bloody entertainments endured, despite the best efforts of the law and religious reformers, the social and economic changes of the nineteenth century doomed what remained of them. The old festive calendar could not survive the grim reality of the six-day industrial age working week. In Bavaria, which had 200 days recognized locally or nationally as festive occasions in 1770, only 85 such days survived by 1830. And by the 1840s some employers in English mining districts recognized only Christmas Day and Good Friday as holidays. Like leisure time itself, even space for ball games and festivals became harder to find. Enclosure and urbanization everywhere usurped open spaces for games, and other such practices, and the ritual violence that underlay much popular protest began to disappear.

Although they were in decline for much of the early modern era, festive occasions, whether in their inherent ritualized violence, or in the mass violence to which they could give rise, added greatly to the turbulence of this age. It is to mass violence, popular protest in the form of intimidation, riots, and rebellion, that we next turn.

FURTHER READING

Bakhtin, Mikhail, *Rabelais and His World*, translated by Helene Iswolsky (Cambridge, MA: MIT Press, 1968).

Bercé, Yves-Marie, *Fête et révolte: des mentalités populaires du XVIᵉ au XVIIIᵉ siècle* (Paris: Hachette, 1976).

Burke, Peter, "The Carnival of Venice" in Peter Burke (ed.), *The Historical Anthropology of Early Modern Italy: Essays on Perception and Communication* (Cambridge: Cambridge University Press, 1987), pp. 113–90.

Cashmere, John, "The Social Uses of Violence in Ritual: *Charivari* or Religious Persecution," *European History Quarterly* 21 (1991), pp. 291–319.

Davis, Natalie Z., "Charivari, Honor, and Community in Seventeenth-Century Lyon and Geneva" in John J. MacAloon (ed.), *Rite, Drama, Festival, Spectacle: Rehearsals Toward a Theory of Cultural Performance* (Philadelphia: Institute for the Study of Human Issues, 1984).

Davis, Robert C., *The War of the Fists: Popular Culture and Public Violence in Late Renaissance Venice* (Oxford: Oxford University Press, 1994).

Dunning, Eric and Sheard, Kenneth, *Barbarians, Gentlemen and Players: A Sociological Study of the Development of Rugby Football* (Oxford: Martin Robertson, 1979).

Elias, Norbert, and Dunning, Eric, *Quest for Excitement: Sport and Leisure in the Civilizing Process* (Oxford: Basil Blackwell, 1986).

Hole, Christina, *English Sports and Pastimes* (London: B. T. Batsford, 1949).

Hutton, Ronald, *The Rise and Fall of Merry England: The Ritual Year, 1400–1700* (Oxford: Oxford University Press, 1994).

Le Roy Ladurie, Emmanuel, *Carnival in Romans*, translated by Mary Feeney (New York: George Braziller, 1979).

Malcolmson, Robert W., *Popular Recreations in English Society, 1700–1850* (Cambridge: Cambridge University Press, 1973).

Marvin, Garry, *Bullfight* (Oxford: Basil Blackwell, 1988).

Mitchell, Timothy, *Blood Sport: A Social History of Spanish Bullfighting* (Philadelphia: University of Pennsylvania Press, 1991).

Violence and Piety in Spanish Folklore (Philadelphia: University of Pennsylvania Press, 1988).

Muchembled, Robert, *Popular Culture and Elite Culture in France, 1400–1750*, translated by Lydia Cochrane (Baton Rouge: Louisiana State University Press, 1985).

Muir, Edward, *Civic Ritual in Renaissance Venice* (Princeton: Princeton University Press, 1980).

Mad Blood Stirring: Vendetta and Factions in Friuli during the Renaissance (Baltimore: The Johns Hopkins University Press, 1993).

Ritual in Early Modern Europe (Cambridge: Cambridge University Press, 1997).

Scribner, Robert W., "Reformation, Carnival and the World Turned Upside-Down" in Robert W. Scribner (ed.), *Popular Culture and Popular Movements in Reformation Germany* (London and Ronceverte, WV: Hambledon Press, 1987), pp. 71–102.

Shubert, Adrian, *Death and Money in the Afternoon: A History of Spanish Bullfighting* (Oxford: Oxford University Press, 1999).

Thomas, Keith, *Man and the Natural World: Changing Attitudes in England, 1500–1800* (London: Allen Lane, 1983).

Thompson, E. P., "'Rough Music': Le Charivari anglais," *Annales: économies, sociétés, civilisations* 27 (1972), pp. 285–312.

Underdown, David, *Revel, Riot, and Rebellion: Popular Politics and Culture in England, 1607–1660* (Oxford: Oxford University Press, 1985).

6   Popular protest

If the antics of youth groups and the festive life of early modern Europeans inflicted considerable harm on humans and animals alike throughout the first centuries of our period, another form of collective action, popular protest, consistently disturbed the era, while drawing on many of the rituals of the festive calendar.

Popular protest could assume several forms in our period. Some of them, as we will see, were nonviolent, but protest often occasioned violence of several types. Bullying and intimidation were widespread in isolated acts of violence directed at individuals by small groups of men and women protesting about some action by their victims. Such acts were often a first step in an agenda of popular violence that could escalate. Civil disturbances in the form of riots – localized collective violence of limited duration – also became possible once protestors moved beyond peaceful agitation. And rebellions – collective violence transcending one locale and enduring for more than a few days – erupted when local protest merged with more general issues, like provincial separatism. Local protest could also escalate into rebellion when it gained the leadership of social elites, such as clerics who enjoyed extraordinary prestige, or aristocrats who had the military training to weld protestors into something like military formations.

The character and genesis of popular protest

Historians of popular protest in our period recognized early on that most of the acts they studied, strictly speaking, were not "revolutionary" movements in our sense of that term. We generally envision protest movements in our own time as aiming at the destruction, or radical modification, of the existing political, social, or economic order. We therefore view such movements as "revolutionary" in nature. Early modern protest movements, on the other hand, reflected the values of an essentially conservative society that accorded great respect to tradition and justified established practices by their antiquity. Hence it was innovation in

184

established economic, political, or religious practices that most frequently elicited resistance from those affected by these changes, and this resistance at times could become violent.

The roots of early modern protests may be found in the extraordinary economic, political, and religious changes overtaking western Europe in the period from 1500 to 1789. Economic change in our period was particularly rapid, as the western European states became part of an international and interdependent capitalist economy approaching an industrial revolution.

Politically, too, this was a period of great change, one in which most western European states increasingly centralized and rationalized their administrative machinery. In large and small states alike this meant even greater involvement of government officials in the business of the state's subjects. Police and justice officials led in this process of intrusion into the formerly isolated rural lives of most western Europeans, and while recent research suggests that administrators often coopted local elites to make this a largely peaceful transition, this was not always a tranquil evolution. At the same time, many cities lost local autonomy that some traced back to medieval charters. Even more disruptive were the fiscal consequences of the development of the early modern state and its principal business, the making of war. Taxes increased everywhere, most markedly in time of war.

Finally, this was a period of jarring religious change. The Reformation's rupture of the religious unity of western European Christians in the sixteenth century confronted both Catholic and Protestant with a religious pluralism neither was prepared to accept. The religious strife of the sixteenth and seventeenth centuries was the result of this division.

Violence, however, was only the last stage of popular protest. Early modern protest had a multifaceted repertoire of action. Resistance to events affecting individuals was the starting point for any collective action, and William Beik has noted that: "Protests began with face-to-face disputes over specific grievances and expanded in widening circles to encompass broader groups and deeper resentments."[1] As particular grievances translated into a general sense of injustice, collective resistance became possible. It usually assumed peaceful forms at first, often what one historian has aptly called "mobilized petitions." In the cities of the Spanish Netherlands, for example, the guilds often took the lead in this. Their corporate status required that municipal government seek their ratification of new taxes and laws. Guild leaders might not merely refuse that consent when called to the town hall, but might actually "remain in

---

[1] William Beik, *Urban Protest in Seventeenth-Century France: The Culture of Retribution* (Cambridge: Cambridge University Press, 1997) p. 27.

place" – in the modern idiom they staged a "sit in" – until they achieved satisfaction. When they did this, of course, the news spread quickly, a crowd gathered, and the risk of a protest's escalation to collective violence increased.

Another form of peaceful protest was simple flight. During the Owingen revolt in Hohenzollern, Germany, in 1584, some seventy-three peasant men abandoned their village on the eve of the harvest. They returned only in November when an Imperial edict promised them immunity until the issues in their protest were settled in law. Sometimes, too, common citizens lodged petitions for redress of their grievances. English farmers repeatedly petitioned for restrictions on landowners' enclosures of pastureland. And peasants might even march to the capital to petition their ruler. The peasants of Rottenbuch Abbey in Bavaria, protesting at the Abbey's attempt to evict a number of them, marched for two days to Munich in 1628 to petition the duke of Bavaria. Although peaceful, their assembly again raised the potential for crowd action. Increasingly, too, in our period, individuals pooled their resources to seek legal redress in court for grievances resulting from social or economic change. But the failure of those expedients could lead to collective violence.

A number of factors drew people together for violent protests. A community often closed ranks in the face of innovation imposed by outside authority that forced neighbors to abandon the interminable internecine conflicts that we examined in Chapter 4. Sometimes community leaders led such protest, and in Spain, for example, it was not uncommon for local officials to lead riots against the billeting of troops. But the mobilization of dissent did not always strictly unify the community. In the response of Black Forest peasants in 1725–45 to the attempts of a local monastery to extend its privileges of lordship at the expense of peasant communal rights, we see that communities did not universally close ranks against a threat. Instead, a complex, violent, three-way conflict between Austrian authorities and moderate and radical peasant factions ensued, known as the Saltpeter Wars.

Much more than simple residential relationship underlay collective violence. Kinship links drew many to collective actions, as is recorded when police and judicial records list the names of accused rioters; the role of family relationships in attracting people to a crowd action is suggested by a seventeenth-century French example. In Abjat, in the French Périgord province, judicial officials responsible for punishing rioters charged 100 residents from that village as well as from nearby hamlets. Seventeen family names appear more than once on the indictment list, and five of them appear more than four times. Fifteen men on the list are identified as the son or son-in-law of another individual on the list.

Ties of friendship could also mobilize individuals for riots both in rural villages and in urban neighborhoods. Women especially seem to have determined the social patterns of neighborhood and village life, managing the household, socializing in the marketplace, and transmitting local oral traditions. Women thus played a key role in drawing on their social connections to rally a crowd. Thus in Rotterdam in the 1780s Kaat Mulder, popularly known as "Kaat Mossel," was a formidable instigator of Orangist crowd actions. A mussel sorter on the docks who distributed the shellfish to the city's fishwives, she had in these women a band of friends who could mobilize their neighborhoods for action. But male sociability also created ties between individuals that could often draw men together for action. In seventeenth-century Germany, for example, the patterns of male friendships established during service with the military entrepreneurs of the Thirty Years' War reappeared among the numerous veterans in the ranks of rioters.

Shared occupational experience drew protestors together as well. Guild unity and traditions of corporate action underlay much popular protest in the Spanish Netherlands, but in areas such as the Dutch Republic, where the guild system was weak by our period, less formal organizations, like those of journeymen, provided social links that could mobilize men for acts of intimidation or riot. Occupational ties transcended the boundaries of single towns or villages, too. Early modern peasants did business over relatively wide market areas and thus had far-flung connections. And even at the level of the individual workshop historians have found bonds that brought men together for collective action.

Women might also play a role in crowd mobilization within workplaces. In areas where protoindustrialization, in the form of domestic manufacturing for merchant capitalists, brought large numbers of women into the workplace, females were very active in fomenting and joining protests. There were a number of such areas in eighteenth-century England, including the handloom regions around Manchester and in Devon, and in the metal-working Black Country where more than half of all nail makers were women. In such areas women figured prominently in protest movements, perhaps, as Hans Medick suggests, because similarities in the male and female work experience produced similar social behavior.[2]

Recreational contacts, too, brought protestors together. No place was more dangerous in this regard than the tavern. As we have seen with

[2] Hans Medick, "The Proto-Industrial Family Economy" in Peter Kriedte, Hans Medick, and Jürgen Schlumbuhm, *Industrialization before Industrialization: Rural Industry in the Genesis of Capitalism*, translated by Beate Schempp (Cambridge: Cambridge University Press, 1981), pp. 61–63.

interpersonal violence, alcohol could inflame tempers and loosen inhibitions. And early modern tavern keepers could be troublemakers; generally more literate and better spoken than their patrons, tavern keepers often emerged as leaders of popular protests. The violence that could burst forth from their establishments was evident in a London riot of 1629. An arrest in Fleet Street on 10 July emptied taverns as rioters turned on the authorities and raised barricades in Fleet Street, The Strand, Saint Martin's Lane, and Drury Lane.

Several other factors facilitated crowd mobilization. Certainly a widespread sense of grievance was essential, but historians have found that rioters also believed they had justice on their side. Tax protestors, for example, often assumed that new imposts were the work of corrupt royal ministers, and that if the monarch only knew of their dishonesty, the taxes would be abolished. The protestors therefore often saw themselves as loyal subjects upholding the old order in defying new taxes or extensions of existing exactions. The latter included the *gabelle* in France, an imposition included in the price of salt bought from the monopoly owners that controlled its sale. This explains why French tax protestors shouted "Long live the King without the gabelle!" and in Spain a frequent refrain was "Long live the King and death to bad government." German protestors habitually justified their actions with appeals to a higher authority such as "natural law" or "Godly law."

Intimidation

At a most basic level, popular protest by small groups might assume the form of bullying and intimidation directed against the property, or persons, of those threatening group interests. The object of such action was to force victims to abandon behavior offensive to the group members. It is impossible to quantify precisely the incidence of such actions because, up to a point, intimidation worked; victims failed to report offenses to the authorities out of fear of further retribution. Nevertheless, historians have uncovered sufficient evidence of such actions to understand the repertoire of this primitive form of protest.

Individual anonymity in such activity was essential for perpetrators to avoid the legal consequences of these actions. But if the intimidation was to have any effect, its victims had to be left in no doubt about the grievances that had called forth their actions. Threats of violence were a fundamental part of protestors' repertoire, a first step in what could become an agenda of escalating violence. Threats could take various forms, both oral and written, and in areas of widespread illiteracy they might even be expressed by primitive drawings scrawled on the walls of the homes of offending parties. The progress of literacy in some areas in our period, however, permitted drafting of anonymous letters that give us documentary evidence of intimidation.

E. P. Thompson studied threatening letters printed in the *London Gazette* by the authorities in the period 1750 to 1820, in the hope of eliciting information on their authors that could lead to criminal conviction under eighteenth-century legislation outlawing such missives.[3] Addressed especially to landlords, employers, magistrates, and public officials, the majority of the 284 letters studied by Thompson threatened these individuals with murder, arson, property damage, mutilation, or other forms of violence. Written typically in the third person and expressing a collective sense of grievance, these letters were almost certainly written by individuals. Nevertheless, they reflect the sense of grievance among residential, occupational, or religious groups, the diverse communities of early modern Europe. Not all threats were formal "letters" in our sense of that word; some were tacked up on an offender's door or tied around a rock and thrown through his window.

The largest set of these eighteenth-century letters dealt with food and subsistence issues like bread prices and marketing practices. One addressed to a flour merchant in 1756 read: "If you don't stop carrin the Flower to Bristoll we will knock you . . . in the Head." Letters of this sort so frequently preceded food riots that they seem to have constituted a sort of informal warning to the authorities to take action on subsistence matters or face violence. Letters also addressed agrarian issues, especially enclosures that cost small farmers access to common and waste lands, and loss of such traditional rights as gleaning. An Essex landlady received this threat in 1773: "Ms. orpen I am informed that you and your family whent before last year and glent up what the pore should have had but if you do this year it is our desire as soon as your corn is in the barn we will have a fire for it is a shame you should rob the poor." Other letters dealt with workplace issues, including working conditions and prices for consumer goods. A journeyman shoemaker in 1787 wrote to a master in his trade: "You damd Insignificant Proud Impearius Rascal your are detested by every one that Works for you . . . but I hope Soone to put an end to your pride by Eliminating the Neighbourhood you live in . . . and if possible would Shove your damd Little Self in to the midst of the Flames."[4]

An anonymous letter addressed to a royal tax official, the receiver of the *taille* in Agen, France, provides an example of threats provoked by the fiscality of the early modern state: "If you continue to persecute people like

---

[3] E. P. Thompson, "The Crime of Anonymity" in Hay *et al.*, *Albion's Fatal Tree: Crime and Society in Eighteenth-Century England* (New York: Pantheon Books, 1975), pp. 255–344.

[4] *Ibid.*, pp. 309–40.

you are doing, and if you do not show feelings of humanity that you have not shown up to now, we warn you that you soon will be a victim . . . those who write you are ready enough to murder you . . . The king would not want any one to persecute the people so harshly. Take heed!"[5]

Threats did not always assume such direct, written form, however. Anonymous property damage contained the implicit threat of escalating violence. Thus enclosing and improving landlords might awake to find their barns burning, their fences destroyed, or their weirs knocked down. Agricultural livestock was always a ready target as well, because owners frequently left animals to graze unguarded. Nocturnal attacks on herds, often by individuals who protected their identities by blackening their faces, might leave sheep and cattle maimed and dogs dead.

Intimidating threats and anonymous violence could overtake individuals, too, as an example from eighteenth-century France suggests. In the village of Soubès, in Languedoc, a complex conflict over land rights between local seigneurs of the Peyrotes family and peasants led to intimidation that echoed local festive ritual and ultimately turned violent. Drawing on the tradition of the charivari, youths with drums, violins, and sundry noise-making objects performed insulting and threatening songs under the seigneur's window in the darkness of Sunday evenings for almost a decade and a half. Shots often accompanied these intimidating serenades to enhance their threatening character. Finally, in 1772, two habitual poachers carried through on the crowd's threats and fired on the seigneur's son, almost killing him. Such intimidation and anonymous acts of terror could escalate, with the growth of a local sense of grievance, to riots.

Riot

Riots might vary in size from a crowd of a few people shouting insults and throwing rocks to actions by thousands causing extensive damage to people and property. Large or small, however, riot represented a serious threat to the political and social stability of early modern Europe, one that the law codes of many early modern states recognized. Numerous issues could mobilize significant crowds that might ultimately turn to more general violence in the form of rebellion.

The legal systems of many European states reflected the danger of riot in the narrow parameters they placed on citizens' rights to assemble. In England, as we saw in Chapter Two, the Riot Act of 1715 increased the

---

[5] Reproduced as Plate 11 of Volume 2 of Yves-Marie Bercé, *Histoire des Croquants: Etude des soulèvements populaires au XVIIᵉ siècle dans le sud-ouest de la France*, 2 vols., (Paris and Geneva: Librairie Droz, 1974). Punctuation added.

traditional penalties for illegal assembly in the wake of the Hanoverian succession. The French monarchy's attempts to limit assembly date at least to the sixteenth century, and by the eighteenth century unlicensed assemblies of four or more persons were forbidden because, as one distinguished jurist wrote, "they can expand to disturb religion, the tranquility of the state, or that of the public."[6] Those armed with guns, or even sticks, attending such assemblies could be judged summarily without appeal by the *prévôtés* of the Maréchaussée, the police courts with a well-earned reputation for swift and harsh justice.

Rioters often drew on rituals already familiar to many from the festive calendar in order to rally protestors, and to lend a certain legitimacy to their actions. Protestors might sing while marching, to the accompaniment of drums, fiddles, and other instruments, in imitation of their activities during popular festivities. They frequently bore symbols of their unrest, too: bread stuck on pikes, green sprigs stuck in their hats like May revelers in some areas, or perhaps bits of colored ribbon affixed to their clothing. Mob violence sometimes even embodied acts associated with the traditional festival calendar. During the disorders of the spring and summer of 1789 French peasants in the Périgord region marched from château to château demanding to be fed. Such action was a mass reenactment of the quests of Holy Thursday, Christmas, and Easter in which youths went from house to house requesting lard, chestnuts, or eggs. In both the riot and the ritual quest, denial led to the crowd storming the homes of those who did not contribute. Rioters in 1789, of course, also sought to burn manorial records and seize the weathervanes that in this region symbolized noble privilege. The enclosure riots in the west of England in the 1620s looked remarkably like skimmingtons. A drummer accompanied rioters as they marched, with an effigy of the offending landowner, to pull down fences in the Forest of Dean.

Despite the gravity and frequency of these threats, however, early modern rulers and magistrates seldom responded with the full force of the law. Perhaps they recognized that most rioters had specific grievances and limited violent repertoires. In any case, as we have seen, the authorities lacked police resources sufficient to take a firm stand against disorder, and the use of regular troops against protests raised problems, too. Early modern officials, therefore, seldom attempted to quell riots and punish large numbers of protestors forcibly. Most riots ran their course in a few days, before many troops could be assembled, anyway. Thus, at most, early modern officials typically tried and executed a few ringleaders as examples when the turmoil died down.

[6] François Serpillon, *Code criminal ou commentaire de l'ordonnance de 1670*, 4 vols., (Lyon: Les frères Perisse, 1767), 1, p. 92.

Riots and rebellions, however, left much better records than bullying and intimidation. Police and government records allow historians to understand crowd composition and the great frequency of these actions. While historical research will certainly never uncover evidence of all acts of riot and rebellion, it does permit scholars to estimate the incidence of such events based on intensive local and regional studies. In France, as in much of Europe, the seventeenth century seems to have been the most violent period. René Pillorget's study of insurrectional movements in Provence in this period turned up records of 268 such actions between 1596 and 1660 and another 110 between 1661 and 1715. A similar study of southwestern France by Yves-Marie Bercé revealed 450–500 riots and rebellions in that region in the years from 1590 to 1715.[7] And one historian's estimate of such events nationwide in the relatively more peaceful eighteenth century through to April 1789 places their number at 5,200. Research in Germany indicates that early modern collective violence was common there, too. In the century and a half between the end of the Thirty Years' War and the end of the eighteenth century, tiny Hesse alone had 55 uprisings, while the larger Margravate of Brandenburg sustained 380.

Although collective protests tended to follow a general pattern, no riot, whatever its origins, was entirely typical. The forms of protest, as Charles Tilly has shown, were learnt repertoires that reflected ambient cultural norms and therefore varied temporally as well as from group to group and place to place.[8] Nor were many riots purely of one cause. Overlaying the original issue of contention might be other concerns as well, as in parts of Germany where food riots might also be expressions of anti-Semitism directed against Jewish merchants. Nevertheless, we can identify a number of basic issues that provoked violent protests in our period.

Early modern Europeans lived in dread of dearth. Such fear was justified. In addition to generally rising prices driven by population growth, harvest failure could produce rapid short-term elevation of prices for the bread that was the fundamental element in the diet of most Europeans, reducing even prosperous artisans to penury and sometimes starvation. Those who did not starve were sufficiently weakened by subsistence problems to become even more vulnerable to disease, and epidemics often followed famines. Periods of dearth and rising prices consequently provoked protest throughout western Europe, and food riots were

[7] Yves-Marie Bercé, *Histoire des Croquants*, and René Pillorget, *Les mouvements insurrectionels de Provence entre 1596 et 1715* (Paris: A. Pédone, 1975).
[8] Charles Tilly, *Popular Contention in Great Britain, 1758–1834* (Cambridge, MA: Harvard University Press, 1995), p. 41, and also his *The Contentious French: Four Centuries of Popular Struggle* (Cambridge, MA: Harvard University Press, 1986), pp. 390–98.

probably the most frequent form of collective violence in our period. The frequency of such violence increased markedly from the late seventeenth century as governments in England, France, Spain, Tuscany, and elsewhere adopted free-market practices and abandoned traditional controls of the grain trade intended to regulate prices and assure supplies.

Governments everywhere recognized the threat to public order posed by shortages, however, and often undertook to provide some relief in times of dearth, either in many Dutch cities, Venice, and Geneva (through distributions from state-owned granaries), or from shipments of flour purchased abroad. Indeed, many subsistence-related disturbances represented a popular effort to elicit such steps, a sort of "collective bargaining by riot," to use the phrase of E. P. Thompson.[9] But if such intervention proved impossible, or was delayed, riot might erupt, especially in the period just before the next harvest, when existing stocks were exhausted and prices high, or in the weeks immediately after harvest, when the crop had not yet reached market but rumors about its quantity and quality were rife.

When they did occur, food riots were not expressions of blind rage. E. P. Thompson was the first to demonstrate the role of the moral economy in motivating popular action. The crowd operated within a popular consensus on what were legitimate marketing, milling, and baking practices for its daily bread, and, most importantly, what constituted a just price in the context of the times. Underlying the whole issue was the concept that food should be affordable, an idea that not infrequently meshed with popular conceptions of personal honor resting on self-sufficiency. In Bavaria, for example, peasants embraced the idea of *Hausnotdurft*, that is, the belief that each household should be able to meet its needs with only the labor of its members on its own farm.

Riots motivated by the frustration of such popular values typically erupted in market centers or along routes on which grain was shipped. They assumed several forms. The classic urban food riot, evident even in the ancient world, was the market riot bred of shortages or high prices. The crowds in this form of riot focused their action on merchants suspected of hoarding grain supplies to drive up prices, or on bakers charging too much for loaves or selling an adulterated product at the price of a normal loaf.

Crowds often pillaged granaries and bakeries for their goods, but they did not always simply carry off what they had seized. Having seized control of grain, flour, or bread, the crowd members often sold the

---

[9] E. P. Thompson, "The Moral Economy of the English Crowd in the Eighteenth Century," *Past and Present* 50 (1971), pp. 77–136.

product to the populace at a "just price," or forced merchants to do so. This act, called *taxation populaire* by the French, is perhaps the clearest expression of the popular moral economy: the crowd did not steal food, but instead sold it at a price considered fair by the crowd – one always lower than that dictated by market conditions. In such cases, the crowd believed that it acted justly, because even when the rioters sold the goods they turned the proceeds of the sales over to the owners; indeed, in some of these actions rioters kept written records of purchases.

Isolated instances of *taxation populaire* have been recorded as early as the fourteenth century, but the frequency of this type of disturbance greatly increased in the late seventeenth century. It was widespread in Andalusia in 1652 when a famine coincided with a debasement of currency. Records of Dutch, English, and French authorities all seem to suggest that this sort of protest was common by the late seventeenth century. It was, for example, a widespread reaction to the Europe-wide crop failures of 1693. And in France's Flour War of 1775 an outbreak of some 300 separate crowd actions in northern France, *taxation populaire* was the most common crowd response. But the circumstances that underlay the Flour War – the coincidence of crop failures with freeing the grain trade from government controls – produced similar unrest in other countries as well. The eighteenth century, in fact, seems to have been the great age of food riots. France, for example, experienced 182 in 1690–1720 but 652 in 1769–90 by one historian's count.

Fatal violence was remarkably limited in these riots, although property damage could be extensive, as crowds broke into granaries and bakeries and pillaged these establishments. Crowd members did mistreat the proprietors of these establishments when they resisted them, but the widespread subsistence rioting in Andalusia in 1652 was not unusual, costing not one life. Occasionally, however, fatal violence did erupt, and an example from Naples suggests that local officials could come in for their share of popular rage that drew heavily on festive ritual.

In May 1585 the electors on the municipal council ordered a reduction in the size of the city's standard loaf of bread. Because bread would continue to sell at its accustomed price, this step constituted a real increase in food prices. Popular anger focused on the elector charged with representing the people on the council, Giovan Vincenzo Storace, a man popularly thought to have been both too friendly with the Spanish viceroy and involved financially with people speculating on the price of grain. So on 8 May 1585 a street crowd seized the sedan chair to which gout confined Storace and carried him backward through the streets, in much the same fashion we have seen cuckolded husbands carried in charivaris. All the while the crowd pelted the elector with various objects, finally killing him, mutilating his corpse and dragging it face down through the streets, as condemned criminals were sometimes conveyed to the gallows. The crowd then cut out Storace's internal organs and carried them through the streets impaled on the tips of its weapons, and there were reports that rioters actually ate his flesh. The crowd eventually tossed the remains of the elector's body near the viceroy's residence with the cry: "Here is bad government." Rioters went on to sack Storace's home and rape the women of his household.

The crowd's retribution visited on a highly placed and wealthy citizen represented a violent inversion of the social hierarchy akin to that we have found common in early modern festive life. Indeed, crowd actions reduced Storace to the level of a beast: he was dismembered as the bull and other beasts were in popular festivals, and his flesh was even consumed, if reports of cannibalism were true. And destruction of his property deprived his heirs of the most visible evidence of his status. Threats of this sort of retributive action in food rioting never entirely disappeared in our period, but other forms of food-related disorder seem to have focused more on the goods in short supply and less on those whom rioters blamed for their woes.

In a second form of food riot, crowds blocked highways or waterways to assure their local food needs by preventing the movement of grain out of their area to large urban markets offering higher prices for agricultural commodities. When they blocked the transport of agricultural products, crowds often seized the commodities outright or sold them off in *taxation populaire*. Historians identify the earliest appearances of this sort of crowd action in the first decades of the seventeenth century, as they developed in response to the increasing market influence of growing urban centers and international trade. They were especially common in the rural hinterlands around great urban centers in times of dearth. In England, for example, they occurred in Norfolk, Essex, Kent, Sussex, Hertfordshire, Hampshire, and the Thames Valley, the regions that supplied the London market, in periods of shortage in the 1630s and 1640s. Sometimes such riots against food transport could be extremely serious, like those that erupted during one of Italy's worst seventeenth-century famines. As grain prices tripled in Rome in 1648, the papal governor in Fermo ordered local grain to be moved to a warehouse for shipment to Rome and deployed troops in position to enforce his commands. Not content with merely interrupting grain shipments, the crowd in Fermo pillaged the governor's palace, stormed the prison where he sought refuge, and killed him.

Another form of violent protest, riot against agricultural innovations, was closely related to food riots. The widely held popular assumption was that enclosures of common land took property out of cultivation and thus reduced the food supply. The enclosure of common lands not only made more difficult the economic survival of smallholders dependent on traditional rights to graze their livestock on commons, but also limited their rights to gather wood, coal, peat, and stone, and to hunt and fish as well. Seventeenth-century Sydenham, Kent, typified the dependence of many rural dwellers on common lands. There, half of the freeholders possessed less than five acres of land, and 40 percent held only a cottage and a garden plot. Rights to commons were essential for such farmers. But other agricultural innovations also threatened traditional land use, especially drainage of fens and creation of deer parks and other game reserves that further reduced resources for the small agriculturalist, and disturbances directed at agricultural change related closely to the local progress of these innovations. Indeed, the mere rumor of change sparked appeals to landowners, threats, litigation, and, as a last resort, riots.

Enclosure of common lands seems to have inspired the most widespread collective violence against agricultural innovation. The fences and hedges that enforced enclosure were the first victims of collective action. Perhaps the most intense period of such riots against enclosure in our period occurred in the years from 1626 to 1632 in the west and center of England, where the cash-starved Stuart monarchy sought to raise revenue by developing the economic potential of the royal forests of Dorset, Wiltshire, Gloucestershire, Worcestershire, and Leicestershire. Accordingly, the crown leased the lands to entrepreneurs drawn chiefly from the court, authorizing them to kill the game on these lands, cut and sell the timber, and subdivide the terrain into enclosed parcels to be let out for farming or stock raising. This process of disafforestation threatened to deprive local smallholders of their traditional rights to common usage of these lands. Even though the crown offered some compensation, their response was a series of riots in which crowds sought to reopen the lands by destroying boundary markings (like hedges, ditches, and fences), pulling down the homes of the enclosers' agents, and physically attacking their workmen. Together these riots were called the Western Rising, although they seem to have remained unconnected local disturbances.

Some of the largest riots occurred in Gloucestershire's Forest of Dean, which had extraordinarily large timber resources, as well as iron and coal deposits that could be mined readily with pits. Local miners particularly claimed rights to the forest, but others benefited from it, too, cutting wood or quarrying stone there. On 25 March 1631 a crowd of 500 men, accompanied by fifes, drums, and banners, marched through the forest destroying enclosures, firing on the home of the encloser's agent, filling in one pit, and throwing cut timber into the Wye River. The Dean riot drew heavily on the rituals of festive life. Several of the leaders called themselves "Skimmington," after the English charivari. The whole event ended, as did popular festivals like Guy Fawkes Night, with the destruction of an effigy – in this case that of Sir Giles Mompesson, the encloser. A larger crowd of some 3,000 returned on 5 April with drums and banners, destroying more enclosures and burning several houses. Smaller riots recurred sporadically for the rest of the seventeenth century.

Another manifestation of the enclosure riot stemmed from contested hunting rights. Throughout early modern western Europe hunting was the privilege of the aristocracy, but in the late seventeenth and eighteenth centuries, in England especially, new laws reinforced this traditional right as the gentry and aristocracy improved their lands to include deer parks and even undertook rearing of game for the commercial market. Landowners defended their interests with armed gamekeepers, spring guns activated by tripwires, and traps for men. These developments interfered with illegal hunting by ordinary farmers and often entailed game destroying their crops. Inevitably, there were conflicts between individuals and game wardens – and riot, too. Both kinds of violence occurred on Cannock Chase, between Stoke and Birmingham, where the earl of Uxbridge, who inherited the tract in 1747, sought to protect his deer from local hunters and to engage in the rearing of rabbits for the urban market. Violence between poachers and gamekeepers was endemic here, but the rabbits, which locals believed destroyed grazing land, were a particular bone of contention. When litigation failed to stop the earl's expansion of his warrens, armed crowds invaded the chase in December 1753 and January 1754, killing perhaps 15,000 rabbits and destroying their warrens. Physical conflict and litigation continued in this area for more than half a century.

On the European continent, too, innovations by seigneurs seeking to increase their manorial revenues by enclosing commons, redrafting land surveys (called cadastres), and raising their peasants' dues provoked appeals, threats, and violence. There was extensive violence in Savoy, for example, for almost 100 years in the late seventeenth and eighteenth centuries. The experience of the La Grange family, which acquired the marquisate of Le Vuache in 1758, is illustrative. The La Granges found themselves in possession of a seigneurie in which the peasants freely cut wood, pastured their livestock, and gleaned on the lord's lands. Their watchmen, intimidated by threats, ignored such practices out of simple fear for their lives. The new lords finally reached the limit of their toleration of peasants' violations of what they claimed as their property in 1781, and local response was violent. Peasants beat a watchman, and when field guards seized five village cows on 27 April in pasture claimed by the seigneur, a crowd of women, armed with rocks and sticks, forced the château gates and recaptured the livestock. Two days later peasants armed with guns, bayonets, and sticks again took their livestock to graze the land claimed by the La Granges and, when the seigneur and his watchmen arrived, drove them off. Another confrontation between the lord and peasants on 6 May on the contested pasture resulted in gunfire, and on 13 May, when the seigneur appeared in the village for mass, a crowd of angry armed peasants greeted him, calling him a coward and a thief. Continued confrontations over hunting and other issues prompted the La Granges to sell the marquisate in 1792.

In addition to agricultural changes, early modern Europeans faced the threatening fiscal and administrative innovations imposed by the centralizing state, and they sometimes raised violent protests against these. The sixteenth, seventeenth, and early eighteenth centuries witnessed antitax riots all over western Europe as governments sought to inflict new burdens on their subjects. As in other forms of riot, the crowd readily identified those they held responsible for the imposts and aimed to punish them. Frequently they succeeded. In part this was the result of the tacit support rioters often enjoyed among officers of local government. Agents of central government regularly noted the suspicious inactivity of local functionaries in the face of such outbreaks. In Santiago de Compostela, Spain, royal commissioners, charged with assessing a new tax for all of Castile in May 1683, met intense opposition from students at the university and the large clerical population that took up the popular cause. Local officials did nothing to control growing unrest, and during the night of 7 May stones and shots hit the residence of one commissioner, Don Juan de Feloaga Ponce de León, and his guards arrested a student with a pistol. When the commissioner attempted to interrogate the student the next day, another crowd assembled and demanded that the young man be handed over to the municipality. Later that day the mob, shouting "Kill, Kill!," stormed the commissioner's house, wounded two servants, killed a horse, and went on to attack the homes of others involved in the assessment. A second attempt to carry out the assessment in January 1684 also provoked a riot.

Elsewhere, tax riots had similar results. Amsterdam experienced three days of antitax rioting in 1748, during which the crowd destroyed the homes of twenty tax collectors, and similar rioting in 1777. And in the small German states, subject to both Imperial levies, which their rulers lacked the power to attenuate, and the imposts of those local governors, taxes could be very high. On top of these the subjects of such states endured special taxes to fund their princes' travels, the dowries of daughters of the ruling family, and, in ecclesiastical states, the consecration of the ruling cleric. Many German riots targeted such extra burdens.

Taxes, however, were just one reflection of the power of the state. By the eighteenth century, the state was assuming ever-greater regulatory powers to confine the poor, police the city, and regulate private and public morality. Such regulation, no matter how well intentioned, could be resented, and many Europeans chose to resist these intrusions of the state into their quotidian affairs. In Spain in 1766 the government of Charles III, which had already promulgated regulations governing vagabondage as well as sites of public misconduct like pool halls, issued a decree banning the wearing of the round hats and capes favored by many men. It did so to facilitate the apprehension of criminals by forbidding articles of clothing that could readily conceal a lawbreaker's identity. Rioting erupted in Madrid on the day the authorities posted the decree, and the disorders continued for more than two weeks, leaving several people dead. The crowd attacked the local prison, too, liberating its inmates and displaying along the street the bodies of the guards and soldiers it had killed.

The Madrid crowd's first two concerns were repeal of the new law and dismissal of the Italian minister, Esquilache, on whom the population blamed the decree. But, as often happened, the crowd soon formed other objectives, most especially lowering food prices. Indeed, even when the authorities restored order in Madrid, riots erupted in sixty-eight other locales where, once again, resentment of government regulations merged with the real physical needs resulting from the poor harvests of 1763, 1764, and 1765.

Religious and ethnic prejudices also produced riots, although sectarian disturbances tailed off markedly after the end of the Thirty Years' War, the age's last great war of religion. Early modern religious riots, as Natalie Z. Davis has emphasized, had their own unique goals and repertoire, at least in France.[10] The aims of religious rioters were several: defending the doctrine of the crowd and denying the validity of the opposing belief system; purging the community of the opposing faith, which crowd members saw as "dirty and diabolic"; and defending the state against false belief by inflicting justice on heresy. Riots frequently developed out of religious observances, festivals, and popular preaching, and crowd members practiced rites of violence that drew heavily on the Bible, the liturgy, and folk traditions. While both Catholic and Protestant rioters took lives, however, their actions, Davis maintains, were different. Catholics, believing that Protestants represented both a danger to their faith and a defilement of society, attacked all their Protestant opponents,

[10] Natalie Z. Davis, "The Rites of Violence" in her *Society and Culture in Early Modern France: Eight Essays* (Stanford: Stanford University Press, 1975), pp. 152–87.

laity as well as clergy, as they sought to purge society of the Protestant threat. Protestants, on the other hand, sought to destroy what they saw as clerical tyranny, so focused their attacks on Catholic clerics. They also exacted great retribution on the physical symbols of Catholicism, destroying entire sanctuaries, relics, and the iconography of the Church of Rome.

Early modern religious rioters lashed out in several different directions. Dissent within a faith was never welcome, which is why anti-Jansenist riots erupted in Catholic eighteenth-century Tuscany. And the confessional diversity of seventeenth- and eighteenth-century England frequently produced riots against Protestant dissenters, especially Quakers and Methodists.

Religious rioters also commonly directed their wrath at those completely outside their faith. For instance, at an Easter season mass in Lisbon in 1506, a crucifix seemed suddenly to shine, and the congregation cried out "Miracle!" One man in attendance, however, voiced doubt, claiming it was only a reflection. His skepticism incurred taunts of "New Christian," that is, allegations that the man was a Jew, only superficially converted to Christianity under pressure by the state and Church. The crowd killed the doubter and burned his body, and the violence expanded into a large riot as two Dominicans, bearing crucifixes through the streets, further excited the populace with cries of "Heresy!" In the next three days rioters killed some 2,000 people in this sixteenth-century pogrom.

In religiously divided sixteenth-century France numerous crowd actions by both Catholics and Protestants contributed to almost three decades of religious civil warfare. The events of Pentecost in Pamiers in 1566 may be suggestive of the character of such riots. The annual observation of Pentecost, traditionally organized by local Catholic youth, featured the selection of "popes," "emperors," "bishops," and "abbots" to lead such festivities as dancing. Local Calvinists had stoned earlier Catholic Pentecostal rites, and this year the Catholics promised revenge. They marched through the streets with a statue of Saint Anthony, and then began dancing, accompanied by musicians. But when the marchers reached the Protestant quarter of town, their song words became "Kill! Kill!" Three days of fighting ensued, in which ultimately the Protestants triumphed.

Religiously diverse England, however, experienced seemingly the largest sectarian disturbance of our period, the Gordon Riots. The origins of these riots are to be found in parliament's passage in 1778 of a Catholic Relief Act that had removed some of the legal disabilities of English Catholics. On Friday 2 June 1780 George Gordon, a peer and president of the Protestant Association, assembled 60,000 of his members in Saint George's Fields in London to present a petition to parliament for repeal of this legislation. They marched peacefully on Westminster, waving flags, sporting blue cockades on their hats, and singing hymns. Once at Westminster Hall, however, their order broke down. Surrounding the hall, they chanted "No popery!" and abused MPs who supported Catholic relief. Part of the crowd then moved off to loot and burn Catholic chapels at the embassies of Bavaria and Piedmont-Sardinia, and other rioters attacked the heavily Irish Moorfields area.

The next day was relatively quiet, but on Sunday 4 June the crowds reassembled and pillaged and burned a Catholic chapel in Moorfields. On Monday this anti-Catholic rioting spread into other Irish districts of London, and crowds began to attack the homes of prominent supporters of Catholic relief. The rioters that day also began to attack non-Catholic sites that were symbols of authority: the homes of the justices involved in attempts to repress the riots, London's prisons, toll gates, and the Bank of England. Municipal government was particularly slow in responding to this disorder, and the riots persisted until Saturday 10 June, when troops finally restored order to the capital. This worst of eighteenth-century British riots, like many early modern disturbances, resulted in extensive property destruction, but even this was restrained, even ritualized. The crowd assailed only selected targets, and Horace Walpole noted that, in pillaging some houses, crowd members threw furniture and goods in the street for burning but did not burn the homes. Rioters drew on early modern festive ritual, too, frequently humiliating the rich and powerful when they fell into their hands, symbolically inverting the social order.

Often closely related to religious rioting were outbreaks of xenophobia that occasionally disrupted the peace. Religion and nationality were intricately linked in our period. Thus in largely Protestant seventeenth-century London foreign Catholics, like the French, the Spanish, and the Venetians, were never completely safe from crowd action. Xenophobia, however, could also incite crowds' actions against their coreligionists. In Spain Catholic fought Catholic in numerous anti-French riots. The seventeenth century was a period of extended warfare between France and Spain, and this may account in some measure for anti-French feeling in the Iberian country. But other issues exacerbated Spanish dislike of the French. The immigrants from the north were the largest foreign community in the country, and they consistently resisted cultural and linguistic assimilation. Moreover, the French controlled crucial sectors of the economy, including many crafts, petty commerce, and service industries in which few Spaniards deigned to work. Often doing work performed by Jews and Moors before their expulsions, the French prospered, and incurred the wrath of the Spanish in frequent riots. The most serious riots were those in the city of Valencia in 1678 and 1691 and in Saragossa in

1694. Demanding expulsion of the French, and often shouting "Long live the king of Spain!" in a primitive expression of nationalism, armed crowds burned French homes and occasionally killed French people.

Religion and xenophobia apart, employment-related issues also sparked frequent collective violence. In much of early modern Europe the law forbade combinations of workers, and while strikes and walkouts did occur, the organizations required to make them successful were secret of necessity. They were also largely transitory, owing to official persecution and the difficulties of organizing in small pre-industrial workplaces where masters commonly worked alongside journeymen and apprentices. As a result, the peaceful strike was not a common weapon for addressing issues of wages and working conditions, and violence was the usual alternative. This might take the form of collective action to destroy an employer's home or business to force a settlement on labor's terms. In 1738 weavers and shear men in Wiltshire achieved their wage and working-condition goals after riots and property destruction. Individuals could be the crowd's victims, too: London coal heavers, on strike in 1768, lashed out not only at employers but also at an official of a rival labor organization opposed to the strike. Strikers armed with cutlasses and clubs stormed his residence swearing to cut out his heart and liver, a threat of the sort of violence we have seen in Naples.

Crowds of workers might damage production equipment and tools as well. Machinery posed a special threat – to which the skilled labor of the age responded robustly – because it jeopardized the wage rates and perhaps very employment of such workers. A mechanical loom for weaving silk ribbons appeared in Danzig in 1578 but local weavers secured its proscription in the city. It came into use in the Dutch Republic somewhat later, but its use there was limited by the demands of weavers. In England its unrestricted adoption led to petitions to the crown protesting against "this devilish invention" on which "one man doth more than seven English men can so as their cheap sale of the commodities [ribbons] beggareth all our English artificers of that trade."[11] The failure of such petitions to restrict machinery contributed to widespread riots on 9 August 1675 in the weaving center of east London and other areas around the capital, and in Middlesex, Essex, Surrey, and Kent. Labor was well organized; weavers wore green aprons and marched to the locations of the looms, burned the devices, and then mostly dispersed. In this extensive disorder one weaver lost his life to a machine owner defending his property.

[11] Quoted in Richard M. Dunn, "The London Weavers' Riot of 1675," *Guildhall Studies in London History* 1 (1973), p. 14.

On the continent organizations of journeymen not only agitated illegally to improve their wages and work conditions, but also fought among themselves. Many of these craftsmen belonged to secret organizations, known as *compagnonnages* in France, which competed for the allegiances of journeymen. The rivalries between the members of these organizations was intense and produced frequent brawls between their adherents. In fact, Bordeaux court records contain evidence of 181 major brawls and small riots of this kind in that city between 1743 and 1790. The problem of these riotous brawls was so great as to be recognized in municipal ordinances in France: "They gather and go out onto the large thoroughfares and . . . abuse those who are not of their sect with blows of heavy canes . . . moreover, they run around in the night with sabers and drawn swords in hand, eventually led to fight by rage and unparalleled fury so as to kill one another."[12]

Still other causes could produce riots in early modern Europe. Political issues provoked rioting at times, even though this was not an age of mass participation in politics. In the Dutch Republic, for example, the ongoing conflict between the republican merchant oligarchy that often dominated the States General, and the Orange dynasty that aspired to establish a powerful and hereditary office of Stadtholder, resulted in recurring riots in the seventeenth and eighteenth centuries. Perhaps the most famous instance of Orangist rioting, however, occurred in August 1672 as French armies invaded the republic in the Dutch War of Louis XIV (1672–79). Blaming the republican leader Jan de Witt, the Grand Pensionary of Holland, for initial Dutch defeats as Prince William of Orange assumed the Stadtholderate, mobs rioted in many Dutch cities. In The Hague the crowd seized de Witt and his brother, then beat, stabbed, and shot them. Mirroring retributive acts that we have examined previously, the crowd mutilated their corpses, and, as in the Storace bread riot in Naples, there were reports of cannibalism. The crowd then strung up the victims' remains upside down from the local gallows. Hanging upside down seems to have been a universal mob penalty for offenses that rioters considered so heinous as to turn the world upside down. We find it the fate not only of these Dutch riot victims, but of others as well. The mutilated corpse of the French Protestant leader Gaspard de Coligny ended up in this fashion after the Saint Bartholomew's Day Massacre in Paris in 1572, as did the remains of victims of the Communeros uprising in Spain in 1520.

Local politics, too, could beget riots, nowhere more than in Germany where the independence of many city-states gave their town councils

---

[12] Montpellier ordinance, 11 May 1730, quoted in Cynthia Maria Truant, *The Rites of Labor: Brotherhoods of Compagnonnages in Old and New Regime France* (Ithaca: Cornell University Press, 1994), p. 117.

almost absolute power. Indeed, in this regard the seventeenth century was a particularly turbulent era. Conflicts between burghers and their magistrates over a range of issues from taxes to malfeasance in office led to numerous crowd actions. Often crowds seized the city hall to induce the magistrates to resign, although in Frankfurt in 1614 the occupiers had to lock local magistrates in the council chamber for five days, all the while stoking the furnace, to coerce the resignation of their hungry and hot officials. In Frankfurt, too, resentment of patrician administrative chicanery mixed with anti-Semitism to prompt the crowd to sack the Jewish ghetto.

In an age of mass illiteracy, when most news passed by word of mouth, mere rumor could occasion unrest, too. Unfounded rumors of new taxes, brigands, and other threats could all stir up popular violence, as the events of May 1750 in Paris illustrate. Famine in 1747 and 1748 had driven large numbers of the poor into the French capital, and the crown soon armed the police with new powers to remove these vagrants from the streets. In addition, a new police administrator encouraged arrests of vagrants by promising bounties – a step that prompted policemen to arrest almost anyone, including children, in order to collect. These arrests, along with government orders earlier in the century to transport vagrants to the colonies, seem to have been the source of rumors that the police were indiscriminately seizing Parisian children. The rumors' explanations of the seizures were sometimes fantastic: one was that the authorities were using children to provide blood for therapeutic baths for a prince with leprosy! Nevertheless, crowds soon began interfering with arrests, attacking police, and beating strangers. A riot engulfed the Marais district on 16 May, and on 22 May six different riots raged, with some crowds 5,000 strong, as Parisians pursued suspicious persons, stoned public buildings, and ransacked gun shops for arms. Among the numerous victims of this crowd violence was a policeman, whose mutilated body the crowd dragged through the streets on 23 May. The power of rumor, however, was even more clearly demonstrated by events six days after the policeman's death in Paris; rumors had by that time reached Tours, where a crowd apprehended four strangers, accusing them of kidnapping children for shipment to Louisiana.

Crowd identity

Contemporary police and governmental authorities recognized the immanent threat popular protests posed to public order, but only in the mid-twentieth century did historians accord it due regard by beginning the systematic study of such acts. Until that study began, most scholars essentially interpreted early modern popular protest from the perspective of those who recorded its outbreak: the police and judicial officials charged with repression of the disturbances and the maintenance of order. From that point of view, most popular protest was an explosion of the blind violence of the lowest orders of society, groups referred to in early modern French police records as social "scum" (*la lie du peuple*). But the work of two generations of twentieth-century social historians on early modern popular protest now enables a much better understanding of crowd composition.

Studies from all over western Europe confirm that the most active group in crowd actions were those whom George Rudé called the *menu peuple*, that is, those who derived their livings from skilled or semiskilled crafts, shops, or small agricultural holdings. These were not the riffraff of the streets but people with fixed residences, who could often post substantial bails to secure their release from arrest, and were generally literate enough to draft placards and simple protest literature. They were very vulnerable to fluctuations in food prices because of their relatively modest incomes, and relied directly or indirectly on exploitation of the pasture or mineral resources of commons for income, too. Moreover, they feared sudden tax increases cutting further into already tight family budgets, and commonly participated enough in the organs of local government to resent new assertions of outside authority in their communities.

On certain issues other orders of Old Regime society might join collective actions. Religious riots could mobilize a true cross-section of most societies, including clerics, attorneys and officials, and even gentlemen. Tax protests could also draw the participation of socially elite groups, and these might even join in food rioting if it was directed at people against whom they bore a grudge. Several Neapolitans of some standing, for example, took part in the food riot of 1585 because of personal grudges against Storace.

Critically impoverished people, in contrast, seem to have been fairly underrepresented in crowd actions, and historians have advanced several explanations for their relative absence. The most common has been that the starving are either too weakened physically or are rendered too passive by the culture of poverty to participate, even in food riots. A far more persuasive explanation was advanced by Cynthia Bouton in her study of the Flour War of 1775.[13] Noting the evolution of western attitudes toward the poor in both Catholic and Protestant areas since the early sixteenth century, she found poor people marginalized, stigmatized by their condition, and increasingly feared by their more prosperous neighbors as criminals and vagabonds. Consequently, most of them were excluded from the

[13] Cynthia A. Bouton, *The Flour War: Gender, Class, and Community in Late Ancien Régime French Society* (University Park: Pennsylvania State University Press, 1993), pp. 110–12.

communal, kinship, occupational, and other bonds we have seen were instrumental in marshaling people for crowd actions.

The gender composition of early modern crowds was as significant as their social make-up. The presence of women in early modern crowds was large and consistent, and one historian has estimated them at a third of the participants of late eighteenth-century English riots. Women even emerge frequently as leaders in crowd actions. Given the situation of early modern women – one in which they were often treated legally as minors – such prominence requires explanation.

The presence of women in food riots stemmed in part from their role within the family. Charged with the household economy, including marketing, they were sensitive to food-price increases. They were also present in the marketplace and street, ready recruits for protest about the cost of subsistence. Indeed, as Olwen Hufton noted: "A bread riot without women is an inherent contradiction,"[14] and women were present in more than 95 percent of the food riots in the Flour War of 1775. But women were active in all sorts of collective violence, and their participation in other crowd actions is not so easily explained.

We have seen that early modern society considered women to be naturally disorderly and ruled by their lower passions. Consequently, they were under the legal tutelage of husbands or fathers, and were popularly assumed to incur diminished liability in law for their actions and be less likely than men to draw down the full force of the authorities in reestablishing order. Such assumptions seem to have encouraged active female participation in riots and are evident in the shout heard in a seventeenth-century Rotterdam religious riot: "Women can do nothing wrong!"[15] And a riot erupting from an auction for a lease to collect a tax on peat in Oudewater, Holland, in 1628, reinforces the view that women took the lead in such events because they expected no retribution for their actions. As citizens turned on the bidder for the lease, a woman cried out: "Let us sound the drum and send our husbands home. We will catch the villain and beat him, as we cannot be tried for fighting."[16] Evidence from all over western Europe also suggests that, if men did not always defer to women in protesting, they were prepared to disguise themselves as women to escape the full weight of the law. In the 1770s male peasants, dressed as women and with faces blackened, attacked surveyors working for a new landlord in eastern France. And in Edinburgh, in the Proteus Riots of 1736 against a royal official and the customs laws and union with England

---

[14] Olwen Hufton, "Women in Revolution, 1789–1796," *Past and Present* 53 (1971), p. 95.
[15] Quoted in Rudolf M. Dekker, "Women in Revolt: Popular Protest and its Social Basis in Holland in the Seventeenth and Eighteenth Centuries," *Theory and Society* 16 (1987), p. 344.   [16] *Ibid.*, p. 345.

that he represented, "Madge Wildfire" led a crowd consisting in large part of men dressed as women.

Rebellion

The first two centuries of our period, especially, were an era in which rebellion repeatedly challenged central government authority throughout western Europe. The frequency of these rebellions, in fact, has generated a substantial historical literature on what has been called the "general crisis" of the late sixteenth and seventeenth centuries, and it underlines the gravity of the riots we have examined.

The danger of these riots was that their violence would become generalized and move beyond the level of localized disturbances. This occurred most typically when local issues merged with broader concerns, often of a provincial, regional, or national scope. The risk to the early modern political and social order increased further, if, in the process of expansion, a protest movement acquired the leadership of social elites with great prestige or military experience. Several examples illustrate the threats inherent in the issues that sparked early modern rioting, and emphasize again the violence of the age.

In the German Peasants' Revolt of 1525 we find the largest rebellion in western Europe in our period, one that led perhaps 300,000 people to take up arms but that essentially was misnamed from the first. This was not simply a peasants' revolt but one that also drew on unrest in urban and mining areas so as to merit being called, as Peter Blickle suggested, a "revolution of the common man."[17] Historians identify multiple causes for this revolt and its large following.

By the second half of the fifteenth century, Germany's population was recovering from the effects of the bubonic plague of the fourteenth century, while its economy was rebounding from the economic effects of that demographic disaster. The increased labor supply seems to have driven wages downward, while demographic growth increased the demand for life's necessities and propelled prices upward. Landowners sought to profit from this situation in a variety of ways that caused peasant discontent. They increasingly appropriated commons for their own use, shortened peasant leases in order to raise rents at renewal and to collect the fees that peasants paid at that time, and attempted to increase peasant labor service and dues.

Peasants experienced increased pressure from other quarters at the

---

[17] Peter Blickle, *The Revolution of 1525: The German Peasants' War from a New Perspective*, translated by Thomas A. Brady Jr. and H. C. Erik Midelfort (Baltimore: The Johns Hopkins University Press, 1981), p. 105.

same time. Clerical institutions, to which they owed the tithe, collected that obligation more rigorously because of inflation. And the rulers of the individual German states pursued policies typical of their peers in this age. Taxes rose to support growing bureaucracies and military establishments, and central authority eroded the traditional autonomy of the village community, or *Gemeinde*, particularly in legal matters in which the state supplanted customary law with Roman legal practice.

Shaping peasant responses to these pressures were a number of ancillary developments. Early modern harvest failure was common, but it seemed more frequent than usual in late fifteenth- and early sixteenth-century Germany. Indeed, in the Alsace region the crop failed fifteen times in the period from 1475 to 1525. Such failures gave credibility to astrological predictions for dramatic events to deliver the peasants from their misery in 1525, and there was a sense of expectation among the peasantry. There was also a tradition of rebellion, particularly in southern and western Germany.

The developments we have traced produced, in part, the Bundschuh Rebellion in Alsace as early as 1439. Similar peasant rebellions erupted in 1493, 1502, 1513, and 1517 in southern and western Germany. To the memories of this rebellious tradition among German peasants must be added the Protestant Reformation, whose main German spokesman was Martin Luther. While Luther certainly condemned the revolution of 1525, the example of his defiance of Rome could only have enhanced peasant willingness to challenge authority of every sort. Rebellious peasants drew on traditional elements that we noted in other German protests. Earlier peasant rebels had justified their resistance with appeals to traditional rights and law, and the rebels of 1525 invoked "God's law" to demand a new order that included an end to serfdom and greater autonomy for local communities.

The rebellion began in early 1525 as peasants in their individual villages first refused dues to their lords, presented grievances to them, and at times undertook negotiations. Violence was a last resort, as usual, but it broke out eventually, its typical targets being the monasteries that represented ecclesiastical lordship in the countryside and the castles inhabited by aristocratic landlords as well as rulers. The peasants burned and plundered these places and sometimes killed their residents. More typically, peasants forced noblemen who fell into their hands simply to swear allegiance to their emerging program.

The rebellion quickly spread, aided by the absence of the forces of the Swabian League in Italy in the service of Emperor Charles V. As the outbreaks spread, peasants enunciated their demands in a number of manifestos, the most concise of which was the Twelve Articles of the Upper

Swabian peasantry that incorporated many local demands and were printed, distributed, and often publicly read. Written with biblical references, the Twelve Articles propagated a program of social, legal, and religious reform. They demanded an end to serfdom, restoration of rights to common lands, the more equitable appropriation of seigneurial dues and rents, and the abolition of feudal death duties on peasant property. Further, they demanded an end to legal innovations, election of parish clerics, lowering of the tithe, and administration of its proceeds by the *Gemeinde*. Such demands generated a revolutionary following that transcended both the rural areas of Germany and the peasant order.

The movement's backbone remained the more prosperous peasants and village leaders, not the homeless poor. But as whole villages rose up, they naturally looked to local market towns for leadership. In one town the mayor might assume leadership, in another the innkeeper, and, as the rebellion grew, more exalted figures joined. The rebels in the Lake Constance region marched under the leadership of a patrician landowner and the administrator of the lands of a wealthy cloister. In the towns and cities craftsmen and small merchants, long excluded from the oligarchies that traditionally ran such municipalities, joined the rebellion, as did those in whom the rebels' spiritual ideas struck a chord. Miners, many of whom farmed as well, also joined in some parts of Germany. Even members of the aristocracy participated. Duke Ulrich of Württemberg, who had been dispossessed by the Habsburgs, sought the restoration of his ducal dignities by joining the uprising. And Imperial knights, losing influence to the rising power of the centralizing states of German princes, often cast their lots with the rebels, as did some clergy.

Repression of the rebellion was slow in coming, but extremely brutal when it came. The Imperial victory over the French at Pavia on 24 February 1525 freed the soldiers of the Swabian League for such service, and in late spring the forces of other German princes reinforced them. The rebels were at a great disadvantage in the face of such force as they attempted to unify their local movements into military units. Weak in artillery, leadership, and training, rebel forces quickly met defeat, and their fighters died in large numbers. At Zabern the forces of the duke of Lorraine were said to have slain 20,000 Alsatian peasant fighters. Elsewhere, princely forces burned villages, executed leaders, and exacted other punishments. Contemporaries estimated that 100,000 died on the battlefields and in the subsequent repression. In the wake of the rebellion, however, many German rulers answered some of the peasant demands; many, too, created legal mechanisms that in the future could channel their subjects' grievances into litigation, not violence.

If a mixture of agricultural and political grievances sparked the

German rebellion of 1525, different issues that we have seen provoking rioting underlay other rebellions. Tax increases were consistent causes of early modern rebellion, and they often drew the support of broad segments of society that confronted the authorities with a vertical alliance of social groups ranging from peasants to noblemen. France experienced the greatest number of such rebellions in the sixteenth and seventeenth centuries, but no fiscal revolt posed a greater threat to the political structure of the early modern state than that of the Catalans in 1640. In this case, resistance to a fiscal exaction combined with Catalan nationalism to produce a powerful separatist revolt.

The early modern Spanish kingdom was the product of the marriage of the Catholic monarchs, Isabella of Castile and Ferdinand of Aragon, in 1469, and under this personal union the components of the realm retained their traditional rights. Part of the kingdom of Aragon, the principality of Catalonia kept its distinct language and culture, as well as limits on monarchical authorities summed up in its *constitucións* and defended by its representative body, the cortes. These traditional rights collided with the policies of the chief minister of Philip IV, Gaspar de Guzmán, the count-duke of Olivares. Dominating Spain from 1622 to 1643 and determined to stem the decline of the Spanish monarchy's power in Europe, Olivares pursued a foreign policy that kept the country at war throughout his ministry.

Financing this war effort became an increasingly difficult task, one that led Olivares to seek greater contributions from the components of the monarchy. But in 1626 the cortes of Catalonia rebuffed his plan for a Union of Arms, a scheme that would have required all of the states of the monarchy to support troops in a common army. To the Catalans, the plan appeared to be one more attempt at their domination by neighboring Castile. The cortes rejected a second attempt by the count-duke to secure military subsidies in 1632.

By 1639 Spain's military situation was worsening, and a French invasion forced the monarchy to maintain an army in Catalonia. At the end of the campaign season, Olivares resolved to force Catalonia to contribute to its own defense by ordering that the army be billeted there in preparation for the spring campaign. The *constitucións* were quite clear regarding what the count-duke planned. They stated that Catalan householders were obligated to provide each individual soldier with only a bed, a table, a light, salt, water, and vinegar; Catalans could not be required to provide anything else, unless authorized by vote of the provincial cortes. Billeting was clearly illegal, because Olivares expected the province to both feed and house troops. Moreover, his call for a spring 1640 meeting of the cortes suggested to many Catalans that billeting was the opening wedge in a renewed drive by the royal minister to impose other exactions on the province.

As we have seen, the quartering of troops frequently led to violence between military personnel and early modern civilians, but in Catalonia in 1640 the principles of taxation and provincial rights were at stake, and violence quickly erupted. It is impossible to ascertain whether soldiers desperate for food, or citizens, struck the first blow, but by early February violent incidents were multiplying, with crowds expressing their provincial loyalties in the traditional cry, "Long live the land [of Catalonia]!" By spring marauding Catalan bands were attacking billeted troops and fleeing into the mountains when pursued. Finally, on the feast of Corpus Christi (7 June 1640), a rebellious mob in Barcelona killed the royal viceroy. This act eliminated the chief symbol of royal authority, and in the summer of 1640 local elites joined the rebellion.

The Diputació, a six-man standing committee of the cortes representing the clergy, the aristocracy, and the towns of Catalonia, assumed leadership of the revolt. Led by a priest, this committee embodied the province's rights under its *constitucións* and its adherence gave the rebellion legitimacy and support from all segments of Catalan society. With such support the Diputació in 1641 deposed Philip IV as count of Barcelona (the position on which royal authority in the province rested), and placed Catalonia under French sovereignty. The crown restored its control of Catalonia only in 1652, after years of warfare and a lengthy siege of Barcelona. But the province was hardly pacified; rebellions erupted in 1688 and 1689, and again in 1705 during the War of the Spanish Succession. The latter uprising finally cost the province many of its historic privileges.

Religion, so often at the root of early modern riots, precipitated one of the last great rebellions of our period: that of the Protestant Camisards of the mountainous Cévennes region in Languedoc in southern France. The number of Protestants (or Huguenots, as members of the reformed faith were known) in seventeenth-century Languedoc was large, and they suffered a myriad of problems in the last two decades of the century. Like their Catholic neighbors, they endured the general regional economic decline that Emmanuel Le Roy Ladurie studied, as well as particularly frequent occurrences of the harvest failures and epidemics that afflicted all early modern Europeans.[18] The wheat-harvest failure in 1685, for example, reduced many to a diet of acorns and grass. At the same time, too, all residents of the Cévennes faced rising royal taxes to fund the wars

[18] Emmanuel Le Roy Ladurie, *The Peasants of Languedoc,* translated by John Day (Urbana: University of Illinois Press, 1974).

of King Louis XIV. But the Huguenots also faced growing religious persecution, culminating in 1685 with the king's revocation of the Edict of Nantes that had permitted the existence of the reformed faith. A new royal edict expelled reformed clerics from the realm, forbade Huguenot worship, closed their schools and churches, and required Catholic baptism of their children. Religious toleration ended, and an intense persecution began.

Huguenot beliefs were rooted especially deeply in the Cévennes, where the conversion of the heavily peasant population had been so thorough that its very cultural life revolved around psalms, hymns, and Protestant ritual. Here, then, the crown's attack on the faith was an attack on a whole culture and way of life as well, and Huguenot despair in the last years of the seventeenth century was intense. This despair made Huguenots receptive to the writings of the exiled reformed theologian, Pierre Jurieu, and others. Drawing on the visions of the Book of Daniel, Jurieu predicted that the final end of papism and a reign of peace and righteousness would follow religious persecution. Writings with this theme were widely disseminated in the region and peasant preachers adopted these ideas, too. Such millenarianism, accompanied by the hysteria of secret religious meetings, contributed to Protestant uprisings in 1689, 1692, and 1700.

The Camisard revolt began in July 1702 when a Huguenot predicant and his followers killed several Catholic clerics involved in the persecution of Protestants. The burden of new royal taxes may also have determined some Huguenots to enlist in the cause, and the result was a mass rebellion. The rebels attacked Catholic churches and clergy in particular and waged a highly successful guerrilla war against royal authority. Restoration of order in the region, in the midst of the War of Spanish Succession, tied down Marshal Villars and a royal army of 25,000 men until 1705. Even with such force, Villars restored peace more by amnesties and de facto toleration than military might.

Containing collective violence

In the last century of our period, the frequency of acts of collective violence began to diminish, a number of developments contributing to this pacification of Europe. Outright rebellion and riot became increasingly dangerous with the growth of disciplined military forces at the command of early modern states. While such forces were never satisfactory for policing, as we saw in Chapter 2, they could be deployed to great effect in the face of uprisings against central authority.

The increasing monopolization of force by the centralized state was not, however, the only reason for the decline of riot and rebellion. The bureaucratized early modern state progressively took proactive steps to eliminate the causes of such unrest. Police authorities kept close track of food prices, and when local shortages drove them beyond the means of many, initiated steps to ship in emergency supplies to meet local needs. At the same time, the spreading agricultural revolution of the eighteenth century resulted in a more productive agriculture. That productivity slowly eliminated subsistence crises that had been at the root of much unrest, England and the Dutch Republic profiting first and then, by the early nineteenth century, much of western Europe.

The centralized states that benefited from this enhanced agricultural productivity also began in the sixteenth century the creation of judicial systems that we have seen providing alternatives to feuds and other conflicts. Winfried Schulze and Hilton Root found that the growing accessibility of royal justice provided the means for resolving much conflict between peasants and seigneurs through nonviolent, legal channels.[19] But where peasant unrest remained unsatisfied by the law and burst into violent rebellion, it increasingly lost elite leadership.

Two generations' modern study of early modern popular rebellions has identified their complexity amply. The work of Roland Mousnier and others has shown that peasant rebellions, for example, cannot be defined in simple terms of class conflict.[20] These historians revealed that peasant revolts were often vertical social alliances in which peasant grievances merged with those of aristocrats and others. The result was mass risings against the fiscality of the growing state. But, by the late seventeenth century, the processes described by Norbert Elias increasingly integrated European aristocracies into the behavioral norms of the court society. The result, as we have seen already, was a diminution of private aristocratic warfare and general rebelliousness. Aristocratic participation in revolts, which often provided early modern peasants with their leadership, disappeared as well.

Finally, the objectives and repertoires of popular protest began to change at the end of our period, reflecting many of these developments. By the mid-nineteenth century, in fact, the collective violence that we have examined was an anachronism in much of western Europe. The work of Charles Tilly on popular protest in England and France provides

[19] Winfried Schulze, "Die veränderte Bedeutung sozialer Konflikte im 16. und 17. Jahrhundert" in *Europäische Bauernrevolten der frühen Neuzeit* (Frankfurt am Main: Suhrkamp, 1982), pp. 276ff., and *Bäuerlicher Widerstand und feudale Herrschaft in der frühen Neuzeit* (Stuttgart-Bad Cannstatt: Fromann-Holzboog, 1980). See also Hilton Root, *Peasants and King in Burgundy: Agrarian Foundations of French Absolutism* (Berkeley: University of California Press, 1987).

[20] Roland Mousnier, *Peasant Uprisings in Seventeenth-Century France, Russia, and China*, translated by Brian Pearce (New York: Harper and Row, 1970).

a description of the process. Early modern protests were parochial, in that their activity almost always had a local focus. Local cultural life also dictated a varied repertoire for these actions, as we have seen. But nineteenth-century state development and the emergence of a modern, capitalist economy with a national or international focus changed all of this. Protest required mobilization on a national scale, by political, labor, or consumers' organizations, and no longer addressed local authority figures but officials of national government. The repertoire of protest changed, too; it became one of mass demonstrations and the general strike.

FURTHER READING

Beik, William, *Urban Protest in Seventeenth-Century France: The Culture of Retribution* (Cambridge: Cambridge University Press, 1997).

Bercé, Yves-Marie, *Revolt and Revolution in Early Modern Europe: An Essay on the History of Political Violence*, translated by Joseph Bergin (New York: St. Martin's Press, 1987).

Bernard, Leon, "French Society and Popular Uprisings under Louis XIV," *French Historical Studies* 3 (1964), pp. 454–74.

Blickle, Peter, *The Revolution of 1525: The German Peasants' War from a New Perspective*, translated by Thomas A. Brady Jr. and H. C. Erik Midelfort (Baltimore: The Johns Hopkins University Press, 1981).

Bouton, Cynthia A., *The Flour War: Gender, Class, and Communities in Late Ancien Régime French Society* (University Park: Pennsylvania State University Press, 1993).

Briggs, Robin, "Popular Revolt in its Social Context" in Robin Briggs, *Communities of Belief: Cultural and Social Tension in Early Modern France* (Oxford: Oxford University Press, 1984), pp. 106–77.

Elliott, J. H., *The Revolt of the Catalans: A Study in the Decline of Spain (1598–1640)* (Cambridge: Cambridge University Press, 1963).

Farge, Arlette and Revel, Jacques, *The Rules of Rebellion: Child Abductions in Paris in 1750*, translated by Claudia Mieville (Cambridge: Polity Press, 1991).

Hay, Douglas, "Poaching and Game Laws on Cannock Chase" in Hay *et al.*, *Albion's Fatal Tree: Crime and Society in Eighteenth-Century England* (New York: Pantheon Books, 1975), pp. 189–253.

Kamen, Henry, "A Forgotten Peasant Insurrection of the Seventeenth Century: The Catalan Peasant Rising of 1688," *Journal of Modern History* 49 (1977), pp. 210–30.

Kaplan, Steven, *The Famine Plot Persuasion in Eighteenth-Century France* (Philadelphia: American Philosophical Society, 1983).

Koenigsberger, H. G., "The Revolt of Palermo in 1647" in H. G. Koenigsberger, *Estates and Revolutions: Essays in Early Modern European History* (Ithaca: Cornell University Press, 1971).

Land, Stephen K., *Kett's Rebellion: The Norfolk Rising of 1549* (Totowa, NJ: Rowman and Littlefield, 1978).

Larqué, Claude, "Popular Uprisings in Spain in the Mid-Seventeenth Century," *Renaissance and Modern Studies* 26 (1982), pp. 90–107.

MacKay, Ruth, *The Limits of Royal Authority: Resistance and Obedience in the Seventeenth-Century* (Cambridge: Cambridge University Press, 1999).

Mousnier, Roland, *Peasant Uprisings in Seventeenth Century France, Russia, and China*, translated by Brian Pearce (New York: Harper and Row, 1970).

Mullett, Michael, *Popular Culture and Popular Protest in Late Medieval and Early Modern Europe* (London: Croom Helm, 1987).

Reinhardt, Steven G., "The Revolution in the Countryside: Peasant Unrest in the Périgord, 1789–1790" in Steven G. Reinhardt and Elizabeth A. Cawthon (eds.), *Essays on the French Revolution: Paris and the Provinces* (College Station: Texas A & M University Press, 1992), pp. 12–37.

Rodriguez, Laura, "The Spanish Grain Riots of 1766." *Past and Present* 79 (1973), pp. 117–46.

Rudé, George, *The Crowd in the French Revolution* (Oxford: Oxford University Press, 1959).

  The Crowd in History: A Study of Popular Disturbances in France and England, 1730–1848 (New York: John Wiley and Sons, 1964).

Scribner, Robert W. and Benecke, Gerhard (eds.), *The German Peasant War of 1525: New Viewpoints* (Boston: Allen and Unwin, 1979).

Te Brake, Wayne P., "Revolution and the Rural Community in the Eastern Netherlands" in Louise and Charles Tilly (eds.), *Class Conflict and Collective Action* (Beverly Hills: Sage Publications, 1981), pp. 27–53.

Thompson, E. P., "The Crime of Anonymity" in Hay *et al.*, *Albion's Fatal Tree*, pp. 255–308.

  Whigs and Hunters: The Origins of the Black Act (New York: Pantheon Books, 1975).

Tilly, Charles, *The Contentious French: Four Centuries of Popular Struggle* (Cambridge, MA: Harvard University Press, 1986).

Tilly, Louise, "The Food Riot as a Form of Political Conflict in France," *Journal of Interdisciplinary History* 2 (1971), pp. 23–57.

  "Food Entitlement, Famine and Conflict," *Journal of Interdisciplinary History* 14 (1983), pp. 333–49.

Truant, Cynthia M., *The Rites of Labor: Brotherhoods of Campagnonnage in Old and New Regime France* (Ithaca: Cornell University Press, 1994).

Underdown, David, *Revel, Riot and Rebellion: Popular Politics and Culture in England, 1603–1660* (Oxford: Oxford University Press, 1985).

7 Organized crime

Criminal justice professionals and the public alike employ the term "organized crime" to denote the offenses committed by those who cooperate in repeated acts of lawbreaking. Early modern Europeans suffered even more than their modern descendants from organized crime and, like them, recognized its signal characteristics. Such criminality can assume many forms, from nonviolent petty theft and sophisticated burglary to armed robbery and murder, and single organizations sometimes engage in several different crime forms. Moreover, organized crime is particularly difficult to extirpate. It enlists many individuals to commit its crimes, but often has many more as its auxiliaries. Such people sometimes have deep roots in society as ostensibly lawabiding citizens, or even in police agencies, yet they receive (or fence) stolen goods, shelter criminals from the authorities, or meet criminals' needs in other ways.

In early modern Europe, an age lacking what we would consider essential modern police services, bands of armed men engaged in organized crime frequently roved unimpeded in western Europe, threatening citizens with sudden violence. Bandits were endemic, employing violence in armed robberies of travelers, farmers, and others possessing wealth. Smugglers also inflicted violence upon the community during this period. Groups of smugglers, like that of Mandrin that we encountered in Chapter 1, were common throughout western Europe. Smugglers waged an ongoing guerrilla war against revenue agents and police, and although they sometimes had deeper roots in their communities than bandits, they were prepared to kill anyone, including their neighbors, who interfered with their illegal trade.

We will find that the dangers posed by these groups slowly diminished in the course of the early modern period. The growing power of the western European state by the late eighteenth century began to rid the countryside of armed bands, and better-patrolled coasts and borders of smugglers. But for much of our period threats from these groups were all too real.

216

Banditry

Banditry was perhaps the chief early modern manifestation of violent organized crime. This criminality of armed men and women inflicted considerable violence on its victims, and attempting to understand it has been a longstanding concern. In the early modern period, as we saw in Chapter 1, police officials and popular authors alike understood it as the work of a distinct criminal subculture, almost a breed apart from that of lawabiding citizens. This interpretation of banditry proved durable indeed, and this perhaps explains why modern scholarly study of the problem began only in the late 1950s with the seminal work of an English historian, Eric J. Hobsbawm.[1]

Hobsbawm drew on often romanticized popular ballads, poems, and legends about armed bands of robbers as the sources for his study. He identified and described social banditry, a form of early modern banditry that he saw as quite distinct from ordinary armed robbery. It was a form of banditry that represented a rebellion of peasant society in periods of economic or political dislocation. The state condemned these peasant social bandits as criminals but they retained the support of the society from which they sprang because it regarded them as champions. They were allegedly noble robbers like Robin Hood's men, resistance fighters and avengers of wrongs inflicted on peasant society by the governing classes. In contrast, they never preyed on the peasantry.

Hobsbawm's study of banditry proved highly controversial, but it stimulated considerable research on the whole phenomenon of banditry in criminal justice and police records, sources quite different from the sources mined by the English scholar. Such research has turned up little evidence of either a bandit subculture or of Hobsbawm's social banditry in western Europe, but, as a result, we now understand better what forms banditry assumed, who bandits were, how they were organized, and where, when, and why they flourished.

Hobsbawm particularly linked his social banditry with the peasantry. While we will find that banditry, even that which engendered Robin Hood myths, was hardly an exclusively peasant activity, it was certainly an overwhelmingly rural one. This is not to characterize early modern cities as safe, crime-free places; on the contrary, earlier chapters have demonstrated their tumultuous nature. Urban armed robbery undoubtedly occurred – the English author Horace Walpole (1717–97) once

---

[1] Eric J. Hobsbawm, *Primitive Rebels: Studies in Archaic Forms of Social Movement in the Nineteenth and Twentieth Centuries* (New York: Frederick A. Praeger, 1959) and *Bandits*, revised ed. (New York: Pantheon Books, 1981). The latter study was originally published in 1969.

narrowly escaped death at the hands of a robber with a gun in London's Hyde Park. But Walpole faced a single assailant. Members of urban robber bands seem to have worked individually or in small groups, and large urban bands were relatively rare because their operations might be detected readily in cities, even by the rudimentary police apparatus of the day.

Most early modern states lacked the police resources to suppress rural banditry, and were able to mount only sporadic campaigns against bandits. Governments would billet troops in areas known to assist bandits; and the Spanish monarchy, Genoa, and Venice offered pardons to bandits who would renounce their life of crime and take up military service. A few states mounted more direct actions, but these sometimes simply drove bandits elsewhere. These typically included extraordinary tribunals and military action. Thus the republic of Venice created a special magistracy with broad powers, the Sindaci Inquisitori di Terraferma, to prosecute bandits in its mainland territories in the late sixteenth century. The republic of Genoa vainly used both the military and special courts with powers of summary justice against banditry along the Ligurian coast in the late sixteenth century. The Spanish monarchy finally achieved some success against banditry in Valencia only when it wielded military might to suppress a rebellion there in the first decade of the eighteenth century – and imposed greater government control of the province in the process. But despite such efforts to bring banditry under control, the problem remained widespread in our period and assumed several forms.

Highway robbery was ubiquitous, and early modern travel books sometimes noted sections of road particularly infested with bandits, just as modern guidebooks alert travelers to highway hazards. Sixteenth-century guides warned that highway robbery was a problem both on the roads approaching great cities and on isolated rural paths. Roads leading to large cities were traveled heavily and attracted robbers eager for the cash, merchandise, and personal property carried on such thoroughfares. In the eighteenth century northern Surrey, near London, was a particular haunt of highway robbers, as were other sites on the approaches to the capital. Cities, moreover, provided important bases for armed robbers. Within their walls dealers in used goods, silversmiths and goldsmiths, and a raft of other merchants unconcerned about the origins of their purchases stood ready to receive stolen commodities. And in the inns and taverns of large towns robbers established associations with accomplices and found refuge from the authorities. Amsterdam, London, Paris, Rome, and larger German cities like Mannheim and Marburg were all centers for armed bands of highwaymen. The case of a French bandit,

Philippe Nivet (1696–1729), provides an example of a bandit operating from an urban base.[2]

Under the pseudonym "Fanfaron," Nivet operated chiefly in northern France, using Paris as his main base and Caen and Rouen as secondary bases from which to commit highway robbery and attacks on prosperous farms and houses. His was a large band – the authorities ultimately arrested sixty-eight members – but the actual robberies were carried out by only twenty of these individuals. The remaining defendants (largely residents of Paris, Caen, and Rouen) were receivers of stolen goods, keepers of inns providing refuge or meeting places for the band, or livery-men who supplied mounts to the criminals. Prosecutors linked Nivet and his associates to thirty-eight armed robberies in the period from 1723 to 1728. Six of these were highway robberies ending in fatalities, and the last of them, which led to the final capture, illustrates how such a band operated.

Nivet's final highway robbery victimized Louis David and his wife, dry-goods merchants of Amiens. In August 1728 the couple were returning home, mounted on fine horses, from the Guibray fair where they had done a large volume of business. Nivet and two accomplices joined the Davids and, posing as merchants themselves, accompanied them to a forest near Rouen. Once in the forest, these bandits slit the Davids' throats, stole their considerable money and jewelry, and rode immediately to the home of a receiver where they broke down the couple's jewelry to render it unrecognizable. Then, to frustrate pursuers, Nivet and his men secured new mounts from an accomplice who ran a livery stable and rode to Vernon, where they again changed transport by boarding the postal coach for Paris. They reached the capital but there police apprehended them, by a stroke of luck, at an inn that was a favorite haunt of Nivet and others of his sort.

While cities provided convenient bases and refuges for armed bands like Nivet's, not all highway robbery occurred near major population centers. Isolated stretches of road were ideal for highway robbery because of the unlikelihood of police interference in crimes in progress. A six-teenth-century guide to English roads named Salisbury Plain, Sherwood Forest, and Newmarket Heath near desolate Wicken Fen as particular danger points. In the Papal States of Italy banditry flourished in the 1590s

---

[2] Archives nationales de France, X²ᴮ¹⁴¹⁵, Parlement criminel, minutes; Bibliothèque nationale de France, mss. Joly de Fleury, vol. 2046, pp. 94–106; and *La vie de Nivet dit Fanfaron qui contient les vols, meurtres qu'il fait depuis son enfance jusqu'au jour qu'il a été rompu vif en Place de Grève, avec Beauvoir son maître d'école, Baramon et Mancion ses complices* (Paris: Jean-Luc Noyon, 1729), reprinted in Lüsebrink (ed.), *Histoires curieuses et véritables de Cartouche et de Mandrin*, pp. 139–55.

along the roads connecting Florence, Rome, and Naples. Much of the 250 kilometers of the stretch between Rome and Naples was so narrow and poor as to require pack mules, not carts, to carry the valuable trade in fine textiles and other products. Merchants and travelers moved in caravans led by guides, often accompanied by armed guards. Despite such precautions, bandits robbed these convoys with some frequency; in August 1592 a successful attack on one guarded by fifteen armed men left four dead. Highway robbery persisted in much of Italy well into the nineteenth century, despite the efforts of the papal government, Genoa, and Venice.

Highway robbery was widespread in the Spanish monarchy, too; in Andalusia, where again some roads were no more than mule tracks, highway robbery was rife and goods were moved by armed caravans in a vain attempt to deter attack. Bandits even infested the great north–south route, the Camino Real, in our period, especially where it passed through mountainous areas. In the Sierra Morena the band of Pedro Guerra relieved the duke of Osuña's caravan of 14,000 *ducados* in goods and specie in 1616. Even on the plain of la Mancha in Castile, Pedro Andres led a band of more than thirty desperados in the 1640s. State action did little to combat such crime, and in the late eighteenth century, when Charles III (r. 1759–88) ordered reconstruction of the Seville–Madrid highway, he also ordered construction of new towns along its route as bastions against armed robbers.

Highway robbers sometimes participated in another widespread form of early modern banditry: armed attacks on isolated prosperous farms and homes. Those at risk particularly feared this crime, which usually involved breaking into an occupied residence after dark, and lawmakers in England, France, and other states prescribed the death penalty for it. Nevertheless, such attacks occurred almost everywhere, and the architectural embodiment of the widespread fear of such assault endures today. Medieval and early modern farms in the lower Rhône Valley of France, parts of the Low Countries, and Catalonia possess gated, walled farmyards that resemble small forts, while in Andalusia and other parts of southern Europe both farmsteads and villages occupy defensible hilltops.

The strategy of armed robbers in assaulting an occupied residence was a universal one. Band members first scouted out potential victims, and one of them, often a woman, might visit a farm posing as a beggar or peddler. Alternatively, one of the thieves might assess the wealth of potential victims while employed briefly as a daily or seasonal worker. Band members also noted opportunities for entry into the home, the proximity of neighbors, and the presence of watchdogs that might sound an alarm.

Having identified their objective, robbers often disguised themselves and mounted their assault after dark, when householders were asleep and easily surprised, and when detection of their crime was less likely. Having taken care to kill guard dogs and post sentries who could warn of anyone's approach, the bandits penetrated the house. Architecture dictated their methods of doing this: they thrust through gates and doors with battering rams, scaled walls with ladders, broke though wattle-and-daub walls, burrowed under the doors of earthen-floored cottages, pried open shutters, or cut through roof thatch. Once inside, they searched for the householders' wealth in coin, plate, jewelry, clothing, and other goods, and violence often ensued. Resistance always elicited brutality. When about a dozen members of the band of François-Marie Salembier broke into a physician's home in La Houlette in the Nord *département* of France in November 1795, they used swords and bayonets to kill the doctor, his in-laws, and six children. Amazingly, they then dined amid their carnage, for the authorities' estimate of their number derived from the utensils they laid out to consume the physician's food and drink.

Victims of this sort of crime met violent ends for other reasons, too. Some recognized neighbors or acquaintances among their assailants and were murdered because of their cognizance. Many more refused to reveal the hiding places of their wealth and sustained torture to extract this information from them. This was the fate of jurist Maarten Schats, a victim of the Stoffel van Reesen band, the most infamous Dutch band of the 1660s. Disbelieving Schats's claim that he kept little cash at home, the robbers beat him and then built a fire in which they burned his feet and other body parts in a form of torture so widespread among bandits in neighboring France that those who used it were dubbed *chauffeurs* ("warmers"). Schats never revealed a hiding place and he died a few days later, on 9 March 1660.

Another form of banditry prevalent in a Europe still heavily dependent on raising stock was the theft of livestock. Such crimes were especially common in pastoral uplands and sometimes produced virtual warfare between bands of thieves and their victims and pursuers. One zone for such conflict was the Anglo-Scottish borderland in the Cheviot Hills and the adjacent moors. In this poor and relatively overpopulated area, stealing of cattle and sheep supplemented the meager proceeds of agriculture for many residents during the first centuries of our period. Victims of thefts here violently resisted bands of "reivers," and clan loyalties dictated that kinsmen help to seek armed redress for thefts.

All of these forms of banditry flourished in those areas and eras in which they encountered the least resistance. Zones near national or provincial boundaries, where bandits might elude pursuers simply by crossing the borderline, featured much banditry. Hence the politically fragmented Italian peninsula supported extensive banditry in the six-teenth century, and bandits in the Papal States sought sanctuary from papal forces in the grand duchy of Tuscany. The efforts of Genoese offi-cials to extirpate banditry foundered in part on their republic's border with no less than six neighboring states. Banditry was also widespread on the borders of the duchy of Milan and the republic of Venice, on the Apennine boundary between the duchies of Modena and Parma, and along the frontier of the papal enclave of Benevento and the kingdom of Naples.

Political frontiers frustrated the law-enforcement efforts of larger states, too. French authorities had difficulty controlling their borders with the kingdom of Piedmont-Sardinia, where Gaspard de Besse operated in the eighteenth century, and in the Pyrenees that marked the boundary with Spain. The latter country's efforts against bandits suffered from brigands' crossings on the Portuguese frontier. In England, as we have seen, the frontier with Scotland was an area of notorious lawlessness, a situation duplicated in the sixteenth and seventeenth centuries in the border zone between Denmark and Sweden, where bands stole tax receipts and attacked farms, manors, and vicarages.

Political frontiers, however, were not the only barriers to imposition of state authority on bandits. The incomplete integration of most early modern states also favored these violent criminals. Perhaps the most extreme case was the Spanish monarchy where the historic kingdoms comprising that Iberian state preserved their traditional privileges long into our period, and royal authority remained weak everywhere but Castile. The *feuros* (*furs* in Valencia), or traditional rights, of these king-doms limited royal authority, and one Valencian viceroy wrote: "It goes without saying that there will be bandits as long as there are *fueros*."[3] In Valencia, for example, these local rights prohibited the viceroy from raising money or soldiers to pursue bandits and thus forced him to use the less reliable provincial militia or the small, fifty-man unit of the viceregal guard to search for bandits. Indeed, viceroys found only one effective weapon to curb banditry prior to the end of the seventeenth century, and it was a tacit admission of their weakness: they granted pardons to bandits in return for military service. In 1680, for instance, one viceroy pardoned 118 bandits who followed Juan Berenguer in return for service in Italy, the Balearics, Gibraltar, and Orán. Only after the War of the Spanish Succession was the monarchy able to assert greater authority outside Castile.

---

[3] Quoted in Henry Kamen, "Public Authority and Popular Crime: Banditry in Valencia, 1660–1714," *Journal of European Economic History* 3 (1974), p. 659.

Elsewhere, other factors limited the ability of the early modern state to deal effectively with banditry. Judicial overlap was one. In the province of Holland alone there were some 200 courts of first instance in the seventeenth century, and although these jurisdictions communicated with each other relatively well, this multiplicity certainly did not increase the efficacy of justice. The same can be said for the numerous French court jurisdictions and the political and judicial fragmentation of Germany.

Banditry prospered further in wartime and in areas affected by war where political and judicial authority broke down. The relationship of war to crime was noted by some of the pioneer English historians of crime. Douglas Hay and J. M. Beattie demonstrated that English property crime went up in the wake of seventeenth- and eighteenth-century warfare, as demobilized soldiers and sailors returned to civilian life.[4] Indeed, they found that violent crime increased most dramatically in the years following the end of eighteenth-century conflicts, and that highway robbery grew by more than 50 percent in some of these periods. Continental countries, lacking England's island security, suffered a greater impact from violence resulting from warfare. Early modern forces of order broke down completely in actual war zones, and even after peace returned they proved entirely inadequate to the challenge of violent crime perpetrated by former soldiers, those avoiding military service, and local residents driven to armed robbery by war's devastation.

Armed robbery bred of war afflicted a number of zones repeatedly. The Italian wars contributed military men and impoverished civilians to bands that swelled further thanks to poor harvests in the 1590s and made the late sixteenth century a particularly dangerous period in Italy. In the sixteenth and seventeenth centuries the provinces of Blekinge, Skåne, and Halland together formed a poor, forested border region contested by Denmark and Sweden in their frequent wars. Here mounted bands of bandits drawn from former soldiers and ruined farmers, numbering perhaps 1,000 or 2,000 men in the 1670s, used armed force to steal local tax receipts from the authorities and money, food, and livestock from the civilian population. These bands earned the hostility of local peasants, yet their activities ended only when Sweden gained the region in 1680 permanently and slowly restored order.

But the preeminent European war zone in our period was the area composed of northeastern France, the Low Countries, and northwestern Germany. The Eighty Years' War for Dutch independence, the Thirty

---

[4] Douglas Hay, "War, Dearth and Theft in the Eighteenth Century: The Record of the English Courts," *Past and Present* 95 (1982), pp. 117–60, and J. M. Beattie, *Crime and the Courts in England, 1660–1800* (Princeton: Princeton University Press, 1986), pp. 199–264.

Years' War, the wars of Louis XIV, the War of the Austrian Succession, the Seven Years' War, and the wars of the French Revolution made this a region of constant troop movement, and the zone of operation for countless armed bands that worked without concern for political boundaries.

The Dutch provinces of Holland and Zeeland found their territories inundated with demobilized soldiers and sailors in the period of the Twelve Years' Truce (1609–21), the years after the Thirty Years' War, and the period following the War of the Spanish Succession. Some of these men joined with local, itinerant poor to form armed bands such as the Hees band of the 1650s, and such violent equivalents of the post-Spanish Succession War period as those of Jaco, Gerrit the Cow, the Glory of Holland and Kees Seven-Deaths.

The southern Dutch Republic, especially the Dutch Brabant, and the northern Spanish Netherlands constituted a zone of intense warfare in our period and therefore of great band activity. Here the lower Meuse valley suffered extensive banditry in the 1630s owing to the activities of former soldiers and its war-ravaged citizens. The Zwartmakers ("Blackeners") spread armed robbery, extortion, murder, and arson across the area and into the Ravenstein region of Germany in the years from 1692 to 1699. Between 1706 and 1708 the mounted Moskovieters also committed highway robbery and farmhouse attacks in this area, as did a band that we will examine more closely later, the Bokkerijders ("Billy-goat Riders"), who flourished intermittently in part of this zone and also in western Germany from the outbreak of the War of the Austrian Succession in 1740 until 1778. The area also sustained the band of Jan de Lichte, whose 100 men robbed houses of food and committed large-scale armed robberies in the southern Netherlands from 1747 until their capture in the next year. But the heyday of armed-band activity in this area opened with its conquest, and that of the west bank of the Rhine in Germany, by French Revolutionary armies in the last decade of the eighteenth century.

The 1790s were a period of intense disorder here. The Brabant Revolution of 1789 disrupted the Austrian regime in the Netherlands; the French invasions brought war to this area, the Dutch Republic, and western Germany; and administrative confusion followed French conquest as the region's new rulers reorganized the Low Countries and the German west bank of the Rhine into French *départements*. Throughout the period policing was weak, false documents for criminals widely available, and military uniforms for disguises abundant. Many other factors also encouraged crime. In this region farms were often prosperous and churches were rich (having been spared the de-Christianization that stripped French sanctuaries of their treasures), so it understandably attracted robbers; one historian identified no less than sixteen bands working in the Belgian *département* of Jemappes alone in the period 1794 to 1799.[5]

Political integration of this region with France meant that some of these bands operated in that country as well: the band of Salembier operated in both France and Flanders, committing perhaps its most spectacular offense in an attack of October 1796 on the farm of Philippe Ballet, a member of the Council of Five Hundred, in which the politician was badly wounded during the robbery attempt. Since many of the bands of the 1790s confronted French gendarmes, their activities occasionally assumed the appearance of patriotic protest in the eyes of some of their contemporaries. This was the case of the Bakelandt band operating in western Flanders in 1798–1802, a period in which the French were putting down a peasant rebellion, the Boerenkrijg. Flemish day laborers, rural artisans, and carters joined deserters to commit armed crimes occasionally directed against French authorities. But the best-known band of this sort was that of Schinderhannes.

Schinderhannes ("John the Knacker"), whose real name was Johannes Bückler, led a considerable band in the prosperous Rhineland, an area whose forests had long been a fruitful hunting ground for vagrants and petty thieves. The French invasion made the Rhineland a magnet for criminals and deserters and the area supported a number of bands. Schinderhannes began with cattle rustling in 1797 but soon graduated to highway robbery, burglary, and extortion. He enjoyed a very positive image among German locals because he seemed to contest French authority; in addition, he frequently attacked Jews. Whether motivated by Jews' perceived wealth and the vulnerability of many of them as traveling merchants, or Schinderhannes's own anti-Semitism, these attacks elicited support among much of the local population. Indeed, the trial of Schinderhannes and sixty-eight of his accomplices in 1803 created a sensation in German public opinion that only grew when French authorities guillotined the robber chief and nineteen of his men in Mainz. But it is difficult to discern social banditry in this band, or in others like it.

The armed practitioners of such crimes came to their offenses from a remarkable variety of backgrounds and for many different reasons, but common denominators among the majority seem to have been poverty and their existence on the social margins of early modern society. The numbers of poor grew rapidly in our period. General population growth was a key element in this increase in the poor as the population of western

[5] Roger Darquenne, *Brigands et larrons dans le département de Jemappes* (Haine-Saint-Pierre: Publications du Cercle d'Histoire et de Folklore Henri Guillemin-La Louvière, 1994), pp. 85–149.

Europe rose rapidly in the sixteenth and eighteenth centuries, excluding many from the opportunity of landholding and inexorably driving increases in the price of life's necessities. Structural economic change, like the enclosure movement in England, further added to the ranks of the economically disadvantaged by depriving them of their tenancies and forcing them into itinerant searches for sustenance. Temporary economic crises wrought by wars, famines, and business cycles only added to the ranks of the poor.

Lacking an understanding of the structural economic changes affecting their society and the root causes of unemployment, early modern officials and the public alike saw the growing number of indigent people as a threat to society's order and stability. They reasoned that able-bodied vagrants, who thronged streets and roads seeking work or begging, deliberately chose not to work, and they drew a close correlation between idleness and crime. Indeed, early modern states equated vagrancy and begging with lawbreaking and in our period criminalized vagrancy. The language of laws concerning the able-bodied poor is remarkably similar across national boundaries, and both the English Vagrancy Act of 1531 and a French edict of 1666 permitted judicial action against all those without visible means of support.

Armed with such laws, early modern states rounded up vagrants, driving them back to their home parishes, shipping them off to military or galley service, imposing forced labor on them, or, increasingly, confining them in houses of correction optimistically intended to teach them a work ethic and perhaps marketable skills. The records of these institutions and the authorities' round-ups of the able-bodied poor provide historians with their chief sources on these indigents and suggest the origin for much of the unease such people engendered among the privileged orders of society.

Vagrants were numerous. We will never know their total numbers exactly because only a portion of them left a record of their existence with the authorities, but the well-documented French experience is suggestive. In the 1768–72 period the French Maréchaussée arrested 71,760 beggars and vagrants, and in 1791 the National Assembly's committee examining poverty (Comité de mendicité) estimated the wandering poor at a tenth of the nation's population. Most numerous were those who had earned their livings from the land but were now displaced, temporarily or permanently, by a multitude of factors, ranging from a surplus of agricultural day laborers to loss of the family farm through debt or the effects of enclosure. Unemployed artisans, servants, and unskilled laborers of all sorts also passed through the authorities' net in the early modern period, as did former soldiers. Indeed, studies on England and Bavaria suggest that as many as one early modern vagrant in ten was a former soldier, an invalided military man, or a deserter. Those arrested by the Maréchaussée and other European authorities were difficult to control, too, because they were extraordinarily mobile, readily crossing both internal and national boundaries.

This body of poor people was in constant flux and could expand rapidly because many early modern Europeans lived on the brink of privation at the best of times. Economic difficulties, even of a seasonal nature, could easily force the domiciled laboring poor into begging. Extended financial problems almost as quickly could move artisans into the ranks of the dispossessed poor. And a personal disaster, like chronic illness culminating in the death of the husband and father, could ruin a craftsman's family in an age without a social-welfare safety net. In addition, those whose work forced them to travel could easily blend into the ranks of the rootless poor in times of economic stress. Called by Germans *fahrende Leute* ("traveling people"), they included entertainers, peddlers, chimney sweeps, tinkers, knife grinders, knackers, and schoolmasters who taught during the winter months but then had to resume itinerant searches for employment.

Material desperation could indeed drive beggars and vagrants – already outside the law thanks to their very status – into property crime, but the popular press and public opinion, which we explored in Chapter 1, vastly overestimated the violent danger they posed, so that most Europeans experienced the fear described by R. H. Tawney in his famous phrase, "the sixteenth century lives in terror of the tramp."[6] Modern research in judicial and police records shows that the risk of violent crime at the hands of most vagrants was much less than their contemporaries feared.

The most obvious danger came from those soliciting alms with threats. Indeed, the very appearance of an able-bodied indigent at the door soliciting alms or shelter for the night was inherently a threat to residents of isolated farms. Such callers might be surveying the premises for a later armed robbery, a band of accomplices might be out of sight near by. Refusal of assistance might incur threats of physical violence or burning of the farmer's home, barn, or crops, and consequently the laws of most states harshly punished such begging with threats. Vagrants seem often to have traveled in small groups, and the appearance of more than one beggar at homeowners' doors only heightened their fears, sometimes intimidating them into not reporting such incidents to authorities unable

---

[6] R. H. Tawney, *The Agrarian Problem of the Sixteenth Century* (London: Longmans, Green and Co., 1912), p. 268.

to provide reliable protection. In fact, villagers in the Lyonnais region of eighteenth-century France told police seeking their aid against a group of beggars engaged in petty thefts: "You are not always here and if we were to aid you in arresting them, they will come back and get us."[7]

Despite the visibility of illegal begging, however, petty thievery, generally accomplished without violence, was the preeminent crime of vagrants. This was unskilled theft to provide for the needs of materially desperate people who stole clothing and merchandise from marketstalls, small farm livestock such as chickens and geese, drying laundry, and whatever else opportunely presented itself. But it was organization of vagrants that early modern authorities most watched for, because some in the ranks of the wandering poor became recruits of armed bands. Indeed, a question commonly posed by French authorities to vagrants was: "Were you associated with some other beggar?"

The link between early modern poverty and armed robbery emerges from the observations of contemporaries. Valencia's expulsion of vagrants in 1586 had a tangible effect on travelers' safety according to one Venetian writing about the Zaragosa region: "One has to travel . . . in great peril from cut-throats who are in the countryside in great numbers, all because at Valencia they have issued an order expelling from the kingdom all vagrants after a certain time limit, with the threat of greater penalties . . . Another reason for traveling by day and with a strong bodyguard!"[8] Poverty led many to armed robbery elsewhere, too, the best-documented links between poverty, vagrancy, and armed bands to be found in the plains of northern France in the eighteenth century.

The wheat-growing plains of the Beauce, Brie, Champagne, and Burgundy were crossed by major highways and dotted by large and relatively isolated farms in the eighteenth century. The fertility of the region's soil made these farms prosperous, but not all shared in that wealth. The peasantry held little land and derived a meager, largely seasonal income from agricultural day labor on the great farms. As a result, poverty was common among the local population, and the ranks of local poor swelled with the arrival of itinerant poor seeking alms or work at the rich farms; indeed, it was said that no province had more vagrants per capita than Champagne.

The area's flat plains, where only scattered forests provided bandits with effective refuge, would appear unsuited to banditry. Yet it had a long history of brigandage stretching back to the medieval period and the

---

[7] Quoted in Olwen H. Hufton, *The Poor of Eighteenth-Century France, 1715–1789* (Oxford: Clarendon Press, 1974), p. 222.

[8] Quoted in Fernand Braudel, *The Mediterranean and the Mediterranean World in the Age of Philip II*, translated by Siân Reynolds (New York: Harper and Row, 1975), vol. II, p. 741.

freebooting Grandes Compagnies that operated there at the end of the Hundred Years' War. Olwen Hufton, an historian of French poverty, detected an intensification of band activity in the last decades for the eighteenth century, as poverty grew and the poor and vagrants turned increasingly to petty theft and even armed robbery. The area almost inevitably produced a number of armed bands, too, and Hufton estimated that perhaps a quarter of the roughly 200 members of Charles Hulin's band in the 1760s had once been confined as vagrants.[9] Hulin's band did a little of everything, including petty theft, highway robbery, attacks on farms, and even an armed attack on the Moulins stagecoach office that netted a large sum. But Hulin's was just one of several major bands in the region, notably those of Jean Renard, Robillard, and Fleur d'Epine. It is the Orgères band of the 1790s, however, that historians know of best.

Led first by Jean Anger (known as "Beau François") and then one Ringette (known as "Rouge d'Auneau"), the Orgères band members bore no resemblance to social bandits, preying on rich and poor alike in acts of petty crime as well as highway robbery and assaults on local farms. They were brutal, and in the ninety-five crimes eventually alleged to them committed seventy-five murders and four rapes. This band also employed a tactic characteristic of bands in the region: they were *chauffeurs*. The betrayal of the band by one of its members produced extensive trial records that revealed the identities of eighty-two people accused of committing such crimes, and we find both local and itinerant poor charged.

Domiciled local people of limited means suffering particularly from the economic crisis of the French Revolution included agricultural day laborers, livestock herders, a few peasant proprietors of small farms, and textile workers. They were joined by others whose occupations were normally those found among the more mobile poor, such as peddlers and traveling merchants, and by local merchants and innkeepers as accessories. The link between these people and material deprivation becomes clearer still when we note that the band's operations most commonly occurred in winter, the period of greatest agricultural unemployment, and that the frequency of their offenses increased as Revolutionary-era economic problems intensified. But the connection between poverty and banditry was not always so direct. Olwen Hufton estimated that perhaps a third to as much as half of the French population experienced poverty in the second half of the eighteenth century, yet clearly only a fraction of those people joined organized bands. For most of those who did, other factors often combined with poverty to propel them into banditry.

Social exclusion in various ways contributed to an individual's decision

---

[9] Hufton, *The Poor of Eighteenth-Century France*, pp. 243–66.

to take up a life of banditry. Sometimes this was the result of a crime, often one of violence, which put a young person beyond the pale of the community and its familial, professional, and social networks. Such a situation usually precluded even menial employment and came about in one of several ways. Some individuals found themselves excluded by legal banishment from their communities as a result of conviction for some offense. Many jurisdictions employed banishment as a penalty in an age generally lacking in penitentiaries that might have provided a noncapital penalty. Thus in 1426 1,200 men, representing 1 percent of the population, were on the list of those banished from Vicenza in the Venetian Terraferma. Another form of exclusion, common in Mediterranean Europe, occurred when an act of bloodshed prompted the perpetrator to "take to the bush" (in France, *prendre le maquis*; in Italy, *darsi alla macchia*) rather than risk a trial. In either case, many such excluded individuals easily gravitated to banditry.

The military-service demands of modern governments also contributed to the ranks of the rootless, as young men fled from conscription agents to seek refuge in the countryside. Many of these men drifted into banditry, too. Alongside these fugitives on the fringes of early modern society existed other groups marginalized by their ethnic or religious status.

Known in the early modern period as gypsies, Bohemians, heathens, and Egyptians, the people today designated as Roma by international agencies were a troubling ethnic group for early modern Europeans. Believed to be descended from a tribe of northern India, the nomadic Roma began to appear in western Europe in the fifteenth century. Dark-complexioned and wedded to a nomadic lifestyle in bands under leaders they styled "captains," "counts," or "dukes," the Roma were a highly visible minority whose men engaged in horse trading, tinkering, and entertainment, and whose women often peddled potions and reputed cures to a credulous population. Their men were often armed, and they quickly became associated with trickery and theft; many early modern states, including France, the German states, and the Dutch Republic, banned them from their territories in principle. In practice the Roma existed almost everywhere, despite the occasional persecutions mustered by early modern states.

Petty crime accompanied Roma bands from Spain to northern Europe. But in the 1680s government crackdowns on the Roma began in much of northwestern Europe, lasting in some areas into the 1720s. These persecutions seem to have triggered a wave of more serious crime by the Roma, who moved beyond their customary petty offenses to attacks on representatives of authority and to armed robbery. The Roma could be specially brutal at times, and because they were a very recognizable minority some of them wished to leave no witnesses to their crimes. On 12 March 1721 five Roma men and a woman robbed an old woman's shop in De Glip, near Haarlem in the Dutch Republic. They worked methodically and brutally; having posted lookouts and stabbed the owner's dog, they broke down the door, strangled the aged proprietor with a rope, and absconded with both goods and cash. The Roma also robbed churches, frequently assaulting clerics in the process. In some areas, like the Dutch Republic, Roma joined in crime with another group marginalized by Christian society, the Jews.

Laws in much of western Europe excluded Jews from landownership, guild membership, and countless other aspects of mainstream social and economic life. Such strictures limited economic opportunities for Jews by relegating them to retailing, laboring in unskilled trades, dealing in live-stock, and lending money, and condemned many men to peripatetic lives as peddlers and stock buyers. Such a lifestyle presented openings for crime: peddling and livestock trading enabled a person to scout for rural wealth, while business (as well as family) connections with coreligionists engaged in buying and selling used goods made it possible to fence stolen merchandise. Jewish property crime in the Dutch Republic grew with waves of immigration in the late seventeenth and eighteenth centuries by economically disadvantaged Ashkenazim attracted by Dutch customs somewhat more tolerant than those of Germany.

Needless to say, established Jewish communities in the Dutch Republic found the organized crime of some of their coreligionists discomfiting; it threatened their own tenuous positions in societies dominated by Christians. Nevertheless, criminality by Jews was extensive, and it assumed several forms. Jews committed various nonviolent urban offenses, including thefts from shops and warehouses, pickpocketing, and burglary. Their violent offenses were largely rural, although organization of these crimes and fencing of their proceeds occurred in the cities where many criminals maintained their families. These violent offenses included armed attacks on farms and churches. Indeed, in the Dutch Republic Jews figured prominently in the latter crime to the extent that Florike Egmond, the historian of Dutch organized crime in our period, sees such offenses as acts of "revenge and rebellion."[10]

By the end of our period, Jews increasingly joined with both Christians and Roma in violent crime. This was the case, for example, with the Great Dutch band of the 1790s that operated under the leadership of Abraham

[10] Florike Egmond, "Crime in Context: Jewish Involvement in Organized Crime in the Dutch Republic," *Jewish History* 4 (1) (1989), pp. 75–100. See also her *Underworlds: Organized Crime in the Netherlands, 1650–1800* (Oxford: Polity Press, 1993).

Picard in several branches across parts of present-day Belgium, the Netherlands, and western Germany. Jews, unified in part by kinship, formed the core of this armed band of approximately 150 members who committed numerous highway robberies and armed attacks accompanied by torture on isolated farms and businesses. Individual cruelties perpetrated by band members included seizing earrings and rings with such violence as sometimes to rip off victims' earlobes and fingers.

Another religious minority troubled the Spanish monarchy. The Catholic monarchs had a substantial Muslim minority in their Iberian lands, the Moriscos, to whom they gave the choice of conversion to the Church of Rome or expulsion in 1502. The conversion of most of these Moriscos as New Catholics was superficial at best, and because they constituted a tightly knit and fast-growing community that represented perhaps a third of the population in areas such as Valencia, Old Catholics feared them. Thus Church and state intensified efforts to hasten Morisco religious and cultural assimilation but that contributed to rebellions in 1500–02 and 1568–70. Poverty, too, drove many Moriscos into banditry before the monarchy expelled some 275,000 of them in 1609.

In Morisco banditry, like some elements of Jewish banditry, we may discern, perhaps, an element of protest. In sixteenth-century Granada the local name for a Morisco bandit was not *ladrón* ("thief"), *bandido* ("bandit"), or *bandolero* ("brigand"), but *monfí* ("a banished or exiled man"), suggesting that Muslims especially saw these bandits as different from ordinary criminals. Indeed, they often regarded them as heroes, perhaps because these bandits were unusual in another way, too. They attacked and robbed only Catholics, including merchants and travelers but especially clerics who represented the proselytizing and exactions of the established Church. Favored by the difficult terrain of the region's mountains and the possibility of escape to North Africa, the *monfíes* proved impossible to control in their native Granada. Even scattering the Morisco population to other parts of the Spanish kingdom after the Revolt of the Alpujarras in 1570 failed to solve the problem – it simply spread Morisco banditry to other areas. Only the final expulsion of Moriscos in 1609 ended this banditry.

Elsewhere, other religious minorities suffered the social and economic effects of exclusion and discrimination and perhaps as a consequence turned to crime. We find this with several groups of Protestants, for example, some of whom concocted an odd mix of crime and religious dogma. This was certainly the case with a series of Anabaptist bands in the Low Countries, beginning with that of Jan van Batenburg after the failure of the Anabaptist attempt to realize the Kingdom of God at Münster in 1535. Batenburg and his associates first sought to capture another city, but then turned to armed robbery. Operating chiefly in the Dutch Overijssel province, these groups also worked in the southern Netherlands and fenced much of their loot in Antwerp. They robbed churches and monasteries, stole cattle and extorted money from peasants with threats of destruction of livestock and cattle.

These Anabaptist bands flourished from the 1540s until the authorities captured and burned a leader in 1580 and his followers scattered. Their lengthy period of operation was the result of several factors. These were secretive bandits, with the internal discipline of communities of belief, who used signs and code words to identify each other and, in later years, retreated to difficult terrain that inhibited pursuit. Their history of persecution, common family ties, and polygamy united them, as did their early belief that their robberies simply appropriated the world's goods for God's elect and visited divine wrath on disbelievers. And as they became more robbers and less zealots in later years, their skills in their trade increased; they knew about firearms and enlisted specialists who broke down jewelry, fenced such loot, and picked locks.

Other Protestant bandits, the Wood Beggars, operated in western Flanders and northern France in the second half of the sixteenth century. The band evolved out of an anti-Catholic Protestant guerrilla movement assembled in the 1560s by local gentry in an attempt to secure the region for the reformed faith. The band's religious fanaticism initially seemed to unify its members, but their faith soon descended into simple anti-Catholic banditry. They attacked Catholic farms and churches for money and clothes, torturing those who refused to turn over valuables and brutally mistreating their victims, like one old man whom they emasculated. The band numbered about 110 when the authorities arrested many of its members in 1568.

Professional or social marginalization could create both the need for material gain and the group cohesion to make band activity possible. This was the case with the Bokkerijder bands that flourished between the 1720s and 1770s on the east bank of the Meuse River in a zone politically divided between the Dutch Republic, the Austrian Netherlands, the Duchy of Jülich, and various autonomous and semiautonomous German seigneuries. The Bokkerijders comprised large numbers of people – the authorities had executed 354 alleged members of the group by 1778. Those arrested were neither members of religious minorities nor rootless vagrants; rather, the band's members usually had homes and families in the area of its operations. Many were skinners. Slaughtering sick animals, disposing of dead cattle, and carrying away the bodies of executed criminals, skinners formed an essential but scorned and marginal group living a largely endogamous existence on the fringes of society. They shared this status with other reputedly "dishonorable people" (*unehrliche Leute*) like executioners, knackers, mole catchers, charcoal burners, and practitioners of other distasteful trades. Early modern German society excluded such people from much of routine social life, and even required that they be buried apart from ostensibly honorable members of their communities. But their trade made skinners mobile, put them beyond much of traditional social control, gave them wide-ranging ties with others of their profession, and instilled in them skill with knives. The nature of their trade also brought them knowledge of many farms and made them familiar figures carrying bundles along rural roads.

All of these factors are essential to understanding how skinners, along with impoverished artisans like spinners, weavers, cobblers, and iron workers, behaved after the end of the War of the Spanish Succession in 1714. Peace diminished the need for the services of all these men, so they used their connections and training in organized crime. Under the cover of night, and with disguises like blackened faces and false beards to conceal their identities, they preyed on their neighbors – and perhaps as a form of social protest – on such symbols of the rural establishment as churches. Often they tortured their victims to learn the location of valuables, and they killed with some frequency. Their name, which translates as "Billy-goat Riders," indicates the fear they inspired in an age in which many still associated the male goat with the devil.

Historians have identified youthfulness as another characteristic of early modern robber-band members. We have seen youths incompletely integrated into early modern society, and the former soldiers, indigents, and marginals drawn to membership of bands of robbers were overwhelmingly youthful, as several samples derived from trial records demonstrate. The Dutch band of Hees initiated twelve- and thirteen-year-olds into minor thievery in the mid-seventeenth century before graduating them to armed robbery; few of these bandits were older than twenty-three at their sentencing in 1661. The late seventeenth-century Valencian band of Berenguer yielded 113 bandits to the authorities; the youngest defendant in the resulting case was twelve, the eldest forty-six, and the great majority in their twenties. Similarly, the French Orgères bandits had an average age of thirty-three, and the average age of members of the Salembier band executed at Bruges in 1798 was 33·8. Modern criminologists recognize youth as a particularly crime-prone phase in the life cycle, and it certainly seems to have been during our period.

Criminologists, as we have seen, also find modern violent crime predominantly a male enterprise, and band membership in our period, too, generally accords with this. Most Christian and Jewish bands had a male majority – the large eighteenth-century French band of Charles Hulin was a third female, for example. Roma bands, communities in themselves, had larger female contingents but their women, like those of Christian and Jewish bands, fulfilled certain roles. Women in all these bands seldom engaged in violence; indeed, only two women in the Orgères band seem to have participated in highway robbery. Rather, women performed ancillary roles. They scouted out possible repositories of rural wealth, for as peddlers or beggars in search of alms they were less threatening than males so might gain admission to rural homes and thus the opportunity to gauge householders' wealth. Women also functioned as decoys, sometimes luring men into the clutches of male bandits. But their primary role seems to have been as receivers of stolen goods. Many women worked in the used-clothing trade, some so skillfully as to restitch stolen apparel into forms unrecognizable to their former owners.

Many women appear to have assumed their accessory role in bands upon the enlistment of a male partner or relative. Indeed, familial relations seem to have been key factors for both sexes in the decision to join a band; we find in the French Arbresle band of the 1780s, for example, several couples, several mothers with daughters or sons, and several fathers with sons.

Only rarely do we find women transcending their traditional accessory role to assume band leadership. Inexplicably, the prime examples of female-dominated bands identified by historians come from the eighteenth-century province of Brittany in France, where at least three such criminal organizations attacked farms, extorted money, and robbed people on the highways. Conjugal and familial ties seem to have been at least the partial basis for these organizations. The band of Marie Lescalier (née Marie-Anne Collen) operated over a vast area of Brittany from the 1730s until her arrest in 1757. Lescalier, born illegitimately in 1697, produced at least ten children with three different men belonging to her band. The band of Marion de Faouët (née Marie Tromel) originated among the six children of the two marriages of Marion's mother, Hélène Kerneau, and their spouses, lovers, and offspring. Marion led the band from about 1741 until her execution in 1755, and the band continued after her death, led by other family members into the 1780s. The whole clan lived in a small cottage in Faouët, sallying forth to rob farms and to commit highway robberies of unusual brutality in which band members often clubbed victims to death. The band flourished so long perhaps because its members were careful to prey on nonresidents of their area – especially travelers – in order to prevent denunciations to the authorities by their neighbors. Centered in Kerfot-en-Yvias, the final band integrated three generations of the Lescop family, whose daughters brought to the band various spouses and lovers representing three additional families. When the authorities arrested the members of this band in 1783, they apprehended nine women and eight men – a rare female majority – with a history of crimes going back thirty years.

Residential patterns also played a role in the formation and sustenance of many armed bands. Neighbors, experiencing the same adverse conditions, often turned to banditry together – as did young peasant males from relatively overpopulated pastoral villages in Italy and Spain. The members of the French Arbresle band all lived in the group's namesake town and one neighboring parish, and many of the Bokkerijders were neighbors. Indeed, whole towns could be engaged either in active banditry or the disposal of its swag, as was the case with the Dutch Hees band headquartered in the hamlet of that name amid the dunes and woods not far from Amersfoort. Presided over by "Father" Mees Rutgers, almost the entire village population seems to have been connected with the band. Breton bands, like that of Marion de Faouët, also had deep local roots, and – like most bands with a strong local identity – avoided antagonizing neighbors. The community roots of many bands made extirpation of banditry especially difficult, even if there was no local sympathy for bandit activities. The juries employed in English and traditional Valencian law often refused to convict neighbors; priests sheltered parishioners; and French and Spanish militias sometimes refused to take armed action against those they had known for years.

Recruited as they were from former soldiers, the poor, the young, social and religious marginals, and groups of relatives and neighbors, bandits exhibited little in the way of large-scale operations and professionalism, or the traits of a criminal subculture imputed to them by legend and the early modern press. Nor did most resemble social bandits. Indeed, historians have found that most bands' size, professionalization, and culture were the very opposite of these images.

Only a few really large bands seem to have existed in northern Europe. One of the largest was that of Louis-Dominique Cartouche (1693–1721), which operated in Paris and its region in the second decade of the eighteenth century, attacking farms and inns and robbing travelers and the Paris/Lyons mailcoach. The trials of Cartouche and his accessories resulted in charges against 742 people, and dragged on from 1721 to 1728. But a large number of those charged with Cartouche, as in other large bands like the Orgères band (80 tried) and the Bokkerijders (512 tried in three different periods), were involved in fencing stolen goods, hiding band members, or aiding them in some other way, and were not active as armed robbers.

Moreover, in northern Europe large bands comprising scores or even hundreds of armed robbers and receivers never assembled their entire companies in one place. They seem rather to have had loose structures, keeping in touch with one another in inns run by their associates or at fairs – both locales in which the authorities were accustomed to encountering unfamiliar faces. In such places bandits arranged operations that required relatively small numbers of men, generally no more than twelve to fifteen. Indeed, looking at Germany, Uwe Danker found no case of more than a dozen robbers undertaking a single job in our period.[11] After their jobs bandits often returned to a friendly inn, divided their spoils, and then dispersed, frequently to work independently until another opportunity for organized crime presented itself.

Only in the Mediterranean littoral and, above all, in the Iberian lands of the Spanish monarchy, do bands seem to have operated as large bodies. In the mountains of the south of Spain, for example, a number of bands seem occasionally to have mustered sufficient strength to operate almost at will in the Yecla area of Murcia in the seventeenth century, lashing out at local officials who interfered with their activities. The band of Martin Muñoz was sufficiently strong to enter Yecla in April 1671 and kill two officials; the band returned as strong as ever in November 1683 with eighty men to storm the town again, free a jailed colleague, and make off with 300 sheep and cattle. In the following year Muñoz moved his operations northward, where his band killed the mayor of Albacete. At least two other bands acted with similar daring and strength in the same region in the 1670s and 1680s.

The large-scale operations of Mediterranean bands notwithstanding, most bands displayed a rather low level of professionalism. As we have seen, armed robbery was partly linked to poverty, and many robbers stole when they found themselves in need or when a chance opportunity offered lucrative gains. Need often drove many vagrants, domiciled poor, and other marginal types to theft, and the nature of the goods stolen by band members indicates that they stole whatever opportunity offered them. Few were as specialized and sophisticated in their craft as Ralph Wilson, John Hawkins, and their associates, who in the 1720s turned to stealing bank bills and other negotiable paper from mail coaches and mail riders on the highways around London. Most armed robbers had graduated from petty thievery and were not too choosy about what they stole, returning to their roots in petty crime when necessary. Thus while Philippe Nivet and his men perpetrated the most brutal and spectacular of highway robberies, they were not above pilfering table utensils from

[11] Uwe Danker, "Bandits and the State: Robbers and the Authorities in the Holy Roman Empire in the Late Seventeenth and Early Eighteenth Centuries" in Richard J. Evans (ed.), *The German Underworld: Deviants and Outcasts in German History* (London and New York: Routledge, 1988), pp. 75–107.

Paris taverns when times were hard for them and the publican looked the other way. The Smorthwaits in England committed highway robbery, burglaries, and coin clipping as opportunities arose. Diego Corrientes, who enjoyed a reputation as an Iberian Robin Hood, stole horses, while the Frenchman Poulailler seems to have worked henhouses as well as the royal highways. Even the most famous English highwayman, Dick Turpin, ended his career as it had begun, stealing livestock in 1739.

Most historians have found little evidence of a criminal subculture among bands, either. But many early modern Europeans saw criminals, and the poor, as members of a vast subculture, like that ascribed to the Orgères band by Germain Bouscant, the One-Eyed Man of Jouy. The information he gave the police led to the band's capture, but it also alleged that the band had a distinct subculture, with its own teacher of crime, a "priest" presiding over distinctive anti-sacraments, and a family life defined by unique rituals and vocabulary. Modern historians of banditry, such as André Zysberg, consider these accounts from the One-Eyed Man apocryphal, but enough distinctive practices did exist among robbers for us to trace the origin of representations of a criminal subculture in popular literature and thought.[12]

A distinctive mode of speaking is central to the picture of a criminal subculture. In truth, speech was different among many of the criminals we are examining. Obviously, ethnic minorities like the Roma could readily switch to their own languages, but many other robbers sometimes employed unique vocabulary. They used distinctive words to denote aspects of their work, but lists of these seldom exceed a few hundred words. Historians find the use of such cant indication not of the criminal subculture we have seen described so fantastically in popular literature, but simply a practical way to express the challenges of survival for the poor and marginal. Not insignificantly, such cant may also have been intended to prevent noncriminals from learning of criminals' activities too easily. Bandits also used nicknames almost universally, probably to frustrate detection, and the French authorities seem to have sent Poulailler to his execution without ever learning his baptismal name. Men typically bore epithets that evoked their origins, usually obvious from their regional accents, such as the Auvergnat, Berrichon, Country Dick, Irish Ned, and Tourangeau. Men's nicknames also described striking physical characteristics, hence Big Nose, Cock-ey'd Jack, or Toothless. Sometimes names were ironic comments on physical attributes, as in the case of the Frenchman known as Little Beauceron, who in reality was a

12 André Zysberg, "L'affaire d'Orgères (1790–1800)," *Mémoires de la Société archéologique d'Eure-et-Loir* 30 (1985), p. v.

giant of a man. Women followed other patterns of appellation; in France, for example, their nicknames frequently came from flowers (The Rose) or sexuality (Goes up to the Room).

Some bands lacking common social or geographic roots sought unity and discipline through certain rites. Thus a few bands operating in the Dutch Republic were reported to have adopted a sort of military rank structure, a practice sometimes used by other bands that enlisted former soldiers. Oaths of loyalty were not unknown among bandits, either, and were applied by English bandits threatened by members who might turn king's evidence against their fellows. But beyond such practices as these, early modern robber bands display little evidence of a distinctive subculture.

Ill-disciplined, loosely organized, and practitioners of unsophisticated crimes of opportunity, bandits of the early modern era little fulfill either the image of Robin Hood or that of the criminal subculture. But banditry was ubiquitous in early modern Europe and contributed to the violence of the era. Also contributing to the violent tenor of life were the activities of smugglers, who often operated in many of the border zones favored by bandits.

Smuggling

Smuggling – the illegal movement of goods across internal boundaries or national borders to escape payment of taxes on them – was widespread in our period. Recent research suggests that by the eighteenth-century it was often a highly organized crime form, especially in England and France, where smuggling was extensive. Violence, as we will see, accompanied this professionalization of smuggling.

The early modern state, in almost constant search of revenues to support its wars, lacked the administrative infrastructure (epitomized today by the Internal Revenue Service and the Inland Revenue) to tax directly the incomes of its subjects. Therefore it resorted to less direct means of raising revenue, imposing import taxes on goods at their point of entry into the country, excise fees on the sale of certain products within the nation, or assessments contained within the price paid by consumers of products, especially salt and tobacco, sold under state monopolies often administered by private enterprise. France, the Spanish kingdom, and Venice, for example, all monopolized tobacco sales, while salt sales under state control were longstanding sources of revenue in both France and Spain.

Such levies represented sizeable contributions to the national budgets of many states. One estimate placed income from the royal tobacco monopoly at about 18 percent of the French monarchy's revenues in 1761, while in that same year the sale of salt, managed by a tax farm of private investors, produced some 28 percent of royal receipts. The burden of impositions of such magnitude encouraged smuggling to avoid their payment, as did the nature of the products typically taxed by early modern governments. Some were products vital to life, like the salt required in cooking, preservation, and agriculture, and impositions on salt were bitterly resented. Others were products in growing demand by consumers, including alcoholic beverages, cheap oriental cotton fabrics, tea, and tobacco.

A number of factors made smuggling a difficult crime to control. Most crucially, perhaps, the crime seems to have drawn in increasing numbers of people by the eighteenth century as Europe's growing prosperity fueled consumer demand for taxed commodities. Indeed, it is clear that smugglers were numerous enough to meet mass-market demands by that time. In England, for example, an estimated 3,000,000 pounds (1,500,000 kg) of illicit tea – more than three times the amount legally imported – annually flowed into the country prior to a decrease in the tea tax in 1745.

Historians discern two kinds of smuggling. One was that of the small operator, working individually or in collusion with family or neighbors. This style of operation flourished particularly among Europe's domiciled rural poor, and spread widely, perhaps because many of these people seem to have felt no onus of guilt at their activities. Many apparently regarded smuggling as a legitimate recourse for the poor, and the clergyman attending one English smuggler about to be hanged reported that: "as to the charge of smuggling, he owned that he had been concerned in that trade for a great many years, and did not think there was any harm in it."[13]

Indeed, smuggling was a natural part of what Olwen Hufton called "the makeshift economy of the poor," thriving especially in poor areas along coasts or near borders.[14] It was extensive in early eighteenth-century Sussex, England, as the formerly prosperous ports of Rye and Winchelsea silted up, the cloth trade of the Weald diminished, the herring fisheries declined, and outdated charcoal-fired blast furnaces producing iron closed down. Justice records indicate that the most economically disadvantaged local residents constituted a large number of the smugglers of the eighteenth-century German Rhineland and the Venetian Terraferma, too. In France whole parishes in impoverished areas often joined in smuggling, as one study of the contraband trade in salt in the west of France

---

[13] Quoted in James A. Sharpe, *Crime in Early Modern England, 1550–1750*, 2nd ed., (London: Longman Publishing, 1999), pp. 150–51.
[14] Hufton, *The Poor of Eighteenth-Century France*, pp. 284–305.

suggests. In Yves Durand's study of 4,788 accused salt smugglers, 59.5 percent were women and about 23 percent were boys and girls aged between five and fifteen.[15] Women and children took part widely in smuggling because they were less suspected of lawbreaking than adult males and also drew lower penalties than men.

Others, hardly indigents, also engaged in smuggling. Soldiers on duty participated with some frequency, like the five French dragoons who rode into Saint-Cyr-en-Pail on Sunday 1 February 1693, leading a dozen horses loaded with salt. They set up their wares prominently in front of the church after mass and sold all day, then stayed to accommodate citizens who preferred to buy under the cover of darkness. Even French religious of all types engaged in smuggling. In Bourg-Saint-Andéol, for example, the authorities found Brother Géniteux, a mendicant friar, selling contraband tobacco in a convent doorway on 27 April 1717. A curé of Tours, when apprehended by the Ferme, was found to have stored a large quantity of salt in the presbytery, along with scales, weights, and sacks for transporting the contraband. In fact, whole communities of monks and nuns practiced the smuggling of salt and tobacco in the first half of the eighteenth century. Everyone in Montpellier, for example, seems to have known that cheap contraband tobacco could be purchased from the sisters at La Trinité convent. Accused salt smugglers included the Capuchins of Agde, Alais, and Pont-Saint-Esprit; the Carmelites of Nîmes and Perpignan; and the Recollets of Bourg-Saint-Andéol and Sommières. Clerics elsewhere imitated their French colleagues. In Spain clerics smuggled salt, while in England John Wesley found that he had to remind rural clerics of the evil of smuggling.

Smuggling pervaded early modern society. Such extensive participation in smuggling, and the apparent dichotomy between a popular culture that found nothing wrong with the practice, on one hand, and the ideology of lawmaking elite groups that decreed smuggling illegal, on the other, prompted the first students of contraband to label it a crime of social protest. Such a characterization, however, has become less tenable as historians' knowledge of early modern smuggling has grown. Smuggling had a second form, the organized crime of large bands. This was professional crime so well organized that some French bands actually paid regular salaries to employees drawn from the ranks of vagabonds, former soldiers, deserters and the domiciled poor. But, as we will see, such organizations also attracted members whom we can hardly characterize as poor social protesters.

[15] Yves Durand, "La contrebande du sel au XVIIIᵉ siècle aux frontières de Bretagne, du Maine et de l'Anjou," *Histoire sociale/Social History* 7 (1974), pp. 227–69.

Noblemen organized much seventeenth- and early eighteenth-century French smuggling, for example, and not all of them were impoverished *hobereaux*. The leaders of a band of French salt smugglers in the 1670s were the Norman noblemen François de Poilley, *bailli* of Mortain and nephew of the bishop of Avranches, and his brother-in-law, François de Romilley, a gentleman of the king's bedchamber. And in central France, in the same period, Louis de Valenciennes, seigneur de Bournoiseau and scion of one of the oldest aristocratic families of the Berry, led a band of as many as sixty salt smugglers under the epithet Joyeuse.

This illegal trade enlisted many affluent lay commoners, too. The high degree of organization required in England for the transport and distribution of large quantities of tea drew wholesale and retail merchants and innkeepers into smuggling networks. Government attempts to root out such smugglers were at first counterproductive. The criminals' response to such state activity seems to have been greater organization, and accordingly some historians trace the appearance of armed bands of professional smugglers on a wide scale to the late seventeenth and early eighteenth centuries. The size, professionalism and armaments of these bands emboldened them, especially in a large country like France that was difficult to patrol. Every province of the country experienced some smuggling of salt, tobacco, or other commodities. National and provincial border areas and river valleys harbored favored routes of the caravans of horses guided by armed men that carefully avoided cities where the authorities were most numerous. These caravans could be large yet, spurred by necessity, they covered great distances quickly. During his career Mandrin led six campaigns, or caravan expeditions, into France from his Savoyard and Swiss bases to sell contraband tobacco and cotton fabric. Each one was bigger than its predecessor, and Mandrin's caravan in 1754 included 100 horses, each carrying 140 pounds (70 kg) of tobacco. His caravans moved rapidly, the fourth expedition covering 480 miles (800 km) in thirty-three days. Other bands made more frequent journeys than did Mandrin's. The band of Orange, made up largely of deserters and led by a figure named Croysat, was never apprehended, despite launching two caravans each year to sell its cotton fabrics and other contraband.

The sales of such caravans were not even always clandestine – Mandrin drew crowds of buyers with a drummer. Another band of fifty smugglers rode into Sarlat on 24 March 1762 in mid-morning, occupied the chief inns, placed sentinels at the town gates, stables and guardhouse, politely advised magistrates to remain indoors for the day, and peacefully sold contraband tobacco until dark.

Such extensive smuggling at first overwhelmed early modern police resources. Geography also worked against the representatives of state authority in controlling smuggling. The long coastlines of western Europe were extremely difficult to patrol in their entirety, and some stretches were ideal for smuggling. The Sussex coast of England was one such zone. A marshy area known well chiefly by its small number of residents, it was at once difficult to police and close to the vast London market. Consequently, it was an excellent point at which to unload illegal gin from the continent and contraband Far Eastern tea arriving in Danish, Dutch, French, and Swedish ships. Similarly, the swampy coast of the Netherlands frustrated revenue agents who lacked smugglers' familiarity with its many inlets and waterways. And the rugged Mediterranean coast of France's Roussillon province sheltered a lucrative trade in contraband tobacco that involved both Frenchmen and Spaniards in violation of the royal Spanish tobacco monopoly established in 1703. The rocky escarpments of the coast made concealment of contraband easy, and the heavily wooded hinterland was difficult to police. In addition, smugglers exploited a clause in the Franco-Spanish reciprocal trade treaty that forbade French authorities to stop and search Spanish vessels of less than fifty *tonneaux*. They cunningly landed tobacco from Lombardy and Piedmont transported to the Roussillon coast in small Spanish vessels, then natives of this former Spanish province, who had retained the right to bear arms when the area passed to France in 1659, moved the tobacco into Spain.

National boundaries, often defined by rugged mountains such as the Alps and Pyrenees, were difficult to police, too, a fact that also encouraged smuggling. Natives of such regions, like Mandrin, used their knowledge of local geography to elude revenue agents and prosper as smugglers. National boundaries, however, were not the only points at which governments collected taxes in the early modern period. Some states were divided for tax purposes, and certain goods incurred imposts as they traversed internal boundaries, or were taxed differently from one province to another. This was the case with salt in France. Recognizing the difficulty of collecting high exactions on salt in coastal areas where the mineral could be distilled from seawater, or in zones containing salt mines, the Ferme that administered the salt monopoly, the *gabelle*, set its prices according to the commodity's availability. In several areas of easy availability, including the coastal provinces of Brittany, Boulonnais, Artois, and Flanders, the population paid no imposition at all on salt. Elsewhere, salt taxes, exactions concealed in mandatory salt purchases through the monopoly, could be considerable. As a result, the same quantity of salt sold for as little as 1 *livre* 10 *sous* in Brittany yet as much as 61 *livres* 10 *sous* in the adjacent provinces of Anjou and Maine. The financial incentive to cross a provincial boundary to acquire low-priced salt for resale in another jurisdiction tempted many people into smuggling. Indeed, a single man, carrying a little over 60 pounds (30 kg) of salt from Brittany deep into the Maine for resale could realize twenty-five times the daily wage rate of an eighteenth-century agricultural laborer for his effort.

It seems clear that, throughout our period, the majority of smugglers were just such small-time operators seeking quick profits by simply eluding revenue agents. In France they concealed salt on children crossing tax boundaries; they staged false funeral processions in which the coffin contained not a corpse bound for burial just on the other side of a provincial border, but salt; they baked loaves filled with salt within a thin crust that would look like bread if their carriers had to undergo inspection at a border crossing; and they posed as travelers, carrying rucksacks with false bottoms concealing contraband salt. Perhaps the most unusual mode of smuggling was the employment of dogs that smugglers kept unfed for several days on one side of a tax boundary then released, with a cargo of salt strapped to them, to find their way to their homes on the other side of the tax border. Whatever the means of smuggling, however, the impact of such small operations was considerable in France, as records from the salt depot (*grenier*) in Laval in the highly taxed Maine province show. Most people in the Laval area bought far less than the salt they needed: an average of 2 pounds (4.4 kg) per person per year in 1772, while sales of salt in neighboring tax-free Brittany averaged 24 pounds (48 kg) per person per year, far more salt than the Bretons required. It is evident that the excess Breton salt purchases went illegally to Maine, because only when Breton sources were cut off, as in 1769 when flooding closed the routes between the two provinces, did the Laval depot's sales increase.

Such tactics and large-scale participation in smuggling made contraband trade virtually impossible to repress entirely, and in an attempt to deter such crime some states – including England, France, and the Spanish kingdom – dramatically increased their penalties for smuggling in the late seventeenth and eighteenth centuries. In France, where the royal declaration of 1674 had established fines and seizures of goods as penalties for salt smuggling, the decree of 1729 established three years' galley service as a minimum penalty and death as the maximum punishment imposed on second offenders working in armed bands of five or more. Judgment, moreover, was at the hands of *Commissions spéciales*, like the one in Valence that tried Mandrin, and that quickly acquired a reputation for being harsh tribunals. England exhibited the same pattern, and many smuggling activities became capital offenses in 1746.

The response of organized bands of smugglers to such enforcement of the law was not always peaceful. They used their arms chiefly against the two greatest threats to their livelihood: informers and agents of state authority. Informers were a particular threat to smugglers, who depended on community silence about their activities, either through intimidation or widespread local participation in smuggling. Indeed, the limitations of early modern policing and forensic skills made informers' information essential to the apprehension of smugglers. Authorities thus offered rewards for information that provided the basis for many of their arrests, including that of Mandrin. Consequently, smugglers and those who supported their activities dealt harshly with informers. Murders were common, and brutal, like that of Daniel Chater of West Sussex and the revenue officer captured with him in February 1748: smugglers cut off both men's noses and genitalia before killing them. And in an attempt permanently to silence a captured member of their band, salt smugglers stormed the jail of Mirepoix, France, but managed only to wound the prisoner badly. Sometimes, too, local crowds, whose members had connections with smugglers, inflicted harm on suspected informers and burned their homes.

But armed smugglers reserved their greatest violence for judges, police, and revenue authorities. In Sussex, England, a virtual war raged between authorities and smugglers in the 1740s, and smugglers murdered revenue officers and soldiers with impunity. In Kent some 200 armed men stormed into Dover in May 1744 in an attempt to free a smuggler and his tea-laden sloop from the authorities. Another armed band captured the customs house in Poole, Dorset, to recover a captured tea cargo, and smugglers elsewhere attacked and burned customs houses.

The English situation was not unique. Tobacco smugglers brought a paroxysm of violence to northern Spain in the 1770s, killing frontier guards and virtually besieging the local administrative center of Puigcerda at times. Indeed, in May 1772 contrabanders actually captured the town and held it long enough to release accomplices imprisoned there. Such violence especially assailed France as well: prosecutors charged some forty murders to Mandrin at his trial, and other smugglers left bloody records. In the southwest three noble smugglers led sixty armed horsemen and thirty armed footmen into Aire on 31 May 1645 to recapture their salt-laden mules that had been seized by the Ferme. When the band of the Norman noblemen Poilley and Romilley, seventy-five men strong (including a number of their vassals, domestics, and peasants from their estates), attacked the residence of a revenue official it resulted in the gentlemen's capture on 23 May 1673. Jean Cottereau, a smuggler of salt from Brittany to the Maine who operated under the false name of Jean Chouan, beat an officer of the Ferme to death with a stick in December 1780 when he met the man at an inn.

Pitched battles were not unknown in France, either. In May 1706 a band of salt smugglers, hauling their contraband in carts the considerable distance from Lorraine into Poitou, walked into an ambush of revenue officials in a wood near Poligny. The smugglers drew their wagons into a circle and fought a four-hour battle that ended with the death or capture of all but two of them and the seizure of about 2 tons (2 tonnes) of salt. Similarly bitter battles raged elsewhere in France. In 1736 smugglers besieged the Valence brigade of revenue officers, while another fight in 1782 engaged fifty-five Roussillon salt smugglers with a Ferme brigade and the royal army.

Already armed, many smugglers found easy the transition to the armed robbery we have examined. The English smugglers of Sussex preyed frequently on wealthy citizens in the 1740s. Abraham Picard and his Great Dutch band dealt in both contraband and robbery. In southern France a band of smugglers, turned armed robbers, used the Devesset wood for sanctuary in the 1760s. Their activities so frustrated the Maréchaussée brigades of Annonay, Privas, and Tournon that the police leveled much of the wood, forcing the band to move elsewhere.

The violence of armed smugglers and bandits did not survive long into the nineteenth century in most of western Europe. Smugglers and bandits found that the growing police power of the state ultimately made their activities increasingly difficult. France led the way in this, followed by England. Indeed, studies of Old Regime policing suggest that by the late eighteenth century a strengthened French Maréchaussée elicited growing cooperation in law enforcement from populations threatened by bandits. As policing became more dependable, its agents confronted less frequently the attitude evinced by Lyonnais peasants who feared band retribution for their cooperation with police when the officers left the area. The Napoleonic regime moved vigorously against bandits in France, the Low Countries, and the west bank of the Rhine with a criminal procedure that suspended the use of the trial jury. Waterloo caused scant interruption in the development of French policing, which was widely imitated in Europe. The capture of Mandrin in fact proved to be something of a watershed event in France. After the 1750s, although small-time operators often eluded the authorities, the monarchy's agents steadily extirpated the large bands of smugglers.

FURTHER READING

Beier, A. L., *Masterless Men: The Vagrancy Problem in England, 1560–1640* (London: Methuen, 1985).
Blanning, T. C. W., *The French Revolution in Germany: Occupation and Resistance in the Rhineland, 1792–1802* (Oxford: Oxford University Press, 1983).

Blok, Anton, "The Peasant and the Brigand: Social Banditry Reconsidered," with reply by Eric J. Hobsbawm, "Social Bandits: Reply," *Comparative Studies in Society and History* 14 (1971), pp. 494–505.

Casey, James, *The Kingdom of Valencia in the Seventeenth Century* (Cambridge: Cambridge University Press, 1979).

Danker, Uwe, "Bandits and the State: Robbers and the Authorities in the Holy Roman Empire in the Late Seventeenth and Early Eighteenth Centuries" in Richard J. Evans (ed.), *The German Underworld: Deviants and Outcasts in German History* (London: Routledge, 1988), pp. 75– 107.

Egmond, Florike, "Crime in Context: Jewish Involvement in Organized Crime in the Dutch Republic," *Jewish History* 4 (1) (1989), pp. 75–100.

    Underworlds: Organized Crime in the Netherlands, 1650–1800 (Cambridge, MA: Basil Blackwell, 1994).

Hobsbawm, Eric J., *Bandits*, revised ed. (New York: Pantheon Books, 1981).

Kamen, Henry, "Public Authority and Popular Crime: Banditry in Valencia, 1660–1714," *Journal of European Economic History* 3 (1974), pp. 654–87.

Pike, Ruth, "The Reality and Legend of the Spanish Bandit Diego Corrientes," *Folklore* 99 (1988), pp. 242–47.

Winslow, Cal, "Sussex Smugglers" in Douglas Hay *et al.*, *Albion's Fatal Tree: Crime and Society in Eighteenth-Century England* (New York: Pantheon Books, 1975), pp. 119–66.

Conclusion

Half a millennium ago, in 1500, European travelers safely reaching any major city must have heaved a sigh of relief, and perhaps uttered prayers of thanks, for having escaped the violence of bandits, marauding soldiers, and other dangerous types who inhabited the rural expanse that still separated urban centers. Indeed, the very aspect of the travelers' destination perhaps convinced some of them that they were approaching a bastion of security in a violent world.

Impressive fortifications still surrounded continental European cities, protecting them from attack by hostile forces and seemingly from the crimes and violence ubiquitous in early modern society. Nuremberg, one of Germany's greatest trading centers, dwelt behind a moat and a double line of thick stone walls almost 3½ miles (5·6 km) in circumference. The walls of Paris were in some places 6 ft (1·8 m) thick and 28 ft (8·4 m) high, buttressed with towers at every 220 ft (66m), and equipped with chains to complete the municipal defense perimeter by blocking the Seine River where it passed through the city. Florence, birthplace of the Italian Renaissance, sought security behind medieval walls 20 ft (6 m) high, with much higher towers along the line of fortification.

Admittance within such city walls, especially at night, was not easy, even for a peaceful traveler, as the great French essayist Michel de Montaigne discovered while touring the defenses of Augsburg, Germany, in 1580. He found that nocturnal arrivals gained admission to sixteenth-century Germany's largest city only by informing guards precisely of their destination within its walls and paying a fee to permit them to enter the city by passing through four gates and an iron barrier before crossing the drawbridge spanning the moat.

Such elaborate arrangements protected a city's inhabitants from external threats, but once our travelers gained admission to the city they found little to encourage them to relax their guard. Streets were unlit. Those abroad after dark on legitimate business carried torches or lanterns to light their way, and arms for self-protection, because most cities mustered only a few night watchmen for policing. Other aspects of the early modern city must also have kept travelers alert for danger. Many were like Nuremberg, where municipal authorities stored torches or lanterns at strategic locations to be lit in case of trouble. The city fathers also provided heavy chain barriers that street captains might draw across to close off key thoroughfares in case of riot or other disorder.

By the second half of the nineteenth century, all of this had changed. Most obviously, governments almost everywhere had removed city walls, often replacing them with broad boulevards. This demolition of city walls primarily reflected new military realities, for such age-old defenses could not withstand modern artillery. But the physical openness of the modern city also reflected new levels of security, both within its limits and in the countryside beyond. Modern behavior was becoming less and less violent, professional police forces patrolled urban streets and country roads with rising effectiveness, and the growing judicial power of the state punished more efficiently those violent offenders whom the police arrested. Indeed, the physical openness and relative security of the modern city demonstrate the results of trends in western European violence that we have traced through the early modern period and that continue to evolve in the early twenty-first century.

Both the 1500–1800 period encompassed by this book, and the two succeeding centuries, witnessed much that diminished western European violence. State power, sustained by its increasing monopolization of force, increasingly imposed greater order and discipline on western society. And as the work of Norbert Elias suggests, human behavior itself seems to have become less violent through the accruing effects of a "civilizing process" that affected ever-growing numbers of Europeans. We have traced the reality of this decline in violence through analysis of the falling rate of homicide in Europe from 1500 to 1800, a trend that continued into the nineteenth and twentieth centuries.

Despite the clear decline in homicide that historians identify, however, the popular misapprehensions about the realities of violence that we noted in Chapter 1 persisted. Like their early modern ancestors, nineteenth- and twentieth-century Europeans continued to fear the unexpected act of violence, as we still do today. The modern media fan fears, just as did the early modern press whose output we examined in Chapter 1. Growing popular literacy and new technologies made possible the inexpensive mass-circulation newspaper of the nineteenth century, which often used lurid accounts of violence to boost sales. This press could create far greater crime panics than could its early modern counterpart through widely disseminated front-page coverage of the sordid careers of violent nineteenth-century offenders like "Jack the Ripper."

Admittedly, the broad retreat of violence that attracted so little popular attention was never constant. Just as we have seen the long-term decline in early modern homicide rates interrupted by temporary increases in murder rates in early eighteenth-century England and Amsterdam, similar interruptions in falling homicide rates occurred in the modern period as well. Rates of modern homicide often increase in times of social, cultural and economic change. Perhaps for men and women of the late twentieth century the most memorable rise in homicide happened as part of a general increase in all crime experienced by western Europe and the United States that began in the 1960s and ebbed only in the early 1990s.

Homicide rates have not dropped at the same pace in every western European country, either. Northwestern Europe, the most urbanized part of the continent, clearly led in the containment of violence. We have seen this decline beginning as early as the sixteenth century in some countries, and by the early twentieth century it produced homicide rates at or below 1 per 100,000 of the population in England, France, Germany, Belgium, and the Netherlands. The less-developed Mediterranean littoral, the early modern center of violent feuds and vendettas, at first failed to experience much decline in homicide, as Italian statistics suggest. Districts in rural southern Italy produced homicide rates as high as 40 per 100,000 in 1881–83. Palermo exceeded 60 per 100,000 in the same period, and even Rome, capital of the unified kingdom, produced almost 40 per 100,000, thanks to an active knife-fighting culture. Nonetheless, by the post-World War II era, Italian homicide rates, and those of other southern European countries, approximated to those of northwestern Europe.

Our survey of early modern trends in containing violence established a foundation for understanding the reasons for this long-term decline in homicide and other brutal behavior. As we saw in Chapter 2, the early modern state was imposing greater order and discipline on its armed forces by the seventeenth century, reducing the violence that soldiers inflicted on civilians and creating a formidable weapon against large-scale collective violence. At the same time, most states began a very slow process of monopolizing force within their borders. One aspect of this process, as we saw in Chapter 2, was improved policing, starting with the creation of regular urban policing in seventeenth-century Paris, and in the establishment of rural police forces such as the French Maréchaussée. In the later years of our period, and in the nineteenth century, most states perfected such forces. The London Metropolitan Police, created in 1829 by Home Secretary Sir Robert Peel, epitomized the modern urban police force, and was much imitated. The transformation of the French Maréchaussée into the Gendarmerie Nationale during the Revolution of 1789 provided a model for similar rural forces like the Prussian Gendarmerie, the Italian Carabinieri, and the Spanish Guardia Civil. A second aspect of this process of state monopolization of force was control of private arms. Beginning most clearly in France, the state's attempts to control private weaponry advanced from confiscation of early modern private artillery parks to virtual outlawing of individually owned handguns in some states in the late twentieth century.

Developments in the early modern justice system that we examined in Chapter 3 also reflected the increasing power of the state. Modern state courts continued the early modern expansion of courts' competence, subsuming the functions of infrajudicial and parajudicial modes of dispute resolution to end privately negotiated settlements as well as individual acts of revenge, duels, and feuds.

The modern state also brought to fruition the early modern search for more efficient justice, and the modern court was far more effective in reinforcing state power than the tribunals of the early modern period. In France the Revolutionary Criminal Code of 1791 and its successors recreated that nation's judicial system, from local justices of the peace to departmental assizes, with the goal of making justice both free and accessible. Urban areas of nineteenth-century Britain received more efficient police courts in place of justices of the peace to deal with less serious violence, and more effective justice developed in other countries as well.

As such courts supplanted private acts of violence in regulating disputes, they also hastened a process begun in the early modern period: the slow diminution of violence in state justice itself. The brutal, public theater of corporal and capital punishments that we examined in the early modern period disappeared, at least from public view, as judicial elites, reflecting a growing repugnance for violence that Norbert Elias found common in their social group, searched for a new penology. Corporal punishment of civilians, already waning in the late eighteenth century, disappeared almost totally in subsequent years; and capital punishment, which we found used with decreasing frequency in the early modern period, continued to decline in frequency while also moving inside prisons (except in France prior to 1939) and out of the public view. Incarceration became the typical punishment for nonlethal violence everywhere, and in the twentieth century the death penalty all but disappeared from western Europe.

Western European courts, at the same time, used the new penology to deal more strictly with violent offenses. Penalties directed at violent offenders increased everywhere, reflecting the gravity that violence was assuming for this society. Assault and battery no longer regularly elicited pardons from judges, and domestic violence became a matter jurists could no longer overlook. England offers a clear example. In 1853 the Act for Better Prevention of Aggravated Assault upon Women and Children placed a limit on husbandly or parental correction of women and children by assigning criminal sanctions for any bodily injury inflicted on them.

Thanks to the growing permeation of even the lower orders of the nine-teenth century by the values of the civilizing process, members of these groups, increasingly appalled by domestic violence, reported such cruelty to the authorities more frequently. Significantly, judges seem to have applied the full rigor of the new laws in response to such reports because the public, in part reacting to the modern sensationalist press, perceived a wave of violence that needed control.

Modern society's general acceptance of values that social elites had adopted in the early modern period affected other sorts of violence, too. The diffusion of those values associated with the civilizing process greatly eroded the popular culture that fostered charivaris and similar rough activities. We saw in Chapter 4 that social elites, embracing new values, began to eschew much of popular entertainment in the early modern period. By the early 1800s much of western Europe experienced the popular triumph of those values, a development Peter Burke has called the triumph of Lent over Carnival.[1] Early modern festive life, where it survived into the industrial age, became a quaint relic of tradi-tional folk culture, not the brutal excess it had once been. Such diffusion of new standards of personal comportment also made violence like the lethal encounter in Gensac that we examined in Chapter 4 increasingly less generalized in society. With the waning of the old popular culture and modes of personal comportment, much of the basis for the ritual group violence and interpersonal violence of the early modern period disappeared.

The police apparatus of the modern state aided judicial authorities in the dissemination of new behavioral standards. The police of the nine-teenth and twentieth centuries were much more effective than their early modern predecessors in advancing the behavioral standards we have associated with the civilizing process, if not always in apprehending violent offenders and bringing them to the bar of justice then. The early nineteenth century really marked the birth of modern urban policing, and the uniformed "bobby" of the London Metropolitan Police was much more than an agent of the law: he was what one historian has termed a "domestic missionary" for urban discipline.[2] Indeed, the London police-man, always literate, attending church in uniform, and subject to unan-nounced inspections of his home by superiors concerned to assure the probity of his domestic life, was intended as an unarmed role model for

[1] Peter Burke, *Popular Culture in Early Modern Europe* (New York: Harper and Row, 1978), pp. 209–43.
[2] Robert D. Storch, "The Policeman as Domestic Missionary: Urban Policing and Popular Culture in Northern England, 1850–1880," *Journal of Social History* 9 (1976), pp. 481–509.

the populace. Other jurisdictions followed London's lead, although most continental forces were far more military than their English counterpart, and invariably bore arms.

The growth of state power, evident in such police forces, arms control, and the expanding power of state judiciaries, increasingly contained the early modern popular protest we examined in Chapter 6. The violence of banditry and smuggling also diminished in the face of such state power. No figure of equal repute followed Mandrin in western Europe, a sure sign that the bands we examined in Chapter 7 were disappearing by the dawn of the nineteenth century. And while the violence of organized crime continued along the Mediterranean littoral into the first years after World War II, and still disturbs parts of twenty-first century society with the activities of dealers in illicit drugs, it is now far less generalized in its extent. The populations of whole regions seldom pursue smuggling activities, for example, as they did in Old Regime France and in coastal zones of eighteenth-century England and the Dutch Republic.

These developments, whose origins we found in the early modern period, have not completely extirpated violence from western Europe. Indeed, the triumphant modern state of the previous century created new forms of violence of hitherto unimagined intensity to ravage the continent. Two world wars, the Holocaust and other acts of genocide, and the lingering threat of weapons of mass destruction are proof of this. But in terms of quotidian threats of violence, modern western Europeans, as we suggested in the Introduction, are far from living in the worst of times.

FURTHER READING

Emsley, Clive, *Crime and Society in England, 1750–1900*, 2nd ed. (London: Longman Publishing, 1996).
  Gendarmes and the State in Nineteenth-Century Europe (Oxford: Oxford University Press, 1999).
Gatrell, V. A. C., "The Decline of Theft and Violence in Victorian and Edwardian England" in Gatrell, Lenman and Parker (eds.), *Crime and the Law: The Social History of Crime in Western Europe since 1500* (London: Europa, 1980), pp. 238–369.
Hughes, Steve C., *Crime, Disorder and the Risorgimento: The Politics of Policing in Bologna* (Cambridge: Cambridge University Press, 1994).
Johnson, Eric E., *Urbanization and Crime: Germany, 1871–1914* (Cambridge: Cambridge University Press, 1995).
Morris, Terence, *Crime and Criminal Justice since 1945* (Oxford: Basil Blackwell, 1989).
Tomes, Nancy, "A 'Torrent of Abuse': Crimes of Violence between Working-Class Men and Women in London, 1840–1875," *Journal of Social History* 11 (1971), pp. 328–45.

Index

Note: italicized pages indicate figures.

New Approaches to European History